OPEN SECRETS

OPEN SECRETS

EXPLORATIONS IN SOUTH WALES

(As broadcast in the BBC Radio Wales 'Sou'wester' and 'Open Secrets' programmes)

Text/Photographs: Roger Worsley
Drawings/Layout: Piet Brinton

First Impression - October 1987

ISBN 0 86383 195 8

Printed by
J. D. Lewis & Sons Ltd.
Llandysul, Dyfed.

This book is dedicated
to the memory of Piet Brinton

PIET BRINTON

One half of the team which made this book possible, was a fine artist, a brilliant musician, professional broadcaster . . . a man who made records of his own music with his own lyrics . . . who was always busy yet always had time for people. His partnership with Roger Worsley in the 'Sou'wester' and 'Link Up' magazine series on Radio Wales led to the popular radio explorations of 'Open Secrets', produced by Dave Simmonds for Radio Wales. It is these programmes which have been used as the basis for this book, and it was intended that Piet should provide the line illustrations, maps and art work for the book to be written by Roger. From the few drawings in this book it will be seen how good an artist he was . . . for Piet was killed in a car crash on 14th March, 1984 not long after they had started to work on the final version for the book. He left a wife and daughter, and a great many grieving friends, aghast at the loss of a colleague and friend.

Roger Worsley

Contents

Page

List of Illustrations   viii
Introduction   1
The Celts are coming   7
The Dean and the Red Lady   29
Hoyle's Mouth Cave Tenby   31
Bluestones and Black Night   34
Field of the Dead   37
Irish Morse . . .   41
Wofull Newes from Wales   45
Big Forts Have Little Forts . . .   50
A Glint of Gold   54
Plumbing Around Carmarthen . . .   60
Adam and the Adders . . .   64
Vanished into the Sand—   66
Wrecking . . .   69
Died and Lay Dead Two Months . . .   76
God's Whiskers and White Boys   81
Drovers and Deathmongers   86
"The Ears and Nostrils of the Dead . . ."   90
The Mad German and the Mines Royal   94
Canals in the Welsh Hills . . .   97
Mister Morris's Colliers' Castle . . .   102
Palmerston's Follies   104
Porthgain   110
The Little Giant and the Gorge   118
'Cardi Bach' and Sophie the Tanner   130
Oystermouth and the Grave of Dr Thomas Bowlder   133
Three Times Widdershins   138
A cure for Arthritis   140
Arsenic and Old Bishops   143
Hooray, Hooray, St. Lubbock's Day . . .   145
A Faithful Hound Remembered   150
Limekilns   154
Taking the Slow Road   159
Tay and Solomon Grundy   166
A Word from your Writer   173
A short place name dictionary   181
Norse place name index   184
Further reading and bibliography   186
Index   190

List of Illustrations

Picture Title/Description   *Page*

Handful of flints, Middle Stone-age — 1
Drowned forest, Marros beach — 2a
Palaeolithic hand-axe — 2b
Pentre Ifan burial chamber—engraving by Colt Hoare — 3
Group of tanged arrowheads — 4
Pair of Bronze-age cremation urns; Fenton/Colt Hoare — 5
Germander Speedwell — 6
Foel Drygarn; Bronze age cairns and massive iron age hillfort with hut depressions — 8
Roman oil lamp — 9
Celandines; saxon treatment for 'Sore eyes' — 10
Gateholm—cropmarks of an early Christian community — 11
St Davids; Stone remembering Hedd and Isaac, the two sons of the bishop of St Davids murdered by Viking pirates in 1080 — 12
Cosheston; air view of strip fields — 13
Roman glass jug; detail of top and handle — 14a
Roman bronze scent vessels — 14b
Misericord, St Davids; a bad dose of seasickness! — 15
Air view of Castell Mawr Iron-age fort, with its funnel shaped entrance and internal division to separate humans from their animals, or as extra defence . . . — 17
Portait of a Crusader? St Davids — 18
Nab Head; Iron age promontory fort, Mesolithic flint floor, St Brides — 20a
Flint microliths from Nab Head — 20b
Bronze age palstave—a battle-axe, first signs of our species military development — 21a
Bronze age fertility stone, St Nons — 21b
Section of ditch around Bronze-age farm — 22
Pine pollen grains X250 — 24a
Roman Samian pottery—the 'Woolworths' of its day! — 24b
Roman glass vase; example of craftsmanship and modern dating techniques . . . — 24c
Carbonised seeds from excavations; einkorn and emmer — 25
Edible fungus *Helvella*, whose spores have turned up on prehistoric sites — 26
Excavation in progress, Knock Rath, Clarbeston, Pemb. — 27
Paviland cave, Gower — 28
Palaeolithic hand axe, our earliest tool — 30
Hoyles Mouth cave, Tenby — 31
Carn Meini from the air — 32/3
Stonehenge detail — 35
Parc y Meirw stone row, drawing by Colt Hoare 1800 — 37a
Eclipse photographed from Parc y Meirw 1985 — 37b
Detail, stone in Gors Fawr circle, with ice . . . — 38
Gors Fawr stone circle in its desolate moorland setting — 39
'Ogham' stone in Brawdy church—drawing; Piet Brinton — 40
St Dogmaels 'Sagrani' Ogham stone — 42
'Vitalianus' Ogham stone, Nevern—an old Roman soldier? — 43

Picture Title/Description	Page
'Maglocunas' stone, Nevern; bilingual memorials like this helped scholars decipher the ancient Irish alphabet	44
Woodcut, a tudor flood titled 'Wofull Newes from Wales'	45
A gigantic flood in Middle Stone-age times left this forest scythed down like so many matchsticks; Marros	46
Spearhead found in the leaf litter of the drowned forest at Marros, evidence of a pre-flood hunter . . .	47
The Bridge Inn, Newgale, 1882; swept away in the great storm and flood of 1895—a whole street vanished	48
Cwm yr Eglwys church before the 'Royal Charter' storm of 1859, when *400* ships were lost in a single night, and the church almost washed away—engraving; Gastineau	49
Shield boss spiral design—drawing Piet Brinton	50a
Reconstruction of Iron-age hut—drawing Piet Brinton	50b
Lively horse on Iron age coin	50c
Carn Alw Iron-age fort with fine *cheveaux de frise*, a funnel shaped entrance as defence against cavalry	51
Uffington's white horse—drawing by Piet Brinton	52
Crundale Iron-age camp, with its tradition of headless horsemen galloping wildly by on Hallowe'en . . .	53
Dolaucothi, the Great opencast in this Roman gold mine	54a & b
Coffin level, seen from inside the workings, Dolaucothi	55
Gorse, whose prickly spines were used by Roman gold miners to capture the specks of precious metal in settling ponds, then burned to extract the gold	56
Roman mortar, whose depressions later acquired a folk tale about five saints and a thunder storm . . .	57
Roman gold bracelet, Dolaucothi—drawing; Piet Brinton	58
Tudor Woodcut showing mining methods very little changed from Roman times . . . and the origin of Gnomes? . . .	59
Group of Pembrokeshire miners and their 'Druke and Beam'	61
Agricola's Druke and Beam 1556—woodcut	63
Grass snake emerges from hibernation, a magical animal	64
Roch Castle—engraving	65
Pennard Castle at sunset, a ghostly place still	66
Wreck of the barque 'Naples' (watercolour by eyewitness)	67
Wrecking; drawing by Piet Brinton	69
Culver Hole, Gower, Piet Brinton exploring	71
Culver Hole; hauling in a fiddle before recording 'Phebe and Peggy'	72
'Phebe and Peggy' at Philadelphia quay 1772	73
Solva burial register remembers poor Joe Harry and the Smalls light tragedy of 1780	75
Smalls light—model made from original's timber	76
'The Smalls Light Tragedy' as filmed for Sianel Pedwar Cymru by Nant Films; 3 stills from the grim documentary recounting the descent into madness of one lighthousekeeper after the death of his companion, as they wait together for relief . . .	78
Carew Castle from the air	81

Picture Title/Description	Page
Carew Castle from across the 'lake' which supplies the tide mill, showing Sir John Perrott's Long Gallery	82
Sir John Perrott, not an easy man to get on with . . .	83
Carew Castle; Arms of Henry Tudor, his son Prince Arthur and the young lad's bride, Katherine of Aragon—fate was to make her the first of Henry VIII's six wives . . .	84a
Sir John Perrott's half-sister, Queen Elizabeth I, seen pictured on an iron fire-back	84b
Carew Castle after its fire and final abandonment; engraving	85
St Edrins church, yard and 'corpse road' from the air	86
Mesur y Dorth, the pilgrims' 'Loaf Measure Stone'	87
Pilgrims' steps, Nevern	88
Pilgrims' cross, Nevern	89
Porthclais with collier, 1898	90
Porthclais in 1871 showing breakwater and trading ships	91a
Porthclais today, quiet and peaceful, its bloodthirsty past forgotten . . . or NEARLY forgotten . . .	91b
Giraldus Cambrensis, the priestly scholar whose gossip tells more than anyone else about what medieval Welsh life was *like*—statue in St Davids cathedral	92
Aberdulais copper works—detail of 'The Bastion'	94
'Before' and 'After' restoration by the National Trust	95a & b
Aberdulais, the most romantic setting for industrial remains, even Turner couldn't resist it!	96
Pembrey Station showing its canal origins	97a
Hawser marks on the 'railway' bridge	97b
Iron tub boat high and dry, Burry Port old harbour	98a
18th C. colliery tramroad crosses Ashburnham canal, later the Burry Port and Gwendraeth valley Railway; now both lie abandoned . . .	98b
Incline Inn, Pont Henry; a wonder of Wales remembered in a pub sign—	99
Pont Henry, top of the old canal incline, now used by trains—'Incline Hotel' looking down on it	100
Iron notice, one of a vanishing breed—Burry Port and Gwendraeth Valley Railway	101
Mister Morris's colliers' castle, Morriston . . .	102
. . . and the view—Landore copper and steel works 1875	103
Stack Rock Victorian fort from the air	104
Exploring Stack Rock fort, which is on its own island and thus in relatively good condition still	105a
Palliser cannon, the Exocet of its day, Stack Rock	105b
Palliser ready for action, 1898	106a
A boxing match eases boredom! Stack Rock in the '90s	106b
Scoveston Fort, still the classic 'Bank and Ditch' defence . . .	107
Thorn Island Fort, Milford Haven—now it's a hotel for those who REALLY want to get away from it all!	108
Porthgain from the air; remains of industry thick on the ground, in an idyllic setting	110
Porthgain at its zenith, steam and smoke when Muck meant Brass, not pollution!	111
Billhead, showing '. . . a view of Porthgain'' 1880	112
Turn of the century bustle, steam and sail jostling, Porthgain	113
Plenty of steam up in Porthgain	114

Picture Title/Description	*Page*
Early newspaper advert, Porthgain produced granite, slate and bricks in its day	115
Porthgain—early days, fine plate shows waterpowered machinery, pugging, mill, buildings in their prime, and first harbour works; no 'road metal' hoppers as yet . . .	116
View from the clifftop, brick, kiln, harbour works	117a
Schooner leaves harbour in rough seas	117b
Isambard Kingdom Brunel—the 'Little Giant'	118
Air view, north end of Treffgarne gorge, showing 18th C. turnpike over the hill past Iron age fort, while in the valley road, rail and river have to squeeze through Precambrian rock—Brunel's old railway to far right	119
Brunel's 1845 line as it is today . . .	121a
. . . and during the museum's recent excavation and survey	121b
'Success to the railway' it says in Welsh and English, when Brunel's broad gauge rails reach Pembrokeshire in 1853	122
Candelabra presented to the mayor of Haverfordwest by the Directors of the South Wales Railway (Pemb. Museum)	123
Excursion to the Crystal Palace by Train—poster	124
Detail from the candelabra—train on viaduct, in solid silver	125
Map of North Pembrokeshire, with Brunel's scribbled note of approximate line of railway to Aber Mawr Bay	126
Detail, Railway timetable showing service on the old Fishguard and north Pembrokeshire line, 1903	127a
Goodwick station, 'Ringing Rock' and her admirers	127b
Site loco and crew in Treffgarne Gorge during the 1905 workings	128
Cardigan Station in its flower-decked heyday	130
Fragment of timetable, two forgotten private lines . . .	132
Oystermouth Church and the grave of Dr. Thomas Bowdler inventor of Bowdlerization	133
Oystermouth church; details of Mumbles Railway in stained glass	134a & b
Oystermouth church; detail of Mumbles Steam Tram	135
Pioneer of the blue pencil; Bowdler's grave . . .	136
Title page of a cleaned up Shakespeare	137
Trellyffaint Neolithic tomb	138
Toad emerging from Hole	139
Meadowsweet, the arthritic's plant	140
Woodcut from Gerarde's 'Herball'—'Queen of the Medowes'	141
Watson's Flue, Clyne Woods, Swansea	143
Sulphurous stalactites, Watson's Flue	144
Parc le Breos Cwm Neolithic tomb, Gower. Excavated by the pioneer of the Bank holiday who also masterminded the protection of ancient monuments, John Lubbock	145
Limekiln hard by Parc le Breos tomb	146
Parc le Breos tomb; detail of gallery	147
Parc le Breos tomb; detail of a side chamber	148
Arms of the Scourfields, with sportive greyhounds	150
New Moat church	151
New Moat; detail, the faithful hound by his master's side?	152

Picture Title/Description	*Page*
Limekiln, Newgale; drawing by Piet Brinton	154
Mynydd y Garreg, limekilns, a classic set	155
Carew Castle, with its limekiln smoking gently	156a
Limeburners and their mules approach the kiln. Woodcut	156b
Gothic limekilns at Tenby designed by John Nash, he of Regent Street and the Brighton Pavilion	157
Limeburners, bottom of social heap, and their miserable hut	158
Old Fishguard and its limekiln; transport by sea much easier and cheaper before road improvements . . .	159
Marychurch, the Haverfordwest Ironworks, makers of fine churns, gaslamps, railings . . . and milestones—	160
Mounting block, Nevern	161a
Llandovery, monument to drunken driving!	161b
Quotation for milestone by Marychurch (Pembs. Record Office)	162a
A fine example of Marychurch still by the roadside	162b
Georgian roads were masterly examples of privatisation. Repairs went to private tender—advertisement	163a
Carmarthen Ironworks drawing for casting milestone Pembrokeshire Museums	163b
Llandysul, a steam lorry about to leave the station	164
Haverfordwest, a traction engine in Victoria place hauling goods from the railway, 1906	165
Bartholomew Roberts, 'Barti Ddu', the world's most successful pirate, born in Pembrokeshire in 1682, died in action against the navy 1722—his fortune of £51 million was never found . . .	166
'Black Barty' 's signature on a threatening letter, 1721 Haslemere Museum	168
The Skyrme memorial, St Mary's, Haverfordwest. Skyrme was Barty's second-in-command; one of the pirates married a Skyrme daughter and bought a South sea isle with his 'Winnings' . . .	169
Haverfordwest as Barty knew it; looking towards the quay and the castle from the old Priory ruins	170
'Boot topping' a pirate ship to protect it from fouling and give it an extra few knots in speed . . .	171
Boat building—lunch break; detail from medieval misericord, St Davids Cathedral	172
Pentre Ifan, our premier cromlech, the most famous archaeological monument in Wales . . .	175
Drunk monk mourns empty tankard; St Mary's, Haverfordwest	176
Blood of the Raven; Rhys ap Thomas arms on tile; the man who put Henry Tudor on the British throne . . .	178
Wooden butter pat; dairy farming has always been one of our most important industries—how much longer? Pembrokeshire Museums	183
Nevern, the Great Cross; Celtic masterpiece—but nearby, a Viking lies buried . . .	185
Brave priest—cadaver tomb of Thomas Danby, who helped young Henry Tudor escape, and changed the course of British history . . . Tenby, St Mary's church.	195
Rudbaxton Church memorial to Hayward family, probable victims of the Black Death, carrying skulls as a grim symbol of that awful scourge . . .	196

Introduction

It's hard trying to think yourself back into history. For one thing, the time scales are so vast; when Man first appears in Britain, there are very few of him, or her, scratching a living with terrible tools hiding from the worst of the weather in caves like Paviland or Hoyle's Mouth. For millions of years nothing much seems to happen. A scatter of flint here, an axehead broken there, a little heap of burned and chewed bones, occasionally a burial . . . it is all that is left of your ancestors, who shared their world with sabre-toothed tigers, mammoths or woolly rhinoceros, but who probably worried as much about their world as we worry about ours! They certainly worried about death enough to bury as we still do, the body aligned with the passing of the sun across the heavens. There may be signs that food and tools were buried too, so the dead man or woman might have all in death that they had had in life; red coloured earths sprinkled over the body imitated life-blood. So lived, for something like 98% of his history, one of the world's rarest animals, now fast becoming the commonest.

About ten thousand years ago, the flicker of history's eye when you consider the millions that had gone before, some new people arrived around here. They still used stone tools, but they had mastered the art of flaking the easily breakable stone to very fine limits, enabling them to form some of the loveliest pieces of technology from prehistory. It is these tools which gave the culture its name—Mesolithic means Middle Stone Age; these men and women were still rare as animals, but they had a few new ideas, and prospered accordingly. Their new flaked flints would make good fish-hooks, saws, knives, scrapers and borers; they lived in the first house, albeit nothing much from our standpoint! It was shelter, and so caves were not the only homes we now had. This, and our fire, probably accounts for Man's oldest friend, the dog, appearing at our sides at about this time, and he has been with us ever since . . . Man and dog must have watched in horror from the hilltops, or fled from the plains and valleys when, in about 5500BC the sea rose and buried the fertile land which is now Cardigan Bay

or the Bristol Channel, all part of a story we still find as the Biblical Flood legend, or as the Sumerian Gilgamesh story, or as the Welsh Cantre'r Gwaelod; flooded and drowned, the forests at Amroth, Marros, Newgale, Abermawr or Newport altered our landscape and our ideas about it, possibly leading to our next few generations living on high ground, well away from those killing waters.

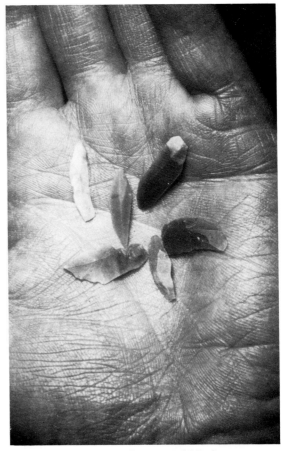

A handful of history—When our Middle Stone-age ancestors were making these superb flint flakes for hunting or fishing, 8000 years ago, Nab Head was miles from any sea.

1

Marros Beach and its drowned woodland—Our middle
Stone-age ancestors knew this as dry land, a rich, dark
oak forest alive with game . . . now it is under water
twice a day. That sudden drowning 7500 years ago has
kept the timber fresh enough to make furniture, or use
in a modern fire . . . beneath where the trees stood
proudly, leaves, bark, twigs, nuts, bramble seeds . . .
all the usual forest litter, but under the sea.

Palaeolithic Hand Axe—The man who made this axe
lived in a Pembrokeshire as cold as Siberia, sharing dry
windswept plains with Mammoth and Woolly
Rhinoceros; disputing the few rock shelters with Sabre-
toothed Tigers and Cave Bears . . .

The next revolution in human affairs arrived
with the men and women of the Neolithic (New
Stone Age), who paddled into our bays and inlets
about 3500 BC. They were not just hunters but
farmers, clearing pieces of forest and making small
fields in which to plant grain or to keep cattle or
goats, sheep and pigs—this activity altered the
landscape for the first time, and we have been doing
it ever since with ever-increasing destructive
power. Neolithic tools were still of stone but magnificently polished and have not just a fine edge but
a superb look and feel to them.

Neolithic farming needed a calendar, which led
to the first 'science', that of astronomy; improve-
ments in productivity led to a food surplus, and the
Neolithic people seem to have used this to feed and
support the astronomer-priests. These powerful
people continually watched the passage of day and
night, getting to know by the position of the sun,
moon and stars what time of year it was and when
terrifying events like eclipses might occur; such
information could be used to tell the farmers when

it was time to plant grain, to put the ram with the ewes (to ensure the lambs arrived at a convenient and known time, saving a lot of walking on the hills ...). The cardinal points on the calendar—longest day, shortest day, equinoxes and so on, were marked with ceremonies still performed to this day; after a dozen changes in religion they are too powerful just to die ... even the officially athiest Communists, after all, keep May Day, once reserved for the pagan goddess Eostre or Celtic Brigid (Bride) or her many prehistoric counterparts. And our ancestors ensured the days would be remembered, along with the rest of the culture of their time, by hiding fact inside story, often violent, always thick with romance, bits of it dripping blood! We forget in this literate society of ours that if you didn't make the young people remember *everything,* then it would all go, every time the old

generation died; and a human life span is terrifyingly short. Those first scientists also had to make sure they kept their painfully gathered knowledge in some form the following generation would, and could, remember. Thus it is that Gors Fawr, Carn Meini and Parc y Meirw stone monuments got their stories, and how people remembered their stories right into this present century.

Pentre Ifan; engraving by Colt Hoare—What you think about history depends on when you live—18th Century Romantic Antiquarians saw Pentre Ifan as a place of bloody Druidic sacrifice—in our computorized age we have invested our remote ancestors with great mathematical powers. We are just as likely to be wrong as the Romantics . . .

Group of barbed and tanged arrowheads—Our Stone-age ancestors were undisputed masters of flaked flint tools, like these magnificent arrowheads (made in about 2500 BC). Even here they are about twice life-size. Yet each razor-sharp point was designed to be used only once . . .

Neolithic religion was concerned with the earth; from the earth came life, crops, food and drink; it was natural to think that from the earth we came and to it we would return, into the womb of the Earth Mother Goddess. She was a powerful being and her likeness has been cropping up ever since in all more modern religions. Her likeness was built in stone and earth, whose central parts remain today as the cromlechs, dolmens and chambered tombs such as Pentre Ifan, Trellyffaint, Parc le Breos Cwm and many dozens of others. Burial was communal in that each tomb was for one family, and as a member of that family died, so the tomb was opened, and their body placed reverently inside, with offerings of food and drink, to await rebirth in the next world. But though there was respect for the newly dead, scant regard was paid to the skeletons of those who had gone before, which are therefore found unceremoniously scattered, when these tombs have been excavated in modern times.

So for fifteen hundred years the first really civilized people Britain had ever seen, lived here in complete peace—not for them the weapons of war, their tools *were* tools. Neolithic people were short, dark-haired, blue-eyed people; they had no cloth, as yet, but wore the skins of their animals . . . but all this was to change drastically. In about 2000 BC they must have been scared and curious to see, arriving on our shores, tall, fair-haired people with heads a bullet shape (Neolithic skulls have a pronounced point at the back); the newcomers were so tall that their coming probably led to the legends of Giants we still have, just as they, the new Britons, saw the pigmy Neolithic people with their little tumps of earth into which they vanished every now and again, and invented Little People or fairies. The main differences between new and old, however, were that the newcomers had mastered the tricky art (or science) of smelting a metal—Bronze, an alloy of copper and tin—and their use of it in warfare. For Man had now reached the stage of his evolution, in which he has been stuck ever since and with ever increasing effect, as a warrior, a fighter for land, security or belief. Neolithic people lived out their long, healthy existence in peace—from now, we would never be without the shadow of war upon us.

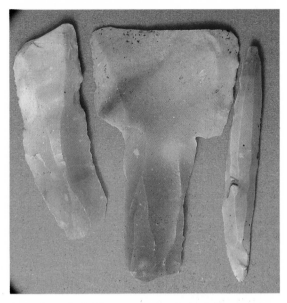

Our remotest ancestors' first fumbling steps in tool-making,—hand-axes for simple hunters (50,000—20,000 B.C.). . .

. . . who only fairly recently found the flakes they wasted were sharper than the core (Middle Stone-age fish hook, knife blade and plane, c6000 B.C.).

Pottery before the wheel; a Bronze-age urn containing the cremated bones of a 19 year old girl who died about 1500 B.C.

Roman pottery, the "Woolworths" of its day, known as Samian to archaeologists; it tends to turn up by the barrowful when Roman sites are being dug!

Top Left: Dinas Island from
Carn Enoc.
Top Right: Bluebell.
Bottom Right: Iron-age Chevaux
de frise defence against
cavalry (Carn Alw).

The first Welsh were proud, fierce warrior-farmers. This fortress on the headland at Dinas is now watched over
by the remote descendants of the Celtic cavalry horses, which were worshipped as gods when not being ridden to
war. Even the gentle Bluebell (*Scylla nonscripta*) was pressed into service. Its bulbs, when boiled, produced a
powerful glue for cementing Iron-age arrowheads to their shafts, a property which the feared Welsh longbowmen
still knew at the dawn of the Gun Age, at Bosworth in 1485.

Bronze age cremation urns—The Bronze age was marked by many changes—the plough, metal-working, weaving cloth . . . and burial in round earthen mounds, often after cremation. These two cremation urns were dug up by the Pembrokeshire historian Richard Fenton of Fishguard in 1800, helped by his friend Sir Richard Colt Hoare (who probably did the drawings).

Bronze age farming was slightly more advanced; they had the plough, while the New Stone Age folk had had to be content with the digging stick. Neolithic pottery was fairly rough, but the new beakers were delicately decorated; Bronze age skills included weaving, so at last we could use the wool supplied by our animals to better effect. But from the landscape point of view, the main effect of the Bronze age invasion, about four thousand years ago, was in land clearance and the new individual burial of the Best People in round tumps of earth, marked on modern maps as 'tumuli', where kings, queens and princes could be buried to survey in death the lands they had commanded and ruled in life; for this society also produced a 'Rich-and-Poor' structure which, again, has been with us ever since. Rich warrior farmers lorded it over the lesser peasants, who toiled, and went to their graves anonymously. Nearly every hilltop has a round barrow on it, sometimes quite a cemetery of them, reminding us of a royal family of long ago.

Now much more land was being cleared, new species of wheat and corn planted, along with plants we now think of as 'wild' but which our ancestors may well have introduced deliberately. The poppy arrived at about this time, possibly as a herb to lessen the pain of warriors' wounds; speedwell also came in, possibly as a wild addition, possibly because its use was suggested for easing the tired feet of travellers—because whereas the Neolithic people had begun making tracks through the forests (like the Golden Way), Bronze Age trade was extensive and required a more elaborate system of tracks, even though most of their trade and, indeed, Man's trade until the railways came, was by sea.

Germander Speedwell—'Speed Well' or 'Traveller's
Joy'—either name tells you what our ancestors felt
about this plant; within living memory there were still
people putting its leaves in their boots to take the aches
out of a long walk . . . did Bronze age travellers see a
sign from the gods in the little booted 'legs' built into
each flower?

And the little 'feet' that appear on speedwell flowers
suggested to early herbalists that the gods might
mean this as a sign . . . years later, medieval doctors
would adopt this idea as the Doctrine of Signatures,
and liverwort would cure liver complaints, lungwort tuberculosis or asthma and so on. Neolithic
people had already introduced a lot of plants not
seen here before (The Rowan and Yew are two of
theirs), but now new, far reaching changes in
vegetation were being wrought by man, and by the
change of climate . . . as the people who finished
Stonehenge, and dragged the Bluestones from the
Preseli Hills to do it, worked in their bigger fields
and brewed the first beer, they might have been
heard remarking that Summers Were Not What
They Were . . .

The Celts are coming

During the one-and-a-half thousand years which followed the Bronze Age mens' coming, the two cultures of stone user and metal user merged to give one of the most brilliant eras the prehistoric world had yet seen. Stars were studied as never before, the great stone circles at Stonehenge and Avebury were finished, mathematical thought seems to have gone on evolving . . . burial habits changed, and the once universal earthen tomb seems to have given way to cremation, though even the urns containing what a delightful Americanism calls the 'Cremains' were still sometimes buried either in the side of a previously constructed tomb, or in urn cemeteries which now only show up on air photographs or occasionally in ditch-digging; even so, these cremations were probably those of the upper crust, the rest of us going alone to our death, alone and soon forgotten, as we always have.

About 600 BC, the villagers would have been startled then terrified by the thundering of hooves which had come right across the plains of Europe— the Celts were coming . . . They invaded the fairly stable Bronze Age civilisations right across from Poland to the Low Countries, down through France to Italy, some coming over the Channel to Britain . . . troops of fierce tribesmen and women sweeping like lightning over the land, borne on horseback. Up to this point the horse had been wild, and wild it still remained in temperament, with wilder men still on its back, their bodies crudely painted in garish dyes and earths, their naked bodies covered in goosegrease, and brandishing weapons made from a new and very tough material. These were the people of the Iron Age.

Iron Age life was short, brutal and gory. Yet this culture produced some of the finest art the prehistoric world had seen. Our Scots, Welsh and Irish ancestors lived fairly brief lives punctuated by incessant fighting. They were head hunters. They built hilltop fortresses whose remains crown every commanding viewpoint—places like Foel Drygarn, Carn Ingli, Nevern, and each promontory at the sea's edge was crisscrossed with banks and ditches to frown out at the many marauding pirates. Every little river valley was lined with small forts like those at Treffgarne. Iron Age technology was not restricted to the new metal, though this was important enough; the first Welsh in Wales had the wheel with which to throw a pot or drive a chariot. Their plough was heavier, so lowland areas came under cultivation and bigger and more extensive 'Celtic Fields' replaced the old forests, fields which are still a significant part of the landscape, where bulldozers, or eighteenth century land clearance, open field or Saxon strip have not overlain them or wiped them out altogether.

The Celts had a talent for design and craftsmanship unique in European art. Their poets were famous. At their great gatherings, fore-runners of the *Eisteddfodau,* tales were told and retold, the holy men, descended in spirit from those first astronomer-priests of the Stone Age, still studied the stars, could fortell events (as one Roman observer noted of the Druids) 'by the Pythagorean reckoning and calculations'—for we now had the odd eyewitness who has left us tantalizing word pictures of our otherwise pre-Historic ancestors. Their knowledge of the stars and of mathematics would not be bettered until Galileo's time, though they now no longer worshipped in the old stone temples but in sacred groves of oak trees. Everything had a name, a story; every night the firesides in our hilltop villages would be humming with the telling-of-tales which was eventually to come down to us, much altered, in poetry, song or legend such as the 'Mabinogi'.

The Romans heard about this land of great rainfall . . . and greater riches—were they not known to them as the Tin Islands? And there was copper, lead, and . . . gold. In 55 B.C. Julius Caesar explored, briefly, and officially put Britain into the Empire . . . but it wasn't until 43 A.D. that we were brought, protesting, into the Roman system. The warlike tribes were forced out of their hilltop sites into 'civilisation' and lowland towns. We spoke our own local dialect, and Latin was the official language. A new religion, Christianity, began to replace the pantheon of gods and goddesses which

the Romano-British people had teeming in the heavens and the underworld; each god or goddess became a saint; old wells whose waters had cured diseases in the name of a pagan deity were now 'St ***'s well', often with the pagan story and ritual, and time of year still intact (St Leonard's Well, St Justinian, St Bride). Carmarthen was a Roman garrison, near the leadmines at Llangunnor or the gold of Dolaucothi. Up in the hills lay camps like Y Pigwn, wet wild places which must have been terrible for the warm-loving Roman garrison! As the centuries rolled by and Roman law lapsed, town centres becoming deserted, excessive taxation and inflation, the movement of middle class families into suburbs or villas, we started to see the end of that civilisation nibbling at our edges . . . warlike tribes like the Vandals, Visigoths, Jutes and Saxons poured into this part of the Roman Empire . . . and it started to crumble. Some time towards the end of the Roman period, a retired Romanised Celtic soldier living at Nevern died and was buried under a stone which still exists—with its moving inscription recording that he was 'Discharged with Honour' and the language is not Welsh, but Irish. In the Dark Age which followed the Roman period, this part of the world became an Irish colony, as our many Ogham inscriptions testify.

After the Romans, then, came a certain amount of disorder, some total chaos, although occasionally there must have been spots where Roman life went on almost unchanged for centuries; but dynasties of local kings took over, and we were now speaking a babel of dialects, Saxon and Latin and Welsh and Danish and Irish and Flemish, a mix which ended, eventually (and after a powerful injection of Norman French) as the language of Chaucer and Shakespeare. West Wales is a cauldron of such linguistic delights, which makes any research endlessly

Roman oil lamp—Fuelled with oil from fish or olive, an example of 2000-year-old mass production—for the Romans were great consumers; they liked good food, central heating, lots of hot water and plenty of slaves to make it all work . . . but the slaves were US . . .

varied. Our various pagan gods and goddesses struggled to survive the coming of the Christian church, and got themselves sainted in the process. In this age, so often called Dark, great churches were built, great men like David preached and thought; David had his spartan cell in Menevia and was always under threat from Danish pirates until Boia, an even bigger rogue than they, took David and his followers under his rough Irish wing, even becoming converted to Christianity in the process, to the fury of his wife and family living in the fort still called Clegyr Boia after him. So now Britain's smallest city and loveliest cathedral stands close by the citadel of their unlikely benefactor.

All around our coastline, Danish names are to be found. Angle, Skokholm, Skomer, Dale, Milford . . . a memory of those fierce warrior sailors who tyrannized the seas for centuries after the Romans left. Their descendants the Norsemen or Normans eventually colonised this country on a more permanent basis, led by the Duke of Normandy; William the Conqueror made a pilgrimage to St Davids in 1081, the year after the Bishop's two sons had been killed by pirates; Britain's westerly coast was still a dangerous place to live; William came past that not quite forgotten Roman soldier at Nevern, which lies on the Pilgrims' way to the great cathedral on the edge of the world . . .

Foel Drygarn—'The Bare Hill with Three Burials'— Bronze age burial mounds from 1500 B.C., surrounded a thousand years later by the great fortress of the first Welsh in Wales, over two hundred huts spilling out down the hillside to make it the most impressive in this part of Britain . . . was it the giant-king Ysbaddaden's castle, home of the lovely Olwen? . . .

Celandines open their bright golden petals only in sunlight, they can 'See'; our Saxon ancestors thought this a sign from God that they'd cure 'Mistiness of the Eyes', and introduced the plant to Britain for medicinal purposes; gardeners now suffer!

Norman life and influence brought new ideas about law and order, as well as French, which would have been a headache to those already here, with their bubbling babel of tongues; the Normans liked building in stone rather than wood, so after their initial Motte and Bailey castles of earth were consolidated, they usually had a topknot of stone added, which in time would become the keep of a castle. For the earliest mottes you have to visit Rudbaxton, New Moat, Wolf's Castle or Eglwys-wrw just to name a few of the hundred or so earthen mounds we have left over from the conquest most of us know best from the Bayeux Tapestry. They seem to have been abandoned fairly soon after the invasion of 1066 and our own smaller one of 1084, and so never had their wooden castle replaced with stone as at Wiston or Nevern, each with its impressive bailey or bank and ditch defence which the Iron Age Celts would have recognised instantly (indeed, many of them would have claimed it as their own, as most of our forts are on prime sites, and have been used again and again). The Dark Ages were over, the medieval period was about to begin; mottes got curtain walls, keeps, gatehouses, walls, towers and all the elaborate panoply of the castle proper. Not just fortresses, but serviceable fortified homes were now the order of the day, for the upper classes anyway,—as usual, peasants were supposed to get along as best they could . . .

Gateholm from the air—In the late evening light you can just make out the collapsed walls and sunken ways of an early Christian settlement from about 600 A.D.—but it has a Viking name . . . *Gata = Holmi* or 'The Island beyond a gap' (a reference to Gateholm's being isolated twice a day by the tide).

11

Hedd and Isaac's memorial, St Davids Cathedral—
The Vikings were here—and murdered the two sons of
the Bishop of St Davids in 1080; William the
Conqueror saw this grave when he came here on
pilgrimage next year . . .

Returning Crusaders brought back ideas as well as
the rabbit and the oboe; Pembroke Castle has well-
made rightangled entrances of a sort designed by
the Infidel to resist a battering ram, copied by the
Marshalls when they got home; the keep now
occupies the site once humped by the motte, when
the castle was '. . . a slender fortress of stakes and
earth . . .' The military men were joined in their
castle building by some of Wales' battling Bishops,
and Llawhaden evolved; the Church Militant was a
reality in those turbulent times, chronicled so well
by Gerald de Barri, 'Giraldus Cambrensis'; he
walked among the turmoil, saw and recorded the
fights and political intrigues, the marriages of his
relations more for land than love, the battles of his
relatives, the kings and princes, as well as the ignor-
ance, bigotry, fear and superstition which was a
part of life for all, high or low born, until fairly
recently.

From now on building was more substantial, the
land saw the lines of castles, the churches, the great
cathedrals; we saw the patterns of agriculture
changing, the strip fields of the Saxons giving way
to the Open Fields of the early medieval period; we
saw trade opening up, the formation of boroughs
and walled towns, built at a time when many nobles
had private armies, when civil war was common-
place, and piracy an everyday affair. The great
Pembrokeshire trio of seaports—Pembroke, Tenby
and Haverfordwest, vying with each other for
centuries as to who would pull in the biggest
amount of trade. There were towns like Kenfig,
which were at one time important, then vanished
under the shifting sand of time and geology. The
town of Newport (Pemb.) was large, bustling and
important long before Newport (Mon.) was any
more than a straggling village, waiting for its turn
to come with coal, the railway and the steamship.

Industry, of course, has been with us since the
earliest days. The stone-axe making Neolithic men,
the Bronze Age traders of faience or jet or amber,
were as much industrialists as those Romano-
British miners who toiled beneath the ground for
lead or gold, cruelly treated by soldiers specially
chosen so they could not speak to their victims . . .
we spoke Welsh, the guards spoke Latin or
Spanish. Iron and glassmaking prospered in

Cosheston from the air—Typical Saxon strip fields around this South Pembrokeshire village, signs of farming from about 600-700 A.D.—sadly, these are now vanishing, modern farming technology hates hedgerows . . .

Roman times along with bricks, pottery and metal-working. Mills worked by wind or water power ground flour or lead ore, crushed furze for cattle-food; some tide mills survived for centuries, getting their power free, as we might still do today, made sturdily in the medieval period to get momentum from the moon . . . you can still see one working at Carew. Industries were essentially local, cottage-based, until the steam engine arrived, clustering everybody within its reach by networks of shafts and pulleys, and the Manufactory had arrived.

To begin with, farming continued side by side with weaving or milling corn, or coal mining, smelting a bit of iron or working some slate or granite . . . local works serving local needs, and small surplusses could be traded with the Captains of the myriads of little ships which were our main source of trade—and gossip!—until they were killed off by the coming of the railway.

Roman Glass Jug

Roman scent vessels—made from bronze, to decorate a lady's dressing-table, two thousand years ago. The Romans came to Britain because of our non-ferrous metals—they called us the 'Tin Islands', mined copper, lead and gold from this part of Wales.

Misery on a misericord—Sea-sickness makes everyone
laugh except the sufferer, and here is that awful joke
carved under a cleric's folding seat in the choir of St
Davids Cathedral. The medieval carvers were given a
free hand in subject-matter as these extra seats (which
allowed mercy to elderly and arthritic clerics during the
interminable services—you LOOKED as if you were
standing, but could take the weight off your feet) could
not be carved with any religious subject matter. So we
have Green Men, quarelling husbands and wives, dogs
fighting over bones, men building boats . . . and the
horror of a stormy journey by sea . . .

A lot of this book will concern itself with sea
trading. Our heavily indented coastline is dotted
with ports, large and small . . . maybe vast like
Milford or tiny like Port Einon or Porthclais.
Inland ports like Carmarthen or Haverfordwest
grew rich and remained so for centuries as ships
large and small plied the oceans of the world for
spices, cloth, wood, food and drink, metals, coal,
candlewax or the hundreds of things we now take
for granted on our supermarket shelves. Look at a
town like Cardigan or Cydweli and you will see
signs of past greatness; good building, fortified, a
rich church, remains of quays for the shipping.

15

These ports prospered from Norman times onwards, often places, like Ogmore, at the lowest fording points of rivers, or where the tide flowed high enough to bring seagoing ships of large burthen, as at Haverfordwest. There would be spread out silks from the Orient, cinnamon and cloves in sweet-smelling casks, wine in barrels, brandy in kegs, silver and carved wood and scented oils, enticing merchant and consumer alike. Also the Tax-man, anxious then as now to get his share, or slightly more than his share, for the Sovereign. A thriving industry grew up to cheat him of his dues, piracy and smuggling became an important part of Welsh industrial life! So came haughty, bad tempered Sir John Perrott, with a great house in Haverfordwest as well as Carew Castle, hauled up before the Privy Council to answer for his alleged piracy and incarcerated in the Tower while he waited . . . he was Queen Elizabeth I's illegitimate brother, so maybe that helped him get away with it, that time . . . There are places with mysterious names, too, like Tobacco Cave near Solva, darkly recessed out of sight with a steep path leading down to it. Nearby, there was deliberate wrecking of fine trading ships on the horribly dangerous coastline— too bad if you were crew or passenger; you could not expect to escape, as the law said at that time that a ship only became common property once *every living soul had perished*. We found a ship like this remembered in song, and did serious damage to the BBC's listening figures by singing it, for 'Sou'wester', to wheezy squeezebox and violin accompaniment, in a wrecker's cave at Culver Hole, Gower.

Industry was the lifeblood of Wales once the Industrial Revolution had got under way, and we had pioneers a'plenty—Trevithick tried out his steam loco on the Penydarren tracks; Siemens pioneered his open-hearth steel process in Swansea, where his little laboratory building should form a fitting tribute to someone who helped make Swansea great. Robert Owen dreamed of social change and planned New Lanark, John Morris was building a castle (of a sort) high on a hill overlooking his copper works in the part of Swansea he named after himself, and we still call Morriston. Not a fort, this, or a grand home for one of the Top Brass, but a set of colliers' flats. Again, it's still there, now looked after by the City Council.

We had lords building canals, we had other lords sabotaging them by letting water out, if they had railway interests! We had Isambard Kingdom Brunel dreaming of great steamships at Milford and leaving us a unique railway system in this part of Wales, a tiny bit of which still exists in its original form at Treffgarne Gorge. Canalliana is not so common as elsewhere in the country, but we had Mrs Kymer's canal, we had a superb set of inclined planes remembered in a pub signboard at Pont Henry, with sleeper blocks and a winding house nearby to tell of its railway days later. Industry grew where motive power or natural resources were to be found. So the 'Mad German' found copper and water power at Aberdulais in Tudor times. The busy Cistercian monks found lead at Talley, iron and coal at Margam; great collieries sprang into use around the Gwendraeth Valley, in Carmarthenshire and right across the lower half of Pembrokeshire; there was iron at Stepaside or granite at Porthgain, bricks, slate, manganese, zinc, silver, all added to the riches of the wealthy, and made work for a lot of poor people without increasing their happiness by very much. New towns sprang up along with the industries—like 'New Town' Milford, planned by men who thought they would grow rich by whale oil, then used for lighting London's streets. Like Neyland, a railway town, or Pembroke Dock (a shipbuilding one), Swansea, a copper town and major port whose river ran polluted green . . . like Llechryd in northern Pembrokeshire, where Ben Hammett decided to build a mad little tinplate works miles from anywhere and, to keep up his own morale, built a mini-canal less than a mile long, and whose fish traps were wrecked by rioters. As industry came, transport increased in complexity and speed, the railways, spawned in their dozens during the great 'Railway Mania' of the 1840s along with the countless companies who fought over who should carry what, or whom. So the Great Western and the South Wales Railway were joined by the Pembroke and Tenby, the Whitland and Cardigan, the Rosebush, the Burry Port and Gwendraeth Valley, the Taff Vale, the Manchester and Milford . . . these and lots more make a delightful litany of tiny companies, mostly vanishing into the 'Big Four' in 1923, and into BR after the second World War.

War, of whatever period, has an archaeology of its own, often recognisable right through all periods of Man's history—the bank and ditch has been with us since Neolithic men put a thorn stockade around their farms to keep out wolves, or the Bronze Age men built boundary ditches with a bank their own side, the Iron Age Celts were terrifyingly efficient at this work, as their countless fortresses, crossdykes and promontory defences testify; Norman motte and bailey defences, the castles of the medieval period, the Victorian forts built against the French, right down to Goose Green and beyond, all have served the same purpose. Modern trends in warfare have left us seaplane hangars in Pembroke Dock, a secret 'spyplane' strip at Treffgarne, a camp for German prisoners-of War at Bridgend ... countless pillboxes now falling under the omnipresent bulldozer, tank traps along the railway line at Cydweli, even a strange concrete Thing near Neyland said to be something to do with the Third World War and Atomic bombs ... it's all archaeology.

Castell Mawr fort from the air—the central bank divided men from animals in this fortified camp built about 300 B.C., with its strong double bank and narrow entrance to slow down a cavalry charge (centre right). The air view shows much change over the centuries; small Celtic fields and long thin Saxon ones enlarged during the Enclosures, and made bigger still for modern machinery.

Angle boasts a fine anti-pirate Pele tower. But of course our Iron Age forts are the stars of this type of military construction, nigh on three hundred of them which will take the enthusiast a healthy lifetime to explore and enjoy, as no two are alike.

Religion, industry and travel, agriculture, warfare, trade; all these and more have left scars on our land, clues for you to follow up; everywhere you walk or ride is richly sprinkled with remains; cromlechs, dolmens, standing stones, forts, field systems; churches, castles and canals, railways and docks, mines and quarries, tracks and milestones and gibbets and suicides' graves, each with its folklore, its own story. 'Great Eastern Terrace' in Neyland commemorates Brunel's enormous steamship, six times bigger than anything else afloat, Llandeilo's Blende street recollects zinc working in the town; Milford's quakers left Starbuck Road and Nantucket Avenue. All these add to your enjoyment of our immensely rich store of history . . .

But . . .

Because we *are* so rich in remains there is a tendency for local authorities, landowners or industrialists to destroy or vandalize casually, on the grounds that ' . . . well, there's plenty more of this stuff, isn't there? . . . 'Why worry about this one? Surely one more or less cannot make any difference?' Well, it can and it does. For one thing, we do not own our land, we hold it in trust for our children, and they will for theirs—it is the ultimate nonrenewable resource. We lose thousands of miles of hedgerow, many old field systems and a lot of ancient woodland every year. The burial mounds, the cromlechs, all need looking after if they are to survive; even the strong banks and ditches of the Celtic hill forts are not putting up with the scraping of the tyres from scrambling motorcyclists. And we might remember that in an age when we seem to be running out of jobs for heavy industry we are, slowly but surely, improving our 'service industry' sector; and this includes holidays and leisure . . . people pay for nice places, they like and value peace and quiet . . . and this is where a lot of these ancient things now lie. They are worth, even in a monetarist way, something—people will not stay in a dead place. They like our landscape. They like our ancient stones, forts and ports, and will pay good money to be shown over them, to stay nearby while they walk an old canal or railway trackbed. So the more we throw away these fine and unique places, the more we are throwing away good money, as well as a priceless heritage for our descendants.

This is part of what being Civilised is all about. Giving us a sense of perspective, keeping our past.

Portrait of a Crusader?—This is how his contemporaries saw him; hardly the massacring villain, scourge of the Infidel . . . but a kindly, rather worried man we might meet anywhere today . . . 13th Century carving, St Davids Cathedral.

A sense of time or How long ago did you say?

Time scales are difficult things to understand, to get into the brain—a month can flash by or seem eternal, a year seems never ending (especially when you're young enough to look forward to your next birthday). A decade is worse, a century unimaginable ... how about a thousand or a hundred thousand? ...

Archaeology is usually dealing with thousands of years; remember?—it was history that never got written down, and has had to be dug up with a trowel—you see the 'experts' at it in their soggy trenches, and ask yourself, 'well, it's all very well, but how do they know it's that old?' Well, how do they? This is perhaps the first problem to try and solve.

Geologically speaking, Man is a new animal—we have only been around for about four million years, and for all but about ten thousand of those we have been a rare animal, eking out a primitive existence apart from the odd cave, scrabbling for nuts, killing passing fish or birds if they came our way, even trapping larger animals like tigers, bears or mammoths with pits or snares ... our tools the simplest bone or stone ... how we survived the Ice Ages I'll never know! This first, long age of Man is called the Palaeolithic, which means 'Old Stone Age'. Several species of hominid were around during that immense time, all of them in small numbers, and they have all but one died out; we are—so far—the exception.

About 8000 BC a group of slightly more advanced people arrived in Britain, using the little flakes from their flint knapping (you can see where they lived and worked at Nab Head), living, in primitive but serviceable leanto huts but otherwise hunting to make a living. They were still a very uncommon animal, and a lot may have got killed during the 'flood' of 5500 or so BC; so the next invaders had to come by boat. These people still used stone tools, but stone ground and polished as well as flaked and knapped. They found a land rich with game, warm, forested with thick oak and hazel scrub, the streams rich in fish, and only a few Mesolithic hunters to share it all with. They seem to have lived amicably enough, and intermarried, pro-

ducing a sub-culture archaeologists know as the Peterborough. Peterborough men and women seemed to inherit from their immediate ancestors of the Mesolithic a liking for travel, and became this society's traders and adventurers, never really settling down to the stay-in-one-place way of life demanded by farming. Neolithic men had axe 'factories' where tough stones were half shaped and roughed out before export to distant lands by the traders—there's one of these axe factories in the Preselis. The small fields were dug with sticks, not ploughs (which had yet to be invented, or an animal tamed enough to pull it when it was). The Neolithic (New Stone Age) people lived on undisturbed and in a state of total peace from about 3500 BC to about 2000 BC, when their calm lifestyle was disturbed slightly by the arrival of people of the Bronze Age, so called because they had mastered the complicated beginnings of metallurgy. And just as the Mesolithic people had mingled by intermarriage with their successors, so the Neolithic folk intermarried with the Bronze Age, or Beaker people (so called because of a distinctive drinking vessel they made, decorated with one particular wing-bone from a blackbird). Some of the older habits, knowledge and custom was absorbed by the newcomers, but their religion, particularly their burial customs, was quite different; whereas the Neolithic people had buried their dead comunally in a long mound of earth, usually with a 'business end' of stone which now forms a cromlech, the Bronze Age people buried the dead individually. But the making of stone rings and lines, its mathematics and symbolism, flourished in the early Bronze Age as never before; Stonehenge and Avebury were finished then, Carn Meini quarried for its Bluestones, and Gors Fawr finished. The bank and ditch was not only being used for defence by Bronze Age people, but placed around their round burial mounds—interestingly, the bank was always placed *outside* the ditch, showing the thinking ... they were protecting us, the living, from what might be the unwelcome attentions of the dead within the barrow.

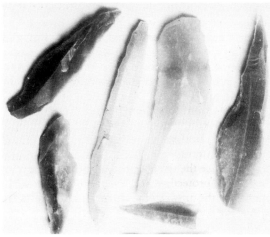

Nab head, St Bride's Bay—A scatter of flints on Nab Head was dropped by people living here 8000 years ago, before the water swept in to make St Bride's Bay. The little promontory fort in the foreground is one of many built in the Iron age (300 B.C.) to protect the coast from pirates. Their fertility goddess Brigantia became St Bride once Christianity arrived, but her feast days survived in Candlemas and Valentine. St Bride's tiny church is on the far right of this air view.

Group of flint implements—from the Mesolithic site at Nab Head; flint is not native to this part of Britain and had to come from Ireland or the chalky areas of Southern or Eastern England. These delicate flakes were made into fish hooks, saws, knives or arrow heads 8000 years ago.

St. David's cathedral, home of our patron saint, centre of pilgrimage and of Celtic Christianity during the medieval period, and still attracting millions of modern pilgrims every year; hiding deep in its valley to avoid pirates in its first days, even the tower was only built as far as the first string-course above the nave level, lest it be noticed by marauding Vikings.

Tall Stones to Make You Remember . . .

. . . A Bronze-age farmer reminding his gods to keep his fields fertile,
four thousand years ago; a retired Roman soldier, "discharged with
honour," whose name is written in the mysterious Irish script, Ogham;
the Dark-age king responsible for this magnificent Celtic cross, and St.
David himself, represented in stone on the screen of his cathedral (Waun
Mawr, Nevern, Carew, St. David's, resp.)

Bronze age Palstave—or battle axe; made by warrior farmers who lived here from about 2000 B.C. onwards; the people who finished Stonehenge, and traded with the Near East . . . a very different Britain from that of the peaceful cromlech-builders . . .

Fertility at St Non's—This stone has stood here for about four thousand years, one of a group set in newly cleared fields in the Bronze age, and intended to send a message to the gods—'please make these fields fertile . . .' Such is the power of custom that it is STILL there, in the age of the combine and the chemical; some are now rubbing stones for cattle, some gateposts . . . but they are still THERE, often with a name catching the ghost of their first use.

Then about 600 BC the Celts arrived, with their horses, their iron smelting, their wheel-made pots and their chariots, their finely woven and well dyed cloth, the women with their hair well done with bone or wooden combs, and plaited about their ears, some carrying a handbag made of moss fibre . . . all of them had their bodies painted amazing colours, many riding horses whose snorting, steaming breath and connection with the fires started by the Celtic warriors, soon got turned by popular imagination into dragons. The Celts are the builders of the fine crop of hill forts we have in this part of Wales. Their improved plough got down to making our first really good fields, surrounding these hilltop castles. Speaking an ancestral form of Welsh, these people were here from about 600 BC

to about 43 AD, and some of them lived on undisturbed throughout the next step in the history of this island—the coming of the Romans.

Now try to put that time-scale in perspective. We can think back to the birth of Christ, about two thousand years ago . . . now, the Bronze Age invasion was as long before the Roman period, and the birth of Jesus, as we are after it. To get back to the first civilisation of the Neolithic arrivals, with their little huts, digging sticks, the first primroses and rowan trees, pottery and lovely polished stone axes, is almost as long again. We have our ideas about history largely because we think only of 'schoolbook' history, largely kings and queens of fairly recent times—the industrial period gets a good showing nowadays, and as for the Victorians and after, they are almost embarrassingly well covered, in more ways than one. We are not an animal that enjoys change, this is one thing history seems to show; it took millions of years to make the better point on the hand-axe, it took thousands to evolve proper ploughs and the first science, that of star-gazing for calendars and navigation. Yet in the years since the last war we have seen ever increasing rates of change, rates for which our minds simply cannot rearrange themselves quickly enough. Now, no sooner do you buy something than it is out of date, no sooner are you familiar with a concept, it is obsolescent. What we are going to do about this once change *really* starts moving, I boggle to think.

But one thing about history is not only the feeling of perspective, but the inevitable thought, 'Oh yes, I've heard this happening before . . .': even our present economic troubles have happened before, and knowing the mistakes people made in previous times ought to help us sort it out now.

*   *   *

Four thousand years ago . . . a ditch was dug to mark a Bronze-age farm boundary; though it gradually silted up, it is still *there*, and could be found and excavated— in its silt lie clues about our ancestors, from fragments of pottery and bone to flint flakes and even pollen grains, telling what lived here when that farm was new . . . And any plant or animal fragments can be dated accurately using the Carbon-14 technique.

Those are the perspectives, but how about the Dates? There they are, written out, but there was no writing for the better part of history, so how do we know we can rely on the Experts? To start with, of course, they didn't know accurately either, all they could do was to dig, and then to presume that something in a deeper level was older than something nearer the surface. An occasional pot fragment or other clue tied a site in Britain with one of the Near Eastern civilisations, and we had a real written date ... or thought we had. The trouble, though, with written history, is that it is so often faked, for one reason or another; political, religious, family or personal gain—paper is unreliable. The absolute dating techniques, when they became available after the last war really made archaeology understandable at last.

Radiocarbon dating is one of the best known, and the earliest. Every living thing has carbon making up part of each molecule—you realise this when you burn the toast! Carbon, the black stuff in pencils and on the burned toast, normally has an atomic weight of 12 units; it's known as Carbon-12. But high up in the stratosphere, powerful atomic particles called cosmic rays hit Nitrogen atoms, which have an atomic weight of 14, and convert them into Carbon-14. Now, this variety of carbon looks, feels, acts just like its lighter brother, but it is not stable, eventually it decays away, giving off a flash of radiation in the process which can be detected by a geiger counter. Carbon-14 is being formed all the time in the upper atmosphere, soon gets converted to carbon dioxide and comes to earth, gets taken up along with carbon-12 in plants during photosynthesis, and the grass, or whatever it is gets eaten by animals, ending up as part of tigers and lions and you and me! So, you and I and every thing on earth, while it is alive, is slightly radioactive with carbon-14. Now, this is not the harmful radiation we hear so much about, it is a very low level of a very weak, natural substance. But it is very useful to archaeologists. When anything, plant or animal, dies, it ceases to take up carbon-14, which slowly starts to decay away, losing half its mass every five and half thousand years or so. So if you had a pound of carbon-14 and left it for 5568 years, then remeasured it, there would be half a

pound left. Putting it more scientifically, the radioactivity dies away to half its value over 5568 years—this is the half life about which we hear so much from the atomic energy people. So, measure the radioactivity of a bone or a leaf or a nut, compare it with results you already have for modern material, and you have an absolute, unfakable date for your bone, or whatever ... This, briefly, is radiocarbon dating, and it is improving all the time.

Thermoluminescence or the glowing pot in the pan

Radioactivity plays an important part, too, in dating pottery by a process called thermoluminescence. This is information carried within the pottery itself. Tiny amounts of radioactivity (largely uranium) in the original clay fire off atomic particles which lodge as energy, to be stored within the clay matrix; when the clay is heated, this 'fixes' the clay and starts the clock. As time goes by, the continual disintegration of the radioactive material results in a build up of this energy, its amount depending upon how long the pot is left unheated ... for a Roman pot it might be nearly two thousand years, until today. Then, when the pot (or powdered fragments of it) is heated to a temperature just below dull red heat, this energy is suddenly released as an eery blue glow, the amount proportional to the date since last firing. It may sound crazy, but it is quite accurate, and there is enough light from, say, a Bronze Age pot to read a newspaper by for a second or so!

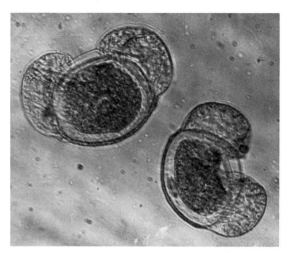

Pine pollen grains—recognisable by their size and shape—but the tree was growing in Roman times, the grains were trapped in a ditch as it silted up . . . Magnified 250 times.

Roman glass vase—Buried glass gets a dullish patina on it which, under the microscope, proves to be bands a bit like tree rings (one season's burial per band) so they can be counted to reveal the number of years the vessel has spent in the soil.

Samian pottery was the 'Woolworths' of its day— every Roman home had lots of this bright red ware, it was used for everything, was easily replaced and so lots got thrown away on every site. This pot has trapped in it information about how long ago it was fired, and a technique called *thermoluminescence* can make it reveal its secret.

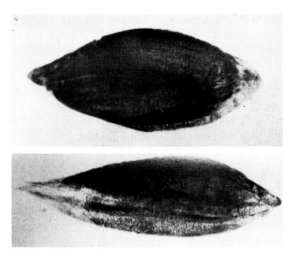

Carbonised cereal grains—of Einkorn (*Triticum, monococcum*, top) from an early Bronze-age hut site and Emmer wheat (*Triticum dicoccum*, bottom) found during excavations in a late Neolithic deposit. Both gave clues about farming technique, our eating habits in the past, and of the dates of the levels in which they were found, thanks to the 'clock' ticking in Carbon-14.

Both grains X5

And there are tree rings . . .

One of the objections which many historians, and nearly all non-historians, have to radiocarbon and thermoluminescence is that the dates they provide are not Absolute—they cannot say 'This pot was made in 3246 BC' but rather 'This pot may have been made about 3230 BC plus or minus forty years'. This objection does not apply to tree ring dating or *dendrochronology*. If you look at a cross-section of a log, its rings go back from 'this year' (on the outside of the trunk) to whenever the tree first grew—for a yew, about a thousand. In that time the climate gave hot dry summers, when the tree didn't grow much, or warmish wet ones, when it grew a lot; the pattern, once analysed (these days by computer) can be recognised in trees from a wide variety of places, and a variety of species too.

Suppose you look at an old tree growing today—you can count back, a year at a time, to about 1700.

If you then find a tree which was cut down, say about 1750, to make the roof timbers of a house, you'll find the same pattern on its *outer* rings, as the *inner* rings on your modern specimen. This tree in turn may take you back, year by year, to 1500, and so on, with patience, as far as your trees can be traced. Using this dating technique on one particular species, the Bristlecone pine of the USA, has proved invaluable to setting up other peoples' chronologies, as this ancient tree lives for anything up to three thousand *years!*

Plants in our past

One of the most fascinating types of detective work which is done in archaeology is the microscopic examination of pollen grains. Pollen lasts a very long time under the right soil conditions, as it has a hard outer case which seems not to decompose or deform, even after thousands of years. Every species of plant has a different shape and size of pollen grain, so that by looking at a magnified sample of ancient soil you will be able to tell what was in flower at that time, and in what quantity. This, in turn, should tell you at what time of year a particular monument was constructed; was it in a grassy clearing or in a wood which has now vanished?; was it damp or dry? Examination of soil samples at various levels in, say, the filling of a ditch, will tell us if there was a change in climate during the time that ditch was naturally silting up. The sudden and unexpected appearance of a plant may indicate that it was introduced deliberately (primroses have been found to have been brought in by the New Stone Age Megalith builders, as was the rowan; poppy and speedwell by the Bronze Age people; hemlock and blackthorn by the Celts; and alexanders, fennel, thyme and a host of culinary and medicinal herbs by the Romans).

Other plant remains which are also found in archaeological 'digs' include seeds and pips, nuts, carbonised grain and charcoal; occasionally you will find an impression of a piece of stem, or a leaf, in some pottery—another clue to add to the heap, trying to make some sense of your ancestors and mine.

25

A Stone age snack . . .—In the right conditions, many kinds of plant fragments remain preserved among prehistoric debris—pollen, charcoal, bone and leaf fragments, even the spores from fungi. This odd object is *Helvella crispa*, which may look awful but is edible and delicious—it seems our ancestors thought so too . . .

Wet sponge cake

We think of pottery as hard, just as it is now when you buy it. After a thousand years or more in the soil, it may look just like pottery still, but it can be the consistency of wet sponge cake; iron objects can have disappeared entirely, be a mere stain in clay or sand, or a conglomerated nodule of stuff which only careful X-raying will reveal as a sword or a plough-share. Wood (as was seen by everyone on the 'Mary Rose' excavation) can be nearly perfect, or so soft it crumbles at a touch. Sometimes there are clues so odd it's hard to take them seriously, like the presence of one particular snail which occurs only where there has been a burial, as it liked feeding off the carcase. It is somewhat gruesomely known as the 'Coffin Snail', and is a very useful animal indeed if the rest of the body, including the bones, has leached away into the soil. The hyphae of a particular breed of fungus, again, indicates that once there was rotting flesh present, another clue to follow up.

Objects which have lasted for centuries under earth or water, can start to drop to pieces quite quickly once exposed to the air. So the next job is conservation where wooden objects, leather sandals, bows and arrows, are slowly leached of salt water, if present, then impregnated with a special water-soluble wax which makes them strong, while the water is removed by freeze drying. Metal objects can be put in an ultrasonic bath to buzz off all the dirt and mess; or they can have a weak electric current passed through an acid bath, when, again, the bits and pieces gradually unstick, leaving the original object in fine condition—if you're lucky!

Finally . . .

We are richly endowed with remains of our ancestors; every year more turn up; we might be forgiven for thinking that no damage can be done by a 'bit of digging about to see what I can find . . .' (this has been said to me on more than one occasion after an archaeological lecture, and it is very disheartening). You see, it is not always the object itself that matters, interesting though this may be; it is where it was found, associated with what bits and pieces in the soil. A coin on its own is just a coin, in its own level of history it is a document. And though it sounds odd to say so, any site, *every* site can only be dug once; put a spade or trowel in the ground and there is no way the soil can ever look the same again, and this is why many digs are only done as a

An Iron age Hut—being carefully cleaned during excavations at Knock Rath, Pembs. A 'dig' isn't just to reveal huts, graves, ditches or fortifications, intriguing though these are—the earth is examined for the minutest detail, down to microscopic level, for the clues it can give to the past of our species.

last resort. We know our techniques are getting better all the time, but if we are not careful, we may have destroyed all the best sites before our descendants come along, and they will have none of the fun we can, which is hardly fair. Metal detectors, used by trained—or, at least, considerate—operators, can be most useful; used on their own they are a menace, as they lead to destruction of much valuable and indeed unique evidence. Treasure hunting is not what archaeology is about. And it's not half so much fun as the Real Thing!

Now to the book; we have barely scratched the surface of this part of Wales to get some interesting sites together; but there is at least one example of each major type, and lists of others you may like to visit. We have tried to tell their story; where they fit in; how to get to them; and who to ask for permission to visit, if they are on private land. Because all land belongs to *somebody*. Some sites are not safe without special precautions—this applies to a number of clifftop or industrial sites . . . and on no account should you ever go below ground unless you have told someone else you are going, and unless you have a hard hat, and a companion.

Good visiting! The Secrets are now about to Open!

The Dean and the Red Lady

. . . Cheery, humourous, bustling, full of elegance . . . seldom without his blue bag, whence, even at fashionable dinner parties, he would bring out and describe, amidst the surprise and laughter of the audience, the last find from a Bone-cave . . .

Thus, one of the people at such a dinner party describes the merry Dean of Oxford, the Rev Buckland, one of many ghosts which whisper around the edges of Welsh archaeology. The Dean was a man of the robust eighteenth century who lived into the pretentious nineteenth, born among the Georgians, a cleric of Victoria; in his time the first great rumblings of evolution would resound, Huxley and Darwin calling down every kind of wrath on their heads for suggesting that the beginnings of the world were not, literally, as described in Genesis. Dean Buckland was in the centre of all this, and you can still visit one of the sites about which controversy raged so long ago, and which is still not entirely dead. This is the cave at Paviland, on Gower.

Thirty thousand years ago, in a coldish gap in the Ice Ages, lived a family of your ancestors and mine —in this little cleft in the Carboniferous limestone they could shelter from the weather, cook, bring up children, on a steep slope overlooking not the sea as now, but a plain—part forest, part grass. Your ancestor would have seen herds of mammoth, woolly rhinoceros, he would have looked down upon the giant Irish elk, a kind of deer eight foot high at the shoulder and with a twelve foot spread of antlers. His cave would have been disputed for ownership by some tough customers, for those were the days of the sabre-toothed tiger, the cave lion and cave bear. The nights would have been full of the harsh call of hyaena, packs of wolves roamed, hunting down the nimble wild horses among the oaks

Paviland cave Gower—The burial place for the 'Red Lady' (who was a man); when 'she' lived and died here, there was no sea, just a slope overlooking a forest spreading as far as the eye could see. If *you* go exploring in places like this, remember what happened to the film crew . . .

and willows. The men and women who lived in this cave might be primitive by our standards, but they thought the same way, their fears are ours still— their skills were amazing, as archaeologists found when they excavated Goat's Hole, as it is known locally; they made scrapers, borers and knives of flint, to help in their hunting down on the plain, they even had small eating utensils called spatulae; they decorated themselves with necklaces of pierced wolves' teeth, reindeer too; even pendants— surprisingly modern looking ones—from the pulp cavity of a mammoth's tooth. The people were scarce animals, our ancestors of the Ice Age; about five hundred people in the whole of Britain . . . but this south-facing cliff edge had several families sheltering from the rain in clefts now called Bacon Hole, Cat's Hole, Long Hole, so for Old Stone Age times this was a highly populated place!

We know what they saw in plant terms, from analysis of the pollen of those which were in flower. Charred bones show what they ate, along with shells from hazel nuts and pips from berries . . . but what of their thinking, their dreams, the things which made them humans? That came with death, and their attitude to it. Death, then as now a frightening mystery, a loss of one you know, and thoughts about the possibilities of rebirth or of other lives than this elsewhere, possibly in the sky . . . all this seems to have occurred to our remote forbears. For in Paviland's little colony, a young man died . . . he was about 19 . . . his relatives buried him as we still bury our dead three hundred centuries later, his body aligned with the passage of the sun across the sky, and the hope that with the rebirth of the sun next day, his rebirth to another life might take place too. His family covered the dead young body with a reddish clay crushed and sprinkled as a representation of life-blood. His corpse was then covered up, and life continued above his head, more meals were cooked, more bones strewn, nuts cracked.

And this is what Dr. Buckland found when he excavated the tomb in 1823. By then Buckland was a noted theologian, wrote copiously (he published sixty-six papers and many books in his lifetime); he

29

had ridden all over the country, great horseback odysseys covering thousands of miles, to make the first-ever Geological maps. He was a respected Fellow of the Geological Society, held the chair of mineralogy at Oxford, and used his flair for show-biz when lecturing:

> ... at this meeting of the Bristol Association, the fire of the evening was a lecture of Buckland's; in that part of his discourse which treated of ichtholites—fossil footprints—the Doctor exhibited himself as a deer, on the edge of a muddy pond, making impressions by lifting one leg after the other. Many of the Grave People present thought our science was altered to buffoonery by an Oxford Don ...

Buckland's little blue bag was soon filled with mammoth and deer and rhino and lion bones, he found the little pendant of mammoth tooth, the beads of wolves' teeth, all the evidence lay before him as he gazed at the skeleton of the young man buried so long before—and his is the classic story of evidence being no good if it arrives before its time. For the good Doctor was a Dean in the days when orthodox religious thinking was still that of the Bishop of Armagh. So when Dean Buckland wrote his book, in which the finds at Paviland were described, he called it Reliquae Deluvianae, relics of the Flood ... for Bishop Ussher had produced, by goodness alone knows what means, a timetable for humanity's beginnings which stated that man was created at 9.30 a.m. on the 26 October 4004 BC. Before Buckland's eyes was indisputable evidence that a man, who was contemporary with animals known to have been extinct for thousands of years, had been buried and the layer in which his body lay, sealed ... Buckland the scientist, Buckland the geologist, knew this. But it was Buckland the Dean who won that mental battle. The writer of 'The Power, Wisdom and Goodness of God as manifested in the Creation' (1836) who only four years before had discovered and named the flying reptile the Pterodactyl, now stated that the young man in Paviland was a young woman, probably of Romano-British age (there is a small fort of that period just above the cave).

I wonder if it was a split in his own thinking which later led the merry Dean to become melancholic and to his nervous breakdown three years after being made Dean of Westminster. His blue bag produced no more amusing items from his diggings, and he died, aged 72, in 1856. His writings were excellent and well researched, humorous and witty, scholarship mingled with an amused view of the world. Yet he could force himself to get the date wrong of the ochre-covered figure, wrong by thirty thousand years—but that he got the sex wrong too is almost unbelievable ... and the young man became, and is still known as The Red Lady of Paviland.

In 1860 the Great Western Railway produced a book to encourage their readers to explore the region by the new railway trains—in it they say of Paviland:

> At Paviland there are two bone-caves, described by Dr. Buckland in 'Diluviae Reliquinae'; in them are found recent shells or bones of elephant, rhinoceros, bear, fox, hyaena, wolf, horse, deer, ox, rats and birds, besides the skeleton of a female, probably coeval with the British Camp on the summit, fragments of ivory, ornaments; these caves are difficult of access from the cliffs ...

The evidence as interpreted by the Dean; but the access description was certainly right. Much more recently a film crew who were making a documentary about Old Stone age Britain got caught by the tide and had to scramble for it, leaving thousands of pounds worth of camera equipment to get filled with salty water. If you should visit the place where the 'Red Lady' lived and died, remember that film crew's troubles and watch out! ...

Hoyle's Mouth Cave Tenby

If you go to Bosherston village in South Pembrokeshire, you will find a large boulder there of granite quite unfamiliar to the area—hardly surprising since it's from Scotland! Climb Carn Llidi near St Davids or explore the rocks of Strumble Head near Fishguard, look at those scratches on the rocks made by glaciers' movement ... those drowned valleys like Solva or Milford Haven ... made by melting waters from the Ice age—and that boulder came down in ice, too.

The men who endured what must have been a chilly existence found some sort of shelter in caves

Hoyle's Mouth Cave—A Victorian couple exploring Hoyle's Mouth before its excavation to reveal the leftovers of men and women who lived here some twenty five thousand years ago. One wonders if the lady ought to be clambering about such places in her delicate condition ...

like Paviland and as their remains were found also during the excavations for Cromwell Road and Trafalgar Square in London, they must have lived there, too, as well as at Hoyle's Mouth! Hereabouts in Pembrokeshire, at Nanna's Cave on Caldey, at Priory Farm and Catshole Quarry, our ancestors

31

watched a land as bleak as Siberia, and their neighbours were animals totally alien to our thinking of British fauna nowadays . . . among the dry tundra grasses and the pines, crashing through stunted bushes of nuts and berries which our ancestors grubbed about in for food, were reindeer, mammoth, woolly rhinoceros, cave bear and cave lion, hyaena and the enormous Irish elk. For about fifteen thousand years the cave was visited by the odd, rare animal Man, eking out his short, harsh existence with his simple tools of bone and stone, making fish-hooks and spear heads and handaxes. If you stood here as he did 25,000 years ago you would have seen scattered hazels, sedges, moss grazed by the reindeer, scattered every now and again by a marauding lion. Moor grass, pine and birch whined in the icy arctic winds which were cold even in the short summer. And you wrapped the skin of some animal around you even tighter to try and keep out the cold. We had at least control of fire, so we had the chance of keeping warm and frightening off other animals. The men who lived here were the culture known as Creswellian, their tools were scrapers, graving tools and a sort of short penknife blade made of stone flakes. The bones of animals were found in among the debris of their floors. These men buried their dead as carefully as we do (see Paviland); they liked ornament and had necklets of wolves' teeth and pendants of mammoth's tusk cut through.

But the climate was changing, and aeons later more men lived here, still miles from the sea but under warmer, wetter conditions and with red deer, ox and pig roaming a richer forest of poplar, juniper and willow, and softer grasses rustled with foxes. This was about 8000 BC, and these final Old-Stone-age men and women must have wondered at a new type of man invading their territory, men with much finer implements of flint flakes, fish-hooks, arrowheads, borers and saws, men who did not need their old cave as they had invented the first man-made house, men who had domesticated the dog . . . hunters too, but the people of the Middle Stone age had moved across from Europe. This low lying area of South Pembrokeshire was to become warmer still, and the Middle Stone-age men's descendants were to roam through golden warm glades of oak and cherry and raspberry, elm and lime smelling sweet in the warm spring sun. They would be the people who would witness that terrible catastrophe when the low-lying rich land was swept into nothingness by a great Flood, whose folk memory comes down to us in Genesis and the Sumerian Tales of Gilgamesh, the Welsh tale of Seithennyn and . . . Atlantis . . .

Carn Meini from the air—Like a giant question-mark on the landscape, this unique outcrop of igneous rock is the source for Stonehenge's 'Blue-Stones'. The 'Golden Way' prehistoric track passes nearby (far left), the faint smudge of an earthen circle can just be made out below the farthest carn. The remains of partly finished stones are still to be found about the quarry site (centre right). Stonehenge is 165 miles to the south, and the stones' transport must be one of the great epics of prehistoric people.

Bluestones and Black Night

Not far from Foel Drygarn is an outcrop of gaunt dark stones which have welded themselves firmly into British folklore. Their journey, their story and the power they seem to have exerted over our ancestors has survived four and a half thousand years in two countries, and the odyssey of their travels is still being argued over by scholars. But anyone who doesn't feel impressed by his ancestors and their feats of engineering, after a visit to Carn Meini (Place of Stones in a pile) is very hard to impress.

Antiquaries, archaeologists and visitors to Stonehenge generally, have long known a story about some of its stones—that they came not from the local Wiltshire Sarsen, but from the Preseli Hills in Pembrokeshire, a hundred and sixty five miles away. The rock is unique, a spotted dolerite easy to distinguish from near relatives by its blueish green colour and its fuzzy specks of white dotted about in it at random. It had enough magic still clinging to it even a century ago that visitors to Stonehenge would hire small hammers from a frowsty 'caretaker' to enable them to hack bits off Europe's greatest prehistoric monument to crush and drink for their ailments—one of the many things Sir John Lubbock and his Ancient Monuments Act sought to deal with!

Now, there is no doubt at all, and nobody disagrees, that the stones originally came from Carn Meini—the only cause of scholarly fighting is how! One group, the geologic school, insists that glacial action took the boulders on their way, and the late Neolithic and early Bronze age men found them lying like stranded whales on the Wiltshire downs and carried them to make the inner circle of Stonehenge. The archaeologists on the other hand insist that Man himself was the agent by which these stones were carried from the bare, windy hills of West Wales to the rolling chalk of Wiltshire, a terrifying journey by land and sea enshrined in folk lore, with a few clues in the history of both sites, and the stone itself, to help give an explanation of why men should have girded together the resources of almost the whole country—for such an effort must have been involved—to get these stones to their present site.

Carn Meini now consists of a rocky outcrop whose deeply fissured rocks lie about in profusion; within sight of this main 'Quarry' are some nineteen other outcrops, and down the hillslope to the south lies a tumbled mass of large boulders, many of which have much the same shape—a slightly oversize 'coffin' oblong with a lump at one end like a club foot. A few of these lie right on the flattened area adjacent to the main outcrop, and one is prostrate at its foot. At sunset the light runs obliquely down this rock and tooling marks can be seen on two of its faces—so at the time it was abandoned, attempts were being made to shape it roughly. To the north-west of this main outcrop a flattened area clear of any stones at all has leading from it a hollow way, cut down in a wide curve to the beginnings of a stream in the valley. When the soil of this hollow way was tested by boring a core out of it (a bit like coring an apple) it showed the particles to be very densely packed by the passage of heavy objects over it.

A little north-east of the outcrop, aerial photographs have revealed a large earthen circle approximately the same diameter as the first phase of Stonehenge. It has yet to be tested by excavation, so it cannot be included as a 'definite', only as a 'probable' or 'possible' in the tangled story of the Bluestones. Other bits of the story come from folklore; when Geoffrey of Monmouth wrote about Stonehenge in early medieval times, his story was that the stones were hurled by Merlin all the way to Salisbury Plain from Ireland—an interesting if unlikely tale! But what is now Pembrokeshire had, in the Dark ages, been an Irish colony, with Irish kings and the Irish language spoken . . . for four hundred years the area around Carn Meini had *been*, in effect, Ireland. So Geoffrey's tale seems to have a core of truth, a glimmer of memory of the real event, as does the strange tale the old lady told at Parc y Meirw.

What are we to make of all this? We know the people of the Neolithic, the New Stone age farmers,

had evolved simple science—astronomy is always the first science to develop in human cultures as it needs no apparatus, just patience and a good pair of eyes!—to aid them in navigation and in computing a calendar for their agricultural activities. All over northern Europe we find alignments of stones, circles, great systems and small ones, all apparently aimed at the same end; to find out where we are in each year, when spring has started, when to plant the corn, when to put the ram with the ewes, and so on. The greatest centres of these activities were in Brittany, in West Scotland (on the Mull of Kintyre) with lesser but important sites in northern Scotland, Yorkshire, Cornwall and—Pembrokeshire. The area around Carn Meini is littered with stone rows and circles, it has a good set of sighting lines for observation of the rising sun or moon or stars, from Preseli Top you can see Ireland, north Wales and Somerset. And here the men of the New Stone age built an observatory. They used the local stone, the dolerite . . . but it is a special stone, it is dark blue, with the fuzzy white spots in it—it looks like a *night sky*, and these early scientists were spending their whole lives studying that night sky, because by then we had enough of a food surplus to employ specialists, full time scientist-priests, if you like. They watched and noted, they then made up tales to tell, full of fact but all nicely wrapped in a cloud of fantasy about princes and beautiful girls, ogres and wild animals, to make those valuable, if somewhat dry, facts memorable—for if they did not, the hard won information about the sky would die with them.

As their information got more complete, they found Preseli was not so suitable as an observatory, as its latitude made the mathematics a bit wonky; by then we seem to have had a primitive grasp of what is now geometry, we knew a bit about Pythagoras's right-angled triangles and used the maths to make our elaborate stone rings like that at Stonehenge, Avebury, Callanish or the local ones like Gors Fawr. The best latitude for the mathematics of

Stonehenge—The tall outer 'Trilithon' stones are of local Wiltshire stone, it is the smaller, inner ring which is made from Pembrokeshire Spotted Dolerite.

their observations to come out was that of Stonehenge, and so it is possible this is the reason for the great journey; the circle on Preseli was abandoned, but those stones, those special speckly blue stones which the gods had made look like a night sky, they could not be left behind . . . and so down the hill they were slid on treetrunks, the way made slippery with willow twigs—in only a little over a mile they would have had enough water, in that stream in the valley, to dam and float each stone on a raft—then down to the Eastern Cleddau and past Picton, Cosheston, Pembroke and Milford to the Channel, across to the Wiltshire Avon, and up that river to within a mile of Stonehenge . . . even though that is a fantastic odyssey, all but two of its 165 miles are on water, so at least the weight of the stones was taken care of.

Have we a jot of evidence for all this? It all sounds too romantic to be true, especially as the geologists don't agree anyway, and it is all five thousand years ago! Well, there are the clues we have already investigated. There are the stones themselves, their very localised distribution. There are the stories, like Geoffrey of Monmouth's. And there is the odd-stone-out . . . because one of the Stonehenge 'Bluestones' isn't a Bluestone at all, but a piece of Cosheston Beds Sandstone from near Pembroke. It isn't

just slightly wrong, from another part of the mountain quarry, say—it is wildly wrong, not even volcanic rock but sedimentary . . . and the Neolithic people were excellent geologists so there is no question of their getting the wrong thing by mistake. What happened?

It is possible there was an accident in the Cleddau, and that one of the precious bluestones was lost, its raft sunk. The fleet must continue (after all, it was using the resources and manpower of much of prehistoric Britain) but by now the priests in charge of this operation were getting obsessed by numbers; things must add up right, or the gods would be angered. So, a piece of the local sandstone, near where the accident happened, was quickly quarried and added to the fleet—now the numbers were correct, then the fleet continued its journey, one enshrined in folklore ever since (part of the Welsh Mabinogi may contain it in the legend of Culwch and Olwen). Meanwhile another bluestone was to be quarried, eventually to replace that sandstone slab so hastily added on the shores near Pembroke . . . and it is still there, waiting for us to see, as for reasons we will never know, the designs for the later phases of Stonehenge made its enormous journey unnecessary.

Well, that's my story and I'm sticking to it . . .

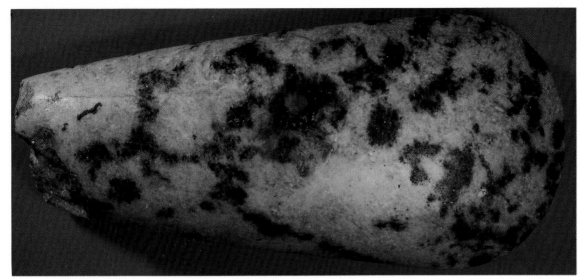

A Masterpiece in Stone . . . A chieftain's ceremonial stone axe polished to perfection, made from the best diorite in the Preselis, 5000 years ago. Courtesy Pembrokeshire Museums.

Waiting for Merlin? Half-finished Stonehenge Blue-stone, dressed and club-footed like its brethren 165 miles off in Wiltshire. When freshly polished, each stone must have looked like a night sky, flecked with stars. (See front cover, Spotted Dolerite in close-up).

Top:
Llech y Dribedd cromlech, near Moylegrove, Pemb.

Lower:
Carreg Samson cromlech, Long-house, Pemb.
The stony centres of what were once great earthen mounds, family graves in which our New Stone-age ancestors buried their dead.

Field of the Dead

Parc y Meirw means just that—Field of the Dead . . . why? I asked an old lady who'd lived in Llanllawer, near Fishguard, all her long life (she was nearly ninety); *why* was it given this curious, shivery name? She didn't know, but they were old stones, she said, up the lane to the mountain about quarter of a mile. What were they like, I wondered; she didn't know. Though she had been born in this cottage, lived in it all her life, brought up her own children, been widowed and was destined to die there, she had never gone up the lane to see the stones. They terrified her. You see, she said, there's a ghostly lady dressed in white, wandering about the fields up there. Didn't want to meet *her*, the old lady said firmly. Four hundred yards, maybe a few more. She never went. An oddly powerful thing, superstition—because a bit of detective work revealed the ghostly lady for what, or who, she was —that story had been around in that area of Pembrokeshire for five thousand years.

For years we have thought of our ancestors as primitive savages, because they were not Christians and didn't have the technology we have now. Their weapons may have been of stone, their fish hooks of chipped bone, but it is their minds we come up against in a lot of archaeological discovery—hold a piece of pottery, look at a stone burial chamber or a stone ring, and you see not only what your ancestor made, but get a glimpse of what he was thinking as he made it. Parc y Meirw is probably one of the oldest scientific instruments in this part of the world —there is nothing savage about it at all.

Top:

Eclipse at Fishguard—Five thousand years after it was built, Parc y Meirw still works. This eclipse was photographed from the stones' site in 1985, the night after the moon had set by sliding down the right-hand edge of Mount Leinster, in the Irish Wicklow Hills . . . the White lady is still wandering.

Bottom:

Parc y Meirw Stone Row—as it was in 1809 when visited and drawn by Colt Hoare; now the stones are half buried in a field boundary bank. They mark one end of a 91-mile-long astronomical 'computor' . . .

The 'Pointed Stone', Gors Fawr—apparently used as a sight to observe astronomical events some time towards the end of the New Stone-age (Neolithic) period, when our ancestors were refining their farming techniques and thus needed to develop a calendar. Gors Fawr is within sight of the Blue Stone quarry at Carn Meini, a piece of which seems to be 'notched' like the sight at the end of a rifle barrel.

The men and women of the New Stone age (or Neolithic) period, who arrived in Britain about 3500 BC, were Britain's first farmers; no longer did they hunt and kill, grub for berries as they felt hungry, follow the herds, chase for hours or stalk through dense forests for their game . . . these people cut trees to clear patches of ground as fields; here they grew grain, had domestic animals around them: they had small villages. Away from their living area was a sacred place set aside for the Dead; we now see the remains of their great stone tombs as the Cromlechs and dolmens with which Pembrokeshire is so well endowed. Now, farming is a science; it needs certain things to be done right, or the whole matter goes wrong. Seeds must be planted at the right time of year, or the resulting plants will not ripen in time for the harvest before the days get too short and winter gets here. For lambs to arrive at a convenient time in spring, the ram should be turned in with the ewes at a set date. All very well for us—we have a calendar. But what happens when you don't have one? This was the Neolithic peoples' problems, and they set about finding out enough about their surroundings to let Nature provide them with one.

The sun is a good marker. From the shortest day on, it rises above a slightly more southerly point on the eastern horizon every morning until the longest day, 21 June, when it stops, then slowly starts its climb up north, and midwinter day again. Know the horizon, then, and you have something to count the days by; this is the basis of all primitive calendars, including the Neolithic one; stone circles like Stonehenge, Avebury, Callanish, or the small local ones like Gors Fawr on the Preseli Hills, were apparently for this purpose. But man was successful; his plants flourished; he had food surpluses, enough to feed men who were not farmers themselves, men who were thinkers, our first scientists you might say . . . Intellectuals. Dreamers, priests, call them what you will, these men made their life's work the study of the sky—not just the sun, but the moon, the stars, their motions in the heavens, their unfailing travels which told us where we were in each year, and occasionally gave us a nasty shock. For sometimes the sun, or the moon, would get a chunk taken out of them or even go out completely, during an eclipse. Frightening enough now, utterly devastating then. The man—or woman—who could predict an eclipse, and also predict its ending and the returning to life of the sun or moon was a powerful person, someone to reckon with.

We have considerable evidence now that our ancestors made a great study of planetary and stellar motion using these stone rings, alignments of stones, and the use of distant objects as foresights (like the sight on the end of a long rifle barrel) to enable them to increase their accuracy in observation, and therefore prediction. Parc y Meirw was one of these, a computor of stone, if you like, to watch for the signs that important things were going to happen in the sky. The sun has been mentioned already, making his steady progress along the sky-line from winter's chill to summer's heat and back

again, regular as clockwork. The moon is nothing like so reliable. It seems to chase about all over the sky. For a start, it does in a month what he sun takes a year over, a trip from northern rising point to southern and back again. But it doesn't get *quite* back to its northern point, no, it is slightly out of true. Next month slightly more again and so on— the moon doesn't get back to its original point on the horizon for eighteen and a half YEARS. Those holy men in this cold field must have had amazing patience to make the original observations with sticks and stone markers before they were sure enough of what they had seen to make the great stone row of Parc y Meirw. For it is a row with a purpose, pointing, showing us the direction to look —in this case for the setting moon. The end of the rifle barrel? Ninety one miles away, over the Irish Sea. And they seem to have included not only the moon's monthly cycle, its eighteen year cycle, but another, only rediscovered fairly recently, a cycle of

Stone Circle, Gors Fawr—The sun, moon and stars, observed with the help of stone rings and rows, make a natural calendar; this part of North Pembrokeshire seems to have been a major observatory five thousand years ago, several other cairn circles, stone rings, rows and menhirs remain to testify to the area's importance both as a good site for observation, and close to the magic of the Blue Stones.

173 days, a tiny 'wobble' of the moon's orbit caused by the differences in pull of the earth and sun's gravitational field. We know this, our ancestors didn't; they just saw the result, and noted it in stone.

Every night, the moon sets in a different place on the horizon, chasing waywardly north and south, north and south again, year after year, nearly, but not quite, getting to the original sighting point. Only when the 'wobble' of the monthly cycle, the 18.6 year cycle and the 173 day cycle coincide and the moon is at its most northerly point, does it set by sliding down the dragon's teeth of Mount Leinster, one of the Wicklow Hills in Ireland. You can see it quite clearly from Parc y Meirw. And when the moon does that, you look down the sight line and see this happen, and you know something very important is imminent. Because only when the moon moves into the ecliptic (the apparent path of the sun through the sky) do those frightening eclipses occur. Parc y Meirw is an eclipse predictor. We found it still works in 1982's autumnal eclipses.

And what about the old lady's story, she who had never been to see the stones, let alone know anything about them or what they were for—none of us did till now. Well, her story gives one clue, the use of the monument the other one. A ghostly lady dressed in white, wandering over the fields at night? The moon. Always a female deity since male Chauvinists gave this heavenly body credit for beauty, waywardness and unreliability, connections with fertility . . . yes, the moon hath raised Her lamp above . . . a set of stones which still work as one of the world's oldest calculators.

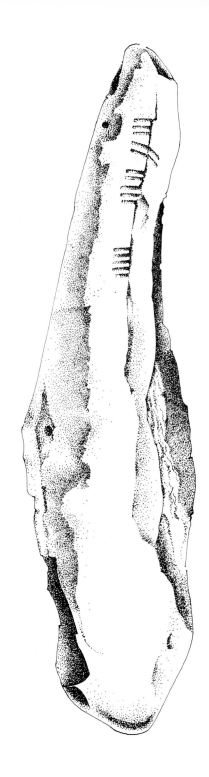

Ogham Stone at Brawdy Church (Drawing, Piet Brinton)—The incomplete inscription is in Ogham only, and says 'M-Q-QAGTE'—Maqi (or son of) Qagte; some, now sadly nameless Dark Age prince buried here at the end of the 5th century A.D. Here you can find two other stones from the same period, plus a fragment of Romano-British material. Brawdy was important when pilgrims visited its many holy wells.

Irish Morse . . .

We think of prehistory as being without writing; but some stones found on the Preseli Hills have curious markings on them, there are Cup and Ring marked stones, enigmatic marks in caves . . . and, on a number of impressive stones in Wales and Ireland, an ancestor of our alphabet; a code for us to crack, from the Dark ages . . .

Pembrokeshire is particularly rich in a rather special 'make' of stone monument, one which is usually rather imposing, which stands (or stood—some have been knocked flat or laid prostrate in church porches for safe keeping) anything up to seven feet high. It originally marked the grave of a rather important person, an early Christian, and you will sometimes find his or her name on the stone in rough Latin script. Sometimes you will also find a rather wistful message from fifteen hundred years or so ago; 'Remember my son'; 'Do not pass by without praying for me' . . . it is hard not to stand there, biting your lip to keep back a tear for a long-dead, long-forgotten human—you will never know them, and yet for a second they seem very close, they and the people who loved them enough to put up this rough memorial.

But there is more to these stones than the simple Latin inscription; a lot of them have small cuts along the edges, hard to see until you have got your 'eye' in (then you'll wonder how you could ever have missed them!); a mix of long and short, upright or oblique, some coming up to one edge of the stone only, some going round their edge and continuing on another face. And they form an alphabet just as modern Morse code does for use in telegraphy. Once historians had noted what was written in Latin, and that some sort of relationship existed between this and the little marks (that the stones are, in fact, bilingual), the marks were translated and the language deciphered . . . and to everyone's surprise, although this is Wales, the language turned out to be Irish.

The script is called Ogham or Ogam (the Irish pronounce it to rhyme with 'Home'). The stones seem to date from the period just after the Romans left, say about 500-700 AD, though a few lie outside those dates; at that time, Pembrokeshire was an Irish colony, we had Irish kings, and spoke the Goidelic version of the Celtic languages, rather than the Brythonic (Goidelic Celtic includes Irish, Scots; Brythonic includes Welsh, Cornish and Breton). At the time the stones were put up, this area was seething with warring tribes, the formation and destruction of mini kingdoms by rival kings and princes, in the turmoil after Roman rule had waned and we had wave upon wave of Picts (who were Scots) and Scots (who were Irish—are you following this?), Saxons, Danes, Welsh tribes from mid and north Wales . . . invasion followed invasion, and this land was a babel of tongues which merged over half a millenium into the beginnings of English (and then only after ecclesiastical Latin had added its peasant equivalent French from the Norman invaders of the eleventh century). What little writing there was comes down to us from the Church whose priests tried to keep a small torch of learning and civilisation going, and in doing so have left us all we have of the history of those times . . . or almost all, for there is Ogham too.

We don't know why this script originated. It may have been designed to write tallies and notes and names on pieces of stick, a script which could be hacked quickly with the sharp edge of the dagger which everyone carried then for personal protection. It may have arisen only for memorials such as these stones. Certainly these are the only survivals. Yet in other parts of Europe it was known and talked about; Greek, Norse and Celtic legend speaks of a writing God, 'OGMA' and that he 'Provided signs for secret speech known only to the learned'. But Ogham is written along a straight line, and the near-Eastern languages such as Sanskrit have words for 'Furrow' or 'Row' which are very like 'Ogham' (Sanskrit's word for 'Straight Road' is AJMA or OJMA). So the Dark Age Irish-speaking priests and wise men who wrote these now fragmentary words may have been known and respected by their contemporaries and must have written a great deal, most of which has now perished. When you stand before an Ogham

41

stone you are seeing what happens in an age of
barbarism, how the human spirit struggles still,
even if it is only to be remembered after death.

There aren't many left; out of 54 stones (30 of
them bilingual in Latin and Ogham) about half
date from 450 AD to 600 AD, with a scatter of later
ones. Thirty seven stones with these strange
inscriptions can be found in south Wales, the
majority—sixteen stones, including the 'Rosetta
stones' which enabled scholars to translate Ogham
in the first place—are in Pembrokeshire in a
cluster. If you get the urge to see Ogham in quantity
then you'll have to go north of the Tweed or to
County Kerry in Ireland where there are over three
hundred; there is a tiny group in Cornwall. But
they are mixed, these other examples, with memorial stones showing their carvers were pagan—the
Picts are known for their pictures, for their depict-
ing animals, patterns, fish, circles, moons and
snakes on their stones . . . Ogham said more.

A stone stands outside the porch at Nevern; as
you read its brief message you are transported back
to the time when the Romans left their former
colony to the mercy of the Vandals and the Visigoths, Saxon, Norseman, Viking, Irish warrior or
Welsh prince. Men of all cultures who had served in
the Roman army must have watched with despair
as the civilised structure started to collapse, as ours
is on the verge of doing and for the same reasons.
One such seems to have been Vitalianus; his name
is on the rough stone in Latin script, and the other
word is 'Emerito', rather poor Latin for 'Discharged with Honour'. So here was a man who'd served
in the Roman army in its last days, who had retired
to live in peace in Nevern, whose grave reminds us
of terrible times with lessons for our own. And that
he was probably Irish is given by the repeating of
his name in Ogham on the top corner of the stone.

Sagrani Stone: St Dogmaels—Bilingual in Latin and
Ogham, a 'Rosetta Stone' for the decoding of the
strange alphabet. SAGRANI *FILI* CVNOTAMI in
Latin; SAGRANI *MAQI* CUNOTAMI in Ogham
'stripes' along one edge . . .

A generation later the area was under the control of a Christian Irish chief called Clethyr, who lived in the fortress above the church—his priest, Brynach, had married the Chieftain's daughter Cymmorth and founded the little Christian cell on the *llan*, or church land across the stream from Clethyr's military activities. St Brynach's church is still there. Vitalianus's memorial was probably there first; there is one piece of a second Roman stone set in the north wall of the present church, so Vitalianus was not alone. Later additions included the chief's own son, and therefore St Brynach's brother-in-law; a stone found during the restoration of the church in the nineteenth Century also has a bilingual inscription, which reads; Maglocuni Fili Clutor (Maelgwn, son of Clethyr) in Latin, then in Ogham Maglicunas Maqi Clutar . . . and there is a clue to the Irishness of Ogham. In Welsh, when Robert had a son, that son was known as 'ap Robert' (which became Probert); Rees or Rhys might have a son who became known as 'ap Rhys (eventually Price). The Scots and Irish form for 'son of' is Mac—witness the Macnamarras, Macbrides, Macbeth and Macduff . . . and here in Nevern poor Maelgwn is son of Clethyr, written as 'maqi'. A small but vital clue.

At about the time Vitalianus's stone was being set up in Nevern, another was pointing its memorial finger at the sky at Bridell, near Cardigan; here the Ogham reads Nettasagru Maqi Mucoi Breci (Nettasagrus, sons of the descendants of Breci). This stone, set up in the late fifth of early sixth century, later had added to it a cross. At Bridell you aren't far from St Dogmaels, where a cluster of inscribed stones was found including one, used as a bridge for a time, by which Ogham was finally unravelled in modern times—it is now inside the church and, word for word, the two inscriptions are the same Sagrani Fili Cunotami and Sagrani Maqi Cunotami. Inside the church at Brawdy are three stones, two of which have Ogham inscriptions; the biggest, over nine feet long, says M-Q- Qagte—whoever he was, he was son of Qagte, but we shall never know his name. Another nearby says Vendagni Fili V----Ni in Latin and simply Vendogni in Ogham; here we know the son but not the father! Mathry's church has a stone for

Vitalianus Stone: Nevern—Vitalianus was probably an Irish-speaking, Christian, retired ex-Roman soldier. His name is in Ogham and Latin.

Maccudicl, son of Caticuus, St Nicholas has a simple stone which says Paanus and a stone for a long dead lady, Tunccetace Wife of Daarus (for women are remembered in these enigmatic stones as well as men). Cilgerran church boasts a fine stone which says, in Ogham Trenagusu Maqi Maqitreni (Trenagusu son of the Descendant of Treni) and in a long Latin sentence which takes two lines:

TRENEGUSSI FILI
MACUTRANI HIC IACIT
Trenegussus son of Macutreni lies here

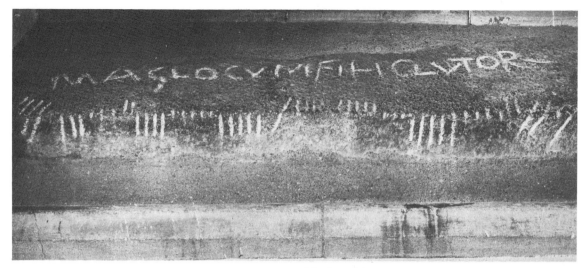

Maglocuni Stone: Nevern—Maelgwn, son of Clethyr, it says in both scripts, Latin and Ogham; Maelgwn's brother-in-law was Brynach the priest at Nevern, so he presumably had the sad job of burying the young prince whose grave has helped modern scholars decipher these enigmatic markings.

Clydai has some fine examples, again inside the church (for which you will need the key). Here you will find Etternus son of Victor; Solinus, son of Vendonius; and Dobitucus, son of Evolengus. At Jordonston and Llandeilo, Llandysilio and St Davids, you will have to hunt hard to find them, but the detective in you will feel a surge of triumph when you run to earth each stone, tinged with sadness for the message it contains, reminding each of us of our transcience and mortality. Most heartfelt, and by far the longest, is an inscription you will have to take the boat to Caldey to see. It has crosses in its faces, and in Ogham it says simply Mag----Dubr---Inb; one trouble with these edge inscriptions is that they get broken off, and this has happened here; it probably said 'the stone of Maglia Dubracubas, son of . . .'; but in Latin follows eight lines giving a call from fifteen centuries ago which even today we feel obliged to think about:

Et Singno Crucis in Illam Fingsi Rogo Omnibus Ambulantibus Ibi Exorent Pro Animae Catuoconi

It's not very good Latin, but its message is stark:

And by the Sign of the Cross which I have Fashioned upon this stone I ask all who walk there that they Pray for the Soul of Catuoconus

we could hardly do less.

44

Wofull Newes from Wales

Every now and again the earth seems to go berserk and break all the rules; tempest, hurricane, earthquake and flood have periodically knocked the confidence out of men who thought they had got the place figured out nicely—folk story is full of it, the Bible points morals from it, and just occasionally archaeology, folk tale and Bible all join forces to tell the same story . . . so it is with the Flood.

If you clamber down the cliff to Marros, or walk along the shingle bank at Newgale, the sands at Whitesands or Newport, or Abermawr you will see something familiar, if shocking, to the navvies who built Cardiff Dock or the garrison of Harlech Castle. If you take a walk on the Scillies, you see hedge banks vanishing down into the sea at high tide. If you read Roman histories, you hear that Caesar's legions could walk where we now take boats, that the Roman forces invading Anglesey to murder the Druids could wade the Menai Straits—something we certainly might think twice about now! Harlech and Cydweli were seaports, now they are cut off from the sea. Medieval writers talk of running cattle across to Caldey, and of ships being wrecked on a sand bar which was walkable at low tide—again, this is impossible now, the sea level has altered. Now, those navvies at Cardiff saw trees, buried deep in clay many feet below the surface, trees with wood so perfect that a lot of it was dug by the men to take home and use for firewood or for carpentry. At Marros and Newgale it is the same story—rows of trees lie side by silent side, like some

Woful Newes from Wales—There have been Great Floods throughout history, this one was in 1604. Some Welsh churches still have marks showing how high the waters lapped . . .

slightly mad railway sleepers or causeway. Again, we are not the first to see this; Giraldus Cambrensis, the Welsh scholar, passed by this way in 1175:-

> We then passed over Newgil sands . . . during the winter King Henry II spent in Ireland . . . the sandy shores of south Wales, being laid bare by the extraordinary violence of a storm, showed the surface of the earth which had been covered for many ages, and discovered the trunks of trees cut off, standing in the very sea itself, the strokes of the hatchet appearing as if made only yesterday. It looked . . . not like a shore, but a grove cut down, perhaps at the time of the Deluge.

There it is, as you might expect; talk of Noah and the Flood—no surprise, coming as it does from a medieval cleric . . . but is he so far off the mark?

All over the world, and certainly around this part of Europe, there are stories in folklore about a universal flood of great violence; many can be traced straight back to the Biblical one—some aren't so easy. The Sumerians, a very ancient near-Eastern people, had their version of the flood story which is so like the Noah one it is almost uncanny. Theirs has the forester-king Gilgamesh meeting an ancient called Utnapishtim, survivor of the Great Flood, when a boat was launched to save all that could be

Marros Beach and the submerged Forest—A pair of oak trees, their roots towards the sea, in among the debris of a forest floor—leaves, acorns, hazels, birch-bark . . . 7500 years ago, some vast earthly heave spewed cubic miles of ocean to drown these coastal lowlands in a few minutes, leaving this mess as archaeology, and countless tales in folklore.

saved: when the boat at last comes to rest on a mountain top, Utnapishtim releases birds, like Noah in the Genesis version, to test if the water has gone. But other lands, other times, tell the same tale. Brittany has a lost land, Kaer ar Iz, drowned during a great inundation, only two people escaping on a white horse. Cornwall had a similar story, the Trevelyan family have the white horse on their family crest as a reminder of their escape. Off Ireland, Scotland and Kent were once rich fields, farms and villages (say the stories) now all drowned. In north Wales the drowned land is called Maes Gwyddno, and here in south Wales it is Cantre'r Gwaelod, the Lowland Hundred.

Once, says the old tale, sixteen fine towns lay in what is now Cardigan Bay. There must have been some danger from flooding, as there were sluice gates to keep the fields and villages dry, to keep the water out . . . and in charge was Prince Seithennyn 'The Third most Drunken Man in Wales . . .' (one wonders who the other two were). Now, poor old Seithennyn, after one booze-up, forgot to close the sluices, the water rushed in, and only two people escaped, a harpist and his assistant, on a white horse as in other versions of the story. The poets set upon him with a will:

> Seithenin, come out and look toward the abode of
>   heroes;
> The plain of Gwyddno is covered by the sea—
> Cursed be the embankment which let in, after wine,
>   the open fountain of the roaring deep.
> Cursed be the keeper of the floodgates who, after his
>   festive mirth,
> Let in the spouting of the desolating ocean;
> After arrogance cometh lasting ruin . . .

runs a medieval poem (trans.) but as recently as 1634 Robert James wrote:

> . . . when the sea doth bate
> Downe from the shore, 'tis wonder to relate
> How manie thousands of thies trees now stand
> Blacke broken on their rootes, which once dry lande
> Did cover . . .

So what was it all, this drowned land, call it Douarnez, Lyonesse, Lethowstow—or Atlantis? At Marros you get some clues. The trees lie with their

Flint spearhead—with a broken tip, found at Marros among the leaf litter and flattened oak trees—did the hunter lose it during the chase? Or drop it in terror at the sound of approaching walls of water? Small details like this, or acorns gnawed by mesolithic mice, bring the place back to eery life as we explore . . .

Bridge Inn, Newgale. 1880—Nothing now remains of this building or its neighbours, buried under the heap of shingle thrown up during 'the Great Storm' of 1895. 'The Bridge' was patriotically re-named 'Duke of Edinburgh' after a visit by Queen Victoria's younger son in 1882. Legend has it that the landlady and her daughter escaped through an upstairs window during the Great Storm, carrying enough gold sovereigns to build the present inn; wisely, it's further inland!

roots towards the sea, their crowns to land; they are—or they were—fine oaks, with one or two beeches, some of them two feet and more through their trunks. They were not rotten at the time they were struck, but in their prime. Underneath them was rich leaf mould, dropped leaves and branches, nuts and acorns (some chewed by mice—how long ago, one wonders?). Birch bark is there, hazel nuts, blackberry leaves, rushes, and all in a remarkable state of preservation. One tree had the rib bone of a whale speared through it by some amazing impact when land was suddenly overwhelmed by the sea. Because this is what seems to have happened. For some time the evidence points to a gradual wetting of the land, plants like rush, trees like alder, indicating that brackish or fen conditions had started to take over from rich, low lying oak woods. Then, suddenly, the whole picture changes, a thick layer

of blueish silt cover the forest, thrown down like so many matchsticks with great violence, the silt being what preserved the forest litter and the trees, bark and fruit, even pollen. This layer is found in all other buried forests in the flood story—and one of the main objections to the Genesis type of flood has been, until recently, that there was no geological force which would raise world sea levels by twenty feet in as many minutes. Now we have the science of plate tectonics and geologists have found

Cwm yr Eglwys—before the 'Royal Charter' storm of 1859 whose force destroyed four hundred ships in a single night, and left this little church with only its western wall standing.

evidence that we are floating above our molten centre on rafts of rock, which are continually emerging from some areas, and vanishing into others to be remelted. Every now and again continents crash into each other—the Himalayas are being thrown up at this moment by the violence of the collision of Africa and Asia. A slip of plates deep in the Atlantic or Pacific oceans might well displace cubic miles of water very suddenly. If this is what happened to Cantre'r Gwaelod, it is a grim thought that if it happened again now, most of the world's capital cities would vanish at a stroke, Thames barrage or no Thames barrage—to quote that ancient author again:-

Their songs of joy turned into a midnight cry

Big Forts Have Little Forts . . .

Up on the Preseli Mountains—we like to call them mountains anyway, even though the highest point is only 1750 feet above sea level!—is a bare, lonely landscape. Heather and bilberries, sphagnum moss and insect-eating sundew plants . . . and the remains of head hunters—

You are never out of sight of an Iron age hillfort, those banks and ditches built to protect Celt from Celt in the turbulent days when Welsh and Irish and Scots were new to Britain and everybody spent their whole time fighting. One of the best is Foel Drygarn (Bare Hill with Three Burials). It's a steep climb up from Croesfihangel, and you can see why the forts were *where* they were; you're in no condition to fight after that scramble! And then there are the defences. Foel Drygarn has two rings of stonework crowning its top, two great banks to discourage intruders. Inside are no fewer than 220 hut circles, in which lived a large Celtic population from about 300 BC onwards. There is a good strong gateway at the eastern end of the fort, and the huts spread outside the defences down the hillside to where the faint banks show where their fields waited for ploughing by patient oxen. As you stand on the summit of the hill you have a lordly view of all that the chieftains who decided to live here saw, two and

Some Celtic Favourites:

Top:
Iron-age ancestors decorated anything from sword handles to fire-dogs, from mirror-backs to shield bosses with voluptuous curving designs . . .

Centre:
Their lives were a riot of colour—brightly dyed woollen clothes, painted bodies . . . even their huts were daubed in garish red, yellow, blue and green clays . . .

Drawings PB

Bottom:
The Celts worshipped the horse—it had won them most of Europe in conquest, their cavalry was feared even by the Romans. Knobbly kneed, beak nosed, sprightly, the horse can be found all over Iron age life in legend, hillside, and coins . . .

Haslemere Museum

50

Carn Alw—a small, fierce fortress with the defence against cavalry which experts call a *cheveaux de frise*, one of the best in Britain. The funnel-shaped setting of stones slowed a charge down to a laboured trot in single file, when defenders in the two guard-houses (seen here as semi-circular stone settings) could easily deal with the intending invaders. But the biggest mystery is why Carn Alw is so heavily defended, yet so tiny that only about twenty people could have lived here . . . was it the home, not for people at all, but for a War God?

a half thousand years ago. You see your neighbours at Carn Ingli and Nevern and Dinas. You stand upon the mounds covering the burials of earlier chiefs, who had known and owned this land a thousand years before the Iron age—it is those three mounds which give the bare hill its Welsh name. You see from here the Golden Road wending its way up the hillside to the south, from St Davids to Gloucester, built even earlier than those Bronze age burials, when stone was just giving way to the first metals, and a brilliant mind was planning a magnificent astronomical temple at Stonehenge, with stones from Carn Meini.

But you see more still; down into the valley to your north-west is a large craggy outcrop called Carn Alw (rocks which echo). This little fort—it only ever had about six huts within its massive defences—has several unique features about it, but it could never have survived so near its giant neighbour without Foel Drygarn's approval or friendship. Yet there it is, very fierce, very strong, tiny, cheekily important. For Carn Alw has a ring-work of dragons-teeth stones forming at one point into a funnel shape, which narrows towards an entrance. This unusual feature is a defence against cavalry—for the Celts had tamed the horse for military purposes, and their journey across Europe from Poland and Silesia half a millenium before Christ brought us iron and amazing art, coupled with unparalleled savagery. The wheel was used to make chariots. It also made possible improved pottery. Iron was mostly used for weapons of war—even their money was shaped like a sword so you could quickly convert your currency into something to fight with! They were headhunters, the great wooden gates of Foel Drygarn hill fort and the smaller but no less impressive one at Carn Alw would both have been surmounted by iron spikes on which were human heads, newly collected. Their wells had human heads dropped down them to appease the gods of the underworld who supplied the water (we still do this, only we have diluted the ritual somewhat; if you've ever thrown a penny into a wishing well, then you are carrying on a two thousand year old tradition—for has not the coin the queen's head on it? . . .); their stories abound with folk losing their heads. When the Iron age itself was forgotten, even the old religion had been superceded by the new, then saints were given to the old healing wells . . . but the loss of heads was remembered in the folk stories. Thus it is that St Decuman, in his well near Pembroke, is remembered as having walked there with head under arm after his beheading, as St Justinian walked across the waters from Ramsey Island, similarly beheaded, similarly carrying his head. The tales of

White Horse—at Uffington, leaping across the Berkshire Downs as he has for over two thousand years, reminder of the importance of horses and horsemanship to our Celtic ancestors, of horse gods and horse legends—he lives by an Iron age fort built on Dragon Hill . . .

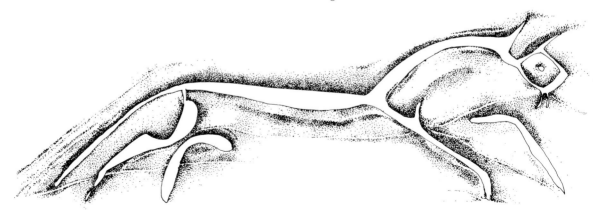

52

Peaceful Porthclais, once set upon by pagan
Vikings intent upon burning David's church.
Henry II, the first Plantagenet king, set out
from here for Ireland with a force of three
hundred ships and "the flower of the nation's
manhood" . . . and here swam ashore *from*
Ireland, Twrch Trwyth, the wild pig of Celtic
mythology who looms large in the story of the
Stonehenge Blue-stones. Iron-age pigs were
worshipped as gods; if Twrch Trwyth existed he
probably looked like this.

History in the Hedge . . .

Top Left: Henry II's favourite, Broom. He knew it as Planta genista, his dynasty became known as the Plantagenets.

Top Right: Henry Tudor searched Bosworth Woods for "the blessed plant" (Herb Bennet), before doing battle with the last Plantagenet king, Richard III.

Far Left: Warriors of all ages knew Woundwort would staunch bleeding . . .

Far Right: . . . but if you were Elf-shot, Stitchwort was the answer.

Bottom Left: Solomon's Seal, for bruised Tudor wives.

Bottom right: Amanita muscaria made Druids think they could fly; its colours are those of Santa Claus and his flying reindeer; dangerously poisonous.

the Mabinogi all have, somewhere, someone who loses his head. These are some of the ghosts to carry with you whenever you explore a hillfort like Foel Drygarn or Carn Alw, echoing once to bloodthirsty battle and slicing swordplay from shaggy horses. Indeed, this part of our history is so enshrined into our folk lore that our stories of warriors fighting dragons—firey, smoke-breathing monsters—may well have come from the Bronze age mens' impression of the arrival of the Men of Iron, the Celts, astride their steaming, puffing little horses . . . must all that smoke not have indicated a fire in the belly? And as for St George and his dragon—he was patron saint of horses, lots of his Welsh sites (including Nicholaston on Gower) have a horsey

Crundale Rath is a fine Iron age fortress north of Haverfordwest, Pembrokeshire. Set into its outer bank is a well with a legend; at midnight on Hallowe'en, the old tale said, the air over the well and the fortress would be filled with terrible cries as gangs of headless horsemen rode by . . . This bloodthirsty story has its roots in Iron-age head-hunting (they often dropped human heads down their wells as offerings to the gods of the underworld); to the worship of the horse; to our Celtic ancestors' celebrations of *their* New Year, which was November 1st, SAMAIN . . . so the old year died on the night of October 31st—Hallowe'en.

connection; look at the Celtic idea of a horse and it is remarkably like our conception of dragons. And the most famous horse of them all? Why Uffington, an Iron age horse cut in chalk . . . on Dragon Hill . . .

A Glint of Gold

Industrial archaeology is generally thought of as being about the workings of the last 100-200 years or so, but of course, industry is as old as Man himself; flint working floors and bellpits for iron ore can be found for Neolithic (3000 BC) and Iron age (400 BC) respectively; there is abundant evidence of ancient industries, travel and trade which come to the surface from time to time in this present effort. But none has a longer nor more varied history, all still clearly visible both on and *in* the ground, than Dolauchothi, the Roman gold workings of Carmarthenshire.

The first people to dig into the hills around Caio seem to have been the Celtic Iron age people, whose work can be seen as a strip across a saddle of hill above Ogofau—it may have been their pioneering which set the Romans off to conquer this part of Wales, settle it with Spanish troops who were already expert at heavy metal mining, and in any case would be the better guards for not speaking the local lingo. A large garrison settlement with baths and barracks was set up by the river Cothi, and soon a huge opencast quarry was dug, at first manually and later by hushing; the ore-containing rocks were very variable in thickness—between a few inches to more than a foot, and were very steeply inclined, so before long enormous caverns were being dug instead, following the veins of gold-bearing rock where they wandered through the mountain, down till they encountered water. Then, primitive screw pumps, worked either by a slave or by waterpower and driven from the surface, got the workings tolerably dry, and very deep working was possible. At the same time adits or levels were dug into the mountain until they met gold workings,

The Great Open Cast—was worked by undercutting then fire setting, allowing the collapse of the side of the hill, which could then be searched for suitable ore, to be crushed to powder and panned for the gold within it . . . the separating pools can still be found on the hillside to the west of the main workings.

both to help drain them by gravity and to facilitate getting the ore out in baskets carried on yokes from the shoulders.

Bottom: Dolaucothi
Coffin Level—So called because it was cut through the rock to be wider at the shoulders (where the slaves' yokes needed more room) than the feet. The Roman engineering is of a very high order, each 'level' is in fact slightly sloping so that it will drain naturally. In deeper workings drainage was by screw-pump. Hydraulic power was used in stamping machinery on the surface, in 'hushing' waste and rock by vast volumes of water released from the reservoir on the hill above the workings—the whole place is served by a superbly engineered aqueduct.

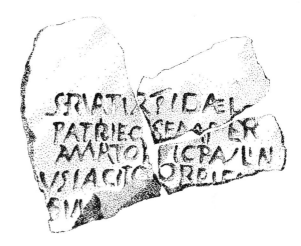

Memorial stone found in the workings, 4th Century.

If you enter the adits you can see how archaelogists came to know some of this. The levels are cut into exceedingly hard rock (which is why it's still safe for you to go in after two thousand years! . . .) and must have needed enormous labour to cut them. So the Roman engineers didn't waste time and effort cutting more than they needed; the tunnels are broad at the shoulder, where the yoke and the men's bent backs needed room to carry the heavy burden out to daylight for its crushing; but they are narrow at the feet—all you needed was a footpath, no more. This characteristic shape has led to the name 'Coffin Level' for these adits. They wind into the hill and eventually end either in a fall, an abandoned working, or in large man-made caves where a lode was worked; formerly these were explorable to a much deeper level, but modern considerations about Health & Safety have led to a lot being bulldozed in. I know it all remains there, but it still seems like vandalism, especially by the National Trust who are present owners of the site.

55

The main method of working, and then crushing the enormous quantities of ore was by slave labour, or by 'Hushing', a word nicely descriptive of the noise which the method must have made. A magnificent leet seven miles long (with a fall of only fifteen feet in that distance) brought water from the Cothi to a truly gargantuan reservoir, half a million gallons at a time then being let loose down the mountain to wash away overburden and new rock broken by the slaves. This formed 'Hush-gulleys' which you can still see cutting into the Welsh mountainside. Then nearby, and also connected to the leet system are steps, wet with waterfalls, cut down the hillslope, which formed pans where the gold could be washed and either settle out or be caught on the hairy spikes of gorse bushes, whose remote descendants still prickle you as you explore the site. The minute flecks of gold were then turned into riches by burning the gorse in great open pits, and the molten metal would run out at the bottom of them to be carried off to Rome at a rate of about a hundredweight a month—it was the richest mine in the empire.

A Roman writer, Pliny, describes the use of 'Ulex, a rough prickly plant' for this catching of the gold (we still have Ulex as the scientific name for gorse), and another writer talks of how the Romans

The rough surface of Gorse spines caught specks of gold in the settling tanks—the plant could then be burned to melt out the precious metal . . . odd to think these lovely plants are probably descended from the products of Roman industry!

went about pumping the deep workings free of water. Diodorus in the 1st Century AD saw a 'Cochlea' or screw pump, where an inclined Archimidean screw in a trough was used to draw water up from those deep soggy levels sixty feet below the surface:

> These screws raise the water by a continuous movement to the outlet of the gallery, drying the bottom of the mine and making it possible to extend the workings comfortably. The Screws are able, with ordinary effort, to throw up in a marvellous manner an immense volume of water; and it draws easily from a great depth a stream that it pours forth at the surface of the earth . . .

When modern gold miners were extending their operations last century and early this century, they found Roman tools and even the remains of one of the waterwheels of wood, used to make this pumping system work; however deep they went, they found the Romans had been there first!

Water was the great problem. Pliny describes the troubles they had:

> The gradient must be carefully controlled . . . there must be a good head of water at the Dressing floor . . . the water is carried in conduits cut into the rock or carried on wooden trestles . . .

He saw mining going on; gold got from the sand of some rivers, streams and ponds, or:

> in other circumstances the miners excavated hollows supported for a time by arches of rock which were afterward allowed to fall in . . . or they sought the ore by means of horizontal tunnels or vertical shafts . . .

He even ventured undergound, and saw the awesome preparations for a 'Hush':

> . . . the coming downfall gives warning that is instantly perceived by a sentinel who is set to watch upon the peak of the mountain. By voice, trumpet and signal he orders the workmen to be immediately summoned from their labours, and at the same moment takes flight himself . . .

The echoes of his warning cry, of the rush of water through the workings, and the immense activities of two thousand years ago, can still be felt at Dolaucothi.

FIVE SAINTS

Five saints, the old stories say, were on a pilgrimage to Saint Davids, when a great hailstorm started; they lay down (the story is vague as to why they were so silly) with their heads on a stone as their pillow, and:

> . . . the droppes of raine were soone congealed into haylestones which were driven with soe muche force on the wearie pilgrims, that they were beaten soe harde against their pillowe that the vestiges they left are still discernable.

The real story of the stone of the five saints which has given its name to Llanpumsaint nearby—the stone on the small mound near a norman motte, was a roman mortar used to grind and hammer bits of gold-bearing rock to force it to give up its valuable metal.

Five Saints Stone—If the gold bearing ore was not crushed mechanically up on the hillside above the workings, it was mashed to powder in mortars, one of which survives with a story of Five Saints using it as a pillow to account for the depressions in its surface.

MODERN TIMES

Where Pliny marked 'Avrvm' on his map of Wales, men have searched for gold ever since. The Norman motte shows we were interested a thousand years ago; medieval monks in the area round Talley grubbed in the earth for riches, and visited Dolaucothi too. Then a gap till 1797 when the diary of John Johnes of Dolaucothi shows him paying a miner 10/- (50p) a yard to sink a shaft—it didn't get far despite the worthy Mr. Johnes upping the amount to 12/6d! The geologist Murchison visited the site and was impressed, as was the Geological survey, whose lucky officer found a nugget of tiny size, still in the museum in London. This was 1840, but fifteen years later the land was gripped in a gold fever; the adventurers of the 'forty-niners', the Klondykers and Aussies, seeing how things would pan out (a gold mining expression we still use as we sing 'Clementine') brought a gold-rush in reverse, and three Australians lived in a little tented camp here, and dug for British gold 'earning enough to support themselves'. In 1871 the 'Mining Journal' reports that further activity there brought a strange engine with the lovely name *'Gnion-Eur-Glawdd'* = 'Fairy of the goldmine'; it was never described so we don't know what it was! Then in 1888 an imposing company, the South Wales Gold Mines Ltd., was formed, a lot of whose woodwork and deep shafts were visible until safety considerations led to their blanking off in recent times. The company had a mill capable of treating 30 tons of ore a *day*, and a Brittan pan like that at Meirioneth's mines—mercury pulverised with the ore to make an amalgam with the precious metal, then burned in a furnace, boiling off the mercury—a highly toxic procedure, one would imagine—to leave behind the gold. They got out only 1½ penny-weight per ton of ore, and stopped in 1892; a Cornishman called Mitchell found a rich vein when he tried the place in 1905, and called it the Roman Lode—though he had to dig down 100 feet to find it.

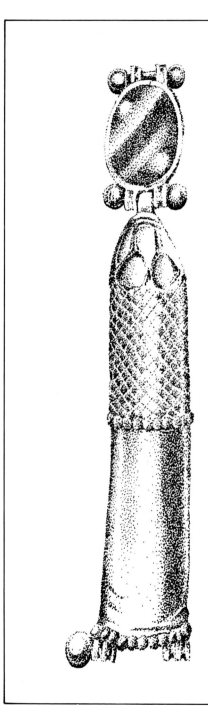

drawing; PB
Gold snake bracelet found at Dolaucothi. Made about 200 A.D.

Its last fling was as Roman Deep Holdings Ltd in 1933, the year we abandoned the Gold standard and Hitler came to power, eventually giving itself the august name of British Goldfields No 1 Ltd.; they made a gold brick from their findings, but again it was the only one. People are still sniffing around the edges of Ogofau and the resting place of the five saints, hoping for that bright glint for which so many men have slaved and died over five thousand years of bloodstained history . . .

Mining didn't change much from Roman times to the early Industrial Revolution of the 18th Century. In this 16th Century drawing Lead miners slide down drifts on ropes or are lowered down shafts to working levels. What light there is comes from hand-held oil lamps, there are horses to help with haulage, and the men wear hooded tunics as primitive protective clothing, and to keep the worst of the water off—it's easy to see where the stories got started of Gnomes bringing riches from the bowels of the earth!

Plumbing Around Carmarthen . . .

They say lead is bad for your health—and I'm sure they are right; breathed from car exhaust fumes or drunk from outdated town waterpipes, chipped by childish teeth from old paint, lead *is* dangerous . . . so much so that some authorities put the Fall of the Roman Empire not so much down to the Vandals, weak emperors and excessive taxation, but to poisoning from their lead conduits, water tanks and pipes. And a lot of it came from around Carmarthen . . .

South Towy, Cystanog, Pistyll Gwyn, Taiaubach, Melin Hill and Nantycerni—romantic names which speak of princes and giants and lovely maids, surely they are the stuff of romance rather than . . . lead mines? But that is what they are. Carmarthen probably owes its status as the westernmost Roman fortified town because of the lead in its hills. And its garrison could be rushed north and east to Dolaucothi if the empire's gold was threatened. So, when you walk among the humps and hollows of Llangunnor, see the Grand Duchess marked on an old record office map, you get echoes not only of the nineteenth Century prosperity, when hundreds of tutworkers and tributers, kibble-fillers and stopers walked out from the town each morning for their twelve hour shift, but of harsh times farther back.

Ovid, a poet of the Roman period, wrote when Christ was only 12 years old:

Not only corn and other fruits for sustenance and store
Were now exacted of the earth, but 'eft they gan to dig
And in the bowels of the earth, insatiably to rig
For riches couched and hidden deep, in places close to Hell . . .

And that is how you feel when you enter the adit of a lead mine. Close to Hell. There is a smell of sulphur on the air, a whiff of garlic too from the arsenic which is also found there. You begin to wonder if the connections between the devil and garlic first arose in a leadminer's mind when he caught that whiff in an adit like Wenallt or Bonville's.

We know, in Wales, how mining and miners have always been kept apart from ordinary folk; we've seen it in the Glamorgan valleys, we've known how our rulers have often spoken of miners as barely human, and this most dangerous of jobs has had its secrecies, its own language even (like those inexplicable workers' names already spoken of! Kibbles? Tuts? . . .) The miner's job was to pluck riches from the grasp of the devil himself, deep in the bowels of the earth—might he not be in league with the cloven hoofed gentleman?—this at any rate was the thinking of medieval people, especially if they caught a quick glimpse of blackened forms emerging suddenly at last light from holes in the ground, talking strange tongues and reeking of garlic. Cornish, Scots and Yorkshire miners will tell you the same. Mining is dark, dangerous and dirty—it is also very lonely, as you are often ostracised by the communities around. This attitude made it easier to ignore the danger, death and suffering of mining communities. Even back in Roman times we have the odd report from a horrified traveller of the working conditions which probably existed around Carmarthen two thousand years ago:

. . . they are held constantly at work day and night without any rest, and carefully kept from any chance of escape. For their guards are foreign soldiers, all speaking different languages so the workers are unable either by speech or a friendly gesture to corrupt those who watch them . . .

This was written in the year Julius Caesar came to Britain to add it to the empire. Another traveller called Diodorus saw our Welsh gold and lead mines, run with ruthless efficiency by the Romans:

They have to get into all sorts of positions and throw to the ground the pieces of ore they deal with; and this they do continually with no cease to comply with the cruelty and blows of the overseer. The young children make their way through the galleries and hollow places and throw up with great toil the fragments of broken stone and bring it up, outdoors to the ground around the entrance . . . there is no-one seeing these luckless people would not pity them because of the excess of their misery, for there is no forgiveness or relaxation at

Druke and beam—Just how little mining techniques
changed over several centuries can be seen from this
photograph, taken at the turn of the Century, of a shift
of miners in one of the many small 'Family' coal mines
in Pembrokeshire. The 'Druke and Beam' winding
gear is just the same as that in 'De Re Metallica''s
woodcuts of 1556.

all for the sick, or the maimed, or the old, or for
women's weakness, but all with blows are compelled
to stick to their labour until, worn out, they die of their
servitude . . .

So, through history, the miner produced the vital
necessities of life in a 'civilised' society while
ignored or put upon by his fellows. Some, mind,
thought enough to write about them. As early as
1387 Ranulf Hugden said of the Carmarthen
mines:

Valeys bringeth forth food
Ond Hilles mettall right goode . . .

and a visit Down Under today often brings a whiff
not only of lead and arsenic but of romance. A book
written in the late medieval period by Julius

Agricola tells of scenes which took place in all metal-
liferous mines like those around Carmarthen. The
veins of ore were hidden deep, you could not expect
to strike it rich every time . . . and once slavery was
abandoned, greed had to be the motive for risking
your life in this way underground! So the Master or
Captain of a mine would have teams of men

working for him, each quite independent, the amount of money they might make depending not only upon their skill and hard work but their luck in striking a rich lode of ore. Agricola describes a stange custom, when a lode was struck, and the archaeology of this custom can still be found.

Areas were worked in Bargains, usually decided (like the North Wales Slate quarrymen still decide who shall have a 'bargain' of slate to split) by pulling straws from the Master's clenched hand. Once a miner had found a lode or vein, a strange ceremony was enacted. The Captain of the mine and his officials walked solemnly to this place, 'men of good repute' said the laws of the mine, and these worthies stood on the edge of the hole, looking at the miner's discovery. The Captain pointed a finger at the miner and asked:

'Which is your Vein?'

The miner replied

'This is my Vein'

'Which digging carries metal?'

'This, I swear it' and the miner pointed to the lode.

The miner was then ordered to approach the winding gear of his little working (like the crank of a wishing well and known locally as a Druke and Beam), to put two fingers of his right hand upon it, then upon his forehead, and say

I swear by God and all the Saints and I call them to witness, that this is my vein; and if it be not mine, may neither this head nor these hands perform their functions . . .

Then the Captain solemnly gave the miner his hefty iron hammer, and the miner threw it as far as he was able, in each direction north, south, east and west from his discovery, and wherever the hammer landed a stake was placed in the ground, to be made more permanent later by a stone boundary mark called a Meer Stone. This area was the property of that miner and his gang, and anything they got up from it was theirs, after the inevitable rakeoffs and taxes had been exacted. The remains of these strange activities can be seen all over the hills around Carmarthen, the adits (or levels into the hillsides), the trials, little heaps of waste giving a clue to buried workings beneath your feet, the

water trickling from drainage levels near the river, even the odd engine house like Clay's.

These miners were free men, of course, apart from the necessity to earn a living. Not so those slaves working under the cruel hand of Julius Frontinus, a name to make anyone around Carmarthen quiver with fear in Roman times. Julius built the great amphitheatre at Caerleon as well as the fierce fortified town to house the legion. He was an expert on water piping and supply of towns, and was totally ruthless in his quest for lead with which to do it. He was the man who crushed the Welsh tribe the Silures and was rewarded by being made Water Commissioner for Rome in 97 AD. His engineer/soldiers found lead in the Mendips, in Yorkshire, Derbyshire, Shropshire, Flint, Denbigh, Cardigan and Carmarthen. No meals for his workers, just work till death intervened. Later, when the Romans were forgotten, men delved into the Carmarthen hills for 2d a day, they pioneered the use of water power and of steam to drain and lift in their holes in places close to Hell. Straggling lines of donkeys took the ore, crushed by the womenfolk and children and those too infirm to go below ground, down to the Quay at Carmarthen where some of it was smelted on the spot, or shipped by sloop to Llanelli. Pioneers. But as descendants of the criminals who were sent to the mines as part of their punishment (a sentence still not unheard of in today's civilised concern for the Proletariat) this provided another reason why the brave men and women of Llangunnor were ostracised, even being buried in separate graveyards . . . for had they not been closer to the Devil than most of us?

WHAT YOU CAN SEE

Along the Llangunnor lane by the river are some levels, now partially blocked by modern rubbish, into which you can crawl (take hard hat, torch, gumboots and at least one friend). This level has the appearance of a Roman Coffin level, though it was much knocked about and used in the great expansion which took place in 1852-1866, when the Vale of Towy and other mines were the biggest employers in Carmarthen. There are pits and shafts all over the hillside, there are mine office buildings at

Bonville's end and a Cornish engine house very like that at Lady Eliza stands jackdawed and noisy in the woods; so once we had steam power here powered by Welsh coal dug by miners of a different locality but just as hardy and brave as Carmarthen's men. Some veins in this area have been worked very recently. Zinc, arsenic and barytes also came from these enigmatic holes in the hills where Merlin once roamed, talking to himself or to his scampering pig . . .

Agricola's Druke and Beam 1556

Adam and the Adders . . .

The locals call it 'Roach', and it is one of the castles which form that amazing Landsker line across Pembrokeshire dividing it into a Welsh northern half and an English (ex-Norman French) half in the south. We are very rich in castles around this area, both of the 'motte' type (see Nevern) and the castle-proper with its keeps, towers and curtain walls. But none has a more curious history than Roch.

It was built by Adam de la Roche—'Adam of the Rock'—and you can see why it got this local name, now remembered in the village's title. A knob of volcanic rock is crowned by this long, thin castle tower, now modernised and lived in, but as recently as 1900 a shell. Adam built this, so the local story goes, in answer to a prophesy. A witch had told this Norman knight his fortune, and it was not nice; he would die, she told him, of an adder bite. Adam was consumed with this thought, and got his masons to design this tall castle to try to defy the witch's prediction. He lived right up at the top of it, never seeing anyone before they had been searched for vipers; having special food brought by special trusted servants, adder-free to a man. The witch had given a time-limit to this incarceration as she had specified the number of years he needed to remain in hiding. The last night approached, and still Adam was alive and kicking, unbit and thinking he had nearly won. Then the last night.

It was blowing a real Pembrokeshire gale—and only we who live here know how hard *that* is—and cold, it was, too. Adam shivered up in his snake-free room and dreamed of roaring fires; he got his servants to bring a mass of logs in baskets, to warm him till the next morning when he would be free.

But one of the baskets of logs concealed an adder, and it bit him, and he was found next morning by his servants, dead, his eyes wide in terror:

'. . . and a look of disbelief on his visage . . .' said the ancient who told this tale. Well, would you believe it? . . .

More prosaically, the castle was used as a beacon in time of Viking invasions; Roch was later owned by the Walters family, whose most famous daughter, Lucy, was the girlfriend of Charles the second (or one of them) and mother of the ill-fated Duke of Monmouth, whose rebellion in 1685 ended in such bloody killings, of 'Bloody Jeffries'' assize . . . Somehow it all seems rather remote from this peaceful bit of Pembrokeshire—

Grass snake emerges from hibernation—Druids and Greek gods alike learned their secrets by having their ears licked by snakes—a snake curls its way up the Tree of Life, whispering corrupting words to Eve . . . to the Egyptians a friend of the sun god, to the Kentucky Holy Rollers a source of ecstasy, relation of dragons, magical animal which symbolized resurrection in the sloughing of its skin . . . and there was the fear of death in its bite . . .

Roch Castle—allegedly built by Adam de la Roche so he was well away from the snakes which, according to the Curse, would be his DOOM . . .

Vanished Into the Sand—

Pennard Castle—sunk in the sand dunes above Oxwich Bay, within sight of another haunted ruin—Oxwich Castle, where walks the ghost of poor Lady Rhys Mansell, murdered by her brawling husband during a quarrel over the proceeds of a ship deliberately wrecked in the bay by false lights—from Culver (see WRECKING).

There is very little remaining above ground of Pennard Castle—you walk over the links . . . it's there, it *must* be there somewhere, the map people have put Olde Englishe there, 'Castle, Rems of' . . . and when you get there, rems it is, with a vengeance! But somehow, once you know the strange story of Pennard (one you can find repeated in some details at Kenfig) the very slightness of the castle is part of the drama.

Once, Pennard stood proudly at the head of a valley, like Manorbier in Pembrokeshire, guarding a landing point against all comers; it is said by the Old Stories not to be a Norman castle at the time of the story, but held by a wild Welsh chieftain Rhys ap Iestyn. He was a friend and colleague of Prince

Llewelyn of North Wales—the last Welsh prince of Wales, killed at Builth in 1282—and seems to have been a bit of a bully-boy; wild, impetuous, extravagant and mean in unpredictable turns, arrogant. The prince had a daughter, Angharad, and Rhys (so the story goes) was rewarded by his royal colleague with the girl's hand in marriage, in thanks for his efforts, his courage and loyalty in

66

battle against the Normans. The wedding was to be at Pennard Castle, there was to be feasting, music and dancing. The only trouble was, nobody seems to have asked poor Angharad's views on it all; and she was not all that keen on Rhys . . .

With the wedding festivities well under way, and young Rhys already downing fair quantities of mead and getting very noisy, Angharad wandered off along the long corridors and draughty walkways of Pennard Castle; the wind mewed gently through the arrowslits and blew little flurries of sand in her face. Then she caught the sound of other music, unearthly, lovely, soft, enticing. From the battlements she saw a group of tiny people dancing to their own musicians in the moonlight, laughing and chatting in some language she did not understand. She watched them, entranced. But some of Rhys' guards had seen them too, and went to tell the Master. By now Rhys was thoroughly plastered and very loud indeed:

I kill them . . . Kill them all . . .

he shouted.

The Barque 'Naples'—was wrecked on 25th January, 1869, near St Davids on her way from Boston, painted by an eyewitness; rockets are being fired to get a line to the survivors . . . but the natives were not always as helpful and friendly; that line of locals could be waiting for loot, and not to care too much how they got it . . .

Angharad tried to stop them, but the soldiers grabbed their weapons and rushed out through the gate into the moonlight—the girl was convinced some terrible tragedy would overtake them all if this was allowed to happen, and entreated her husband-to-be to call his men back. Rhys didn't listen

I fear no one of this world or any other

he roared.

And waving a mug of mead in one hand and a sword in the other, Rhys staggered out to do battle with the mysterious little folk in the dunes. And as Angharad watched, aghast but helpless from the turret above the gateway, the little people vanished, leaving a slight whiff of sulphur on the night air. From the dunes a voice spoke, unearthly, grave, soft, menacing. Rhys stood swaying, uncertain now, with the air ashiver, and heard:

> Proud and arrogant Chief, you came intent to destroy our sport, music and dance—we wished you no harm yet you would kill us; we danced in the moonlight and you would spill our blood on the sand. Therefore the sand is thine enemy. Thy city and thy castle, proud lofty castle though it is, shall be no more . . .

and all at once the moon was covered by clouds, a ferocious storm blew up and the town, and the castle, vanished, ruined, and nobody ever lived there again . . .

That's the story as the old people tell it. History is less dramatic but follows the same story—the little people, as they vanished, had said darkly:

> *'Thy battle, brave chief shall not be with Man but with sand . . .'*

and so it has been. For a castle of its date (thirteenth century) it was only occupied for a relatively short time span—about 250 years, and then only intermittently, and it never saw military struggle, only a battle against the encroaching sand, which by the sixteenth century had destroyed it. Now its only visitors are lizards, herons and the occasional golfer whose ball has gone wide. And if you go there on a moonlight night—They Say you might still hear mournful music from the tufts of grass in the dunes, as Angharad died young, her bullying husband did not know her long, and she still haunts this castle buried deep in the sand of the curse . . .

Reminders of Sea Trade . . .
Top:
Alexanders and fennel, growing at Abercastell, where they have flourished since being brought here by the Romans 2000 years ago along with many other herbs and culinary plants. The Romans liked "Parsley of Alexandria" in salads and stews (it's the ancestor of celery), and fennel with fresh mackerel.

Bottom:
Scurvy grass, *Cochlearia officinalis,* much prized by our sailors (legal and illegal) as a sovereign remedy for the dread disease of scurvy, caused by vitamin C deficiency. The lack of green fruit and fresh vegetables on the long voyages often led to most of the crew being afflicted by this awful scourge, but a mouthful of this plant acted like magic . . . it was even picked to be sold on London's streets . . . King George III liked some for breakfast.

Noah and the Drunken Prince . . .
A piece of oak branch hacked with an axe, lying in some leaf litter; the axe, however, is made of stone, and the forest is now at the bottom of the sea. The trees were knocked down like so many matches during some great catastrophe in the Middle Stone-age,—Noah's Flood perhaps? Could this be the Sumerian "lost land of Gilgamesh, the Forester King", or was it the land drowned when Seithenin, the drunken prince, forgot to close the sluices? It is one of Wales', and the world's, greatest mysteries.
Below: St. Bride's Bay was once dry land (Dinas Fach, Solva).

Wrecking . . .

Some of my wartime years were spent wrecking; that is, enjoyable if ghostly walks along the seashore after storms, finding Bits. A lantern here, a shoe, a piece of brass on some driftwood, a lifebelt with a name . . . German gasmasks were different from our own so there was an exciting *frisson* about such a find . . . one still had its German attached, a sickening morning as the poor man had been in the sea some weeks and I learned by experience that the Coastguard gave you 7/6d (35p to you post decimal types) for every body discovered along the sea's edge. It was not worth it.

Wrecks were a source of income to coastal communities, so much so that in some areas false lights lured ships to their doom, the crew and passengers being murdered as everything worth taking was grabbed from the storm . . .

drawing by PB

69

Then we had our wreck—I mean 'our' wreck; staying to recuperate from the blitz, with a Gower Aunt, her cottage on the edge of a cliff overlooking a snug cove in the bay which, one stormy night, became the grave of a brave little ship on the run from the Nazis; Dutch, she was, and ran the gauntlet of mines and Eboats, not to mention our own defences, to get to Swansea and safety, but the storm came up and blew her into Port Eynon. The Captain and crew were got off safely by breeches buoy, and by the time I visited her next but one low tide, the vultures had been through like locusts (if metaphors may be mixed in this way) and there wasn't a piece of moveable metal that had not gone; and what was not moveable was smashed. People gone mad, one thought . . . but here was I, and what for? To dream again I suppose . . . until I was interrupted by seeing gramophone records all over the deck of one cabin, awash and pulverized. As I stood there, tears in my eyes, the Dutch captain himself came back on board for a last look around; he spoke no English and I no Dutch—my only foreign language was German at that point, a little tactless to try it out in the circumstances. But he searched about and eventually found one record which was, if not undamaged, at least unbroken. He gave it to me, together with his badge; we smiled, and I never saw him again. If he reads this now, he may be intrigued to know that that record —Lotte Lehmann singing a piece of Wagner, started me off on a lifetime of collecting gramophone records; Miss Lehmann, still salty after her immersion in the sea, has been joined by thousands of others, all enjoyed, all with memories of one sort or another. But this isn't the place to muse nostalgically. It is to talk about, and to introduce wrecking.

Wrecking has always been part of life on the coasts of Cornwall and on those of Pembrokeshire and Gower. Terrible seas combine with contrary wind and tide-races to sweep sailing ships (and even as we have seen, ships with good modern engines) off course and onto the rocks. And the rocks are needle sharp, piercing even iron hulls as if they were paper. Underwater archaeologists reckon there are hundreds of thousands of wrecks of all ages around this coastline. Many met their doom in storm or tempest, like the one I saw—many more

were deliberately lured to smash themselves on the rocks, by the placing of false lights in places where a Master would expect to see something, and make a turn too early or otherwise put his ship into its death agonies.

Nobody lived to tell the tale, of course, for two reasons; if once the story got about, Captains might be more careful next time they saw a light in your area . . . and there was a peculiarity in the law which stated that a ship only became Wreck (that is, plunderable, belonging to nobody, a total loss) after 'every living thing on board was dead . . .' This meant rats, cats, people, goats, sheep . . . once everything and everybody was dead, the ship was yours, and a lot of isolated communities lived off this savage law for years. Any survivors of the wreck itself had to run the hopeless gauntlet of trying to scramble ashore hindered by the waves and by villagers standing awaiting them with cudgels and heavy sticks and knives. They were either thrown back or killed first on dry land, their jewels being taken by the drastic if simple expedient of cutting off a finger if it had a ring on it, hacking away an ear on which dangled an earring . . . Then, suitably mutilated in the cause of enrichment, the corpse was thrown back.

The Authorities knew about it of course; but there wasn't a lot they could do. They had first to find the men who lit the false lights; catch them at it; or find the stuff from the wreck, which after the death of all the people on board was legitimate plunder anyway, unless it had excise duty to pay (like silks, or brandy, or baccy). And in the general atmosphere of corruption which prevailed, how were you to get anybody to admit they knew anything . . . brandy for the Parson, baccy for the Clerk . . .?

There are one or two instances of wrecking so blatant, bloodthirsty or dramatic they have become part of local folk lore, so these can be recounted as examples. If you visit the cliffs near 'my' wartime wreck in Overton Mere, Gower, you find a curious structure built into a fissure there, almost invisible unless you go specially to find out. It has odd holes in the masonry of which it is made, which has led some experts to call it a pigeon house. But its construction gives the lie to this; it is near the sea, it has a small door reached by a scramble up an oily rope, then inside you see daylight through two or three windows at staggered intervals up the wall. According to local stories it is a wrecker's light, duplicating, wrongly, the lights for the entrance to Swansea Bay, which a mariner sailing up the channel would be expecting; seeing it, he would turn several miles too soon but, instead of finding Swansea and safety, he could not swing about, especially in bad weather, before he ended up on Oxwich Bay, where his arrival was—expected . . .

Now this can only be supposition. No record survives of what Culver Hole is or what it might have been used for. Its geographical position, the local traditions of wrecking and one other story make it likely, that's the most we can say. The one other story is that of the ghost of Oxwich Castle.

Oxwich, like Culver, has a pigeony look about some of it—there is an elaborate pigeonhouse in the grounds; we don't know where the original Oxwich Castle was, but this one dates from fairly late on, certainly about sixteenth century; the place was built as a fortified mansion by a local family whose fortunes nobody could ever fathom out—so the rumour grew that it was from smuggling and/or wrecking, the Mansells grew rich. Oxwich was compared to Raglan for its splendid and lavish decoration and the number of its rooms. What look like battlements along the top of one wall are in fact the lower halves of windows in what was a long gallery rather like the one Sir John Perrott built at Carew, probably from the proceeds of piracy! Sir Rice Mansell got a similar reputation, building on such a scale; the tower is the culmination of this extravagance, six stories high it was, and richly decorated sets of rooms within it for him and his illfated wife and family . . .

Sir George Herbert, Vice-Admiral of the Crown arrived . . . there had been a wreck, very rich too, he'd heard; where was the cargo, the loot, the duty-payable booze and spice and silks? This is one version; another is that Herbert, too, got a lot of his living from wrecking . . . but this is not reliable. Officially, he was there on behalf of the elder daughter of King Henry VIII—for then we were in that short but bloody rule of Queen Mary. There had been a lot of fighting with France, with whom

Culver Hole is very well hidden from the landward side, and is still quite hard to get into; with a good fire going within, those holes would have looked convincingly like the Mumbles light. But by the time you'd found out it wasn't, it was too late to turn the ship about, and she'd be wrecked . . . and the crew didn't survive to tell the tale . . .

Spain had persuaded Mary to declare war, and next year we would lose Calais as a British 'possession'. The two men, Herbert and Mansell, got heated when Herbert attempted to force himself into the castle to look for the loot—they started fighting, first with swords then with anything that came to hand, even throwing chunks of castle at each other; in this fight Mansell's wife, fearful that if this affray got out there might be horrible consequences (for the years of Mary were frightening for all classes), tried to calm things down. She was herself shouting for peace between the two snarling, fighting men when a stone hit the poor lady on the head and killed her instantly.

The booty was never seen again; what happened we can only guess. But soon afterwards Rice Mansell died broken hearted, and the ghost of Lady Anne Mansell still walks the palatial house she did not live to enjoy, and in which she died trying to keep the peace. Or so they say, anyway . . .

One of the treasured memories of doing the 'Sou'wester' programme was seeing the expressions of mixed bewilderment and disbelief on the faces of the summer visitors, and some locals, when Piet and Rog took to the coast of Gower carrying rope, a tape recorder, a violin and a squeezebox concertina; few walkers of the coast path and cliff-top take these impedimenta; but there was a purpose to this apparent abnormality. We were about to try to recreate a bit of history, that of the loss of *'Phebe and Peggy'*, a story of death and destruction shrined in song.

We have already visited Culver Hole, probably a wrecker's false light to lure great ships to their deaths along with their crews. But is all this talk of wrecking and murdering of survivors in the realms of fiction, of Cruel Coppinger and 'Face the Wall, my Darling as the Gentlemen go by . . .'? Could such barbarism ever really have happened? One bit of evidence gave stark proof, and we were moved to carry all that musical hardware on a country walk in consequence.

Haul the fiddle aloft, me hearties . . .—Piet Brinton taking a violin on board Culver Hole on the day we recorded the terrible tale of 'Phebe and Peggy', remembered in a pop song written in Solva in the 1770s. Violins come into this story in another way—the wreck of 'Phebe and Peggy' so upset a Liverpool violin maker (who'd settled in Solva) that he changed his profession overnight and started to design light houses . . .

72

'Phebe' at Phildelphia Quay   woodcut dated Oct 1772

During a great storm on January 8, 1773 an American ship, the *Phebe and Peggy*, was wrecked in Porth y Bwch Bay, St Elvis, Solva; now Solva was a well known port in those days, she may have been trying to reach it, or been blown off course in the treacherous currents of St Bride's Bay, graveyard of thousands of fine ships. She was said to be en route from Philadelphia to Newry and Liverpool with passengers and a rich cargo . . . she never reached her destination, and still lies off the murderous rocks of the Pembrokeshire coast. The burial register of Solva church tells of three brave men—Henry John, William Woolcock and Peter Richard—who went to the rescue of the passengers and crew of *Phebe and Peggy* and were drowned, along with the people they were attempting to save; 'all boats capsized in the tumultuous seas and every soul perished . . .' said the papers.

But local feeling was so outraged by what happened below on those deadly rocks and inlets and foam-flecked grey cliff edges, that a song appeared, in broad-sheet form, soon afterwards. It tells, in everyday language no less horrible for its ordinariness, what probably happened on the hideous night of January 8, 1773.

This is part of it:

THE WRECK OF THE PENNSYLVANIA ('PHEBE AND PEGGY')

A ship was built in Philadelphia,
The Capital of Pennsylvania;
When she bore out all for the channel,
New Christmas Day she took her farewell.
With merry hearts they sailed for Newry,
First land they spied was the isle of Ramsey;
They set their compass to the North-West—
The hurricane came from the South-West;
Into St Brides Bay she was well recorded,
Where many a thousand souls were drowned.
The night came on, she met the races,
She struck a rock down near St Elvis.

Four Lusty Men came out from Solva,
And eighteen more from Philadelphia;
One was single, three was married,
The boat turned round and they was drowned.
There was some wives, there was some children,
Abroad the ship their cry was dismal,
The weakest sort was left to drowndy,
I hope the Lord here show'd them mercy.

Madam Elliott she was drowned,
Five Hundred guineas in her pocket.
An' ol' Luke Davey and John Phillips
They robbed the lady in a minute,
And for her rings they cut her fingers
And split her ears all for her jewels.
These country mobs they be like villains,
They stripped the ladies of their jewels,
And after they had robbed the ladies,
They left them there like Stinking fishes.
Till Gentlemen came bury the ladies,
In Brawdy Church down near St Elvis.

Now when you rises in the mornin'
Pray to God to Give you Blessing—
Nobody knows but at Sun Rising,
What may befall before the Evening . . .

A bit of folk history, shrined in song, sold at street corners two hundred years ago where consciences suddenly rebelled at our treatment of fellow beings. It must be said that no record remains in Brawdy's burial register of those ladies, gallantly interred by 'Gentlemen' . . . and the song mentions four men drowned in the rescue (or, more likely, by their erstwhile friends on shore); the record only gives three names. But it is not an isolated occurrence, this plunder of a ship, as a visitor to Pembrokeshire in 1791, Mrs. Morgan, wrote in her diary:

DRUIDS TOWN

. . . tie our horse chaise to the bowsprit of a vessel that was lately wrecked, not long since, upon this coast. She was a transport laden with ordnance stores from America, and appeared on the northwest side of St Brides Bay and exhibited such signs of distress as attracted the attentions of the inhabitants of the coast in the neightbourhood of St Davids, and induced them to watch its progress with the expectation of dividing the wreck. Fresh associates joined them, and advanced towards the cliffs at Druidstown, where a considerable number of men and Women assembled.

As they were the very lowest order of the community and had toiled so far solely with the hope of plunder, it may well be conceived that they lost no time in boarding the vessel and loading themselves with her contents as soon as she was accessible. They were the more eager because they knew that the Gentlemen of the country are extremely vigilant upon such occasions and fly without delay to the relief of the Distressed; for the double purpose of rescuing them from the devouring waves and protecting them from the rapacity of those who are waiting among the rocks, to ravish from them the little the sea has spared.

The multitude were in complete possession of their prey. A very considerable quantity of the gunpowder was landed from the stranded vessel. Many of the plunderers had loaded themselves with as much of the booty as their friends threw from the wreck; by such means much of the powder was scattered on the beach and on the rocks. In this scene of general confusion, one of the villagers on the vessel, either irritated at the eagerness of those on shore, and at the waste that it occasioned, or out of mere unthinking wantonness, swore a dreadful oath that he would presently give them enough to satisfy them all. He then snatched up a musket and dashed it against a rock; a single spark was sufficient to produce a most tremendous explosion.

The strand and the rocks were instantly rapt in fire and smoke and many of the unhappy victims who bore about them the means of their own destruction were blown into the air. Several were killed on the spot, some so disfigured that their bodies could not be distinguished. Others died lingering deaths at different intervals of time. And some now live, wretched and miserable spectacles of their own rashness and inhumanity . . .

Mrs. Morgan's Tour to Milford Haven, 1791

The sea is not always the calm and lovely thing we come to holiday by. It is a cruel and sinister place also . . . many professional sailors hate it, fear it, and it is little wonder the tales that come from its depths are often Gothic in the extreme . . . if you have the stomach for it, read on for the grim tale of the Smalls Light—

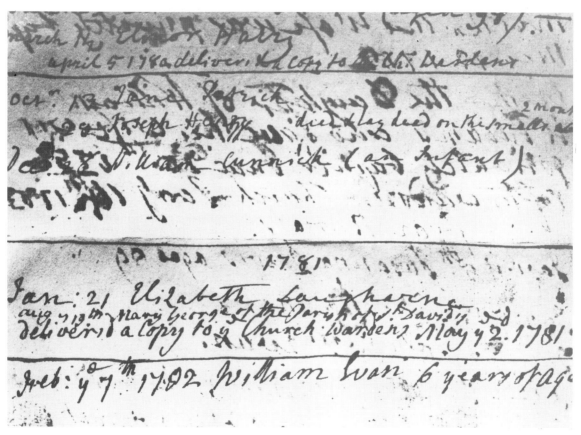

Solva: Burial Register for October 1780—Though very hard to decipher, the central entry reads:—'Octr 28, Joseph Harry, died and lay dead on the Smalls 2 month'.

Courtesy Pembrokeshire Record Office

75

Died and Lay Dead Two Months . . .

THE SMALLS LIGHT AFFAIR

Old sailors sit by the sea, staring out misty eyed, pipe in hand, and tell tall tales to boggling-eyed boys. Much of it is romantic eyewash, but perhaps it is a good thing, we should have had fewer Drakes and Frobishers and Nelsons if everybody thought the life unromantic! But some of those tales are *true* . . .

Like the little mounds at Freshwater West, the graves of sailors from ships drowned there. Like the story of the *Ardmore*, which vanished with all hands on a trip between Ireland and Bristol in 1940, and not a thing more was heard of her until recently, when a diver going much too deep for safety came up from a terrible depth . . . with two of her teacups. Like the *Sultan*, which went down with all hands, as the official report states, 'Including the Ventriloquist'; one imagines him standing on deck trying to say 'Agandon Shick' and 'Take to the Lifegoats' without moving his lips. A showbiz tragedy luckily averted by the steamer which unloaded the whole of Barnum and Bailey's circus onto Milford Dock in 1898, straight from America. Every cove has its tale of shipwreck, bravery, tragedy and, sometimes, grim comedy. But it is always at this junction between land and sea that accident and wreck occurs; and it was here that lighthouses grew.

There are some seven thousand miles of coastline skirting Britain, some of it the most dangerous in the world: the Romans built Pharos beacons; in medieval times some placed lights on dangerous spots to warn mariners while others did so to cause wrecks, of course, like some mentioned in this book already or wicked Sir John Killigrew of the Lizard whose light of 1619 was to wreck many ships. Early light keepers risked kidnapping by pirates or wreckers—there's a tale of one such, when the lightkeeper's daughter on Longships had to stand on the Bible to reach the lamps her kidnapped father had not been able to ignite. Lighthouses have the romance and horror of total isolation which makes the late Roy Plomley's Desert Island quite alluring —we shudder to listen to the tale of Flannan isle

Smalls Light—Victorian model made, as was the 18th Century original, in Solva. From a postcard dated 1902 —the jaunty flag flying from the light says 'READY AYE READY' . . . the model was made from some of the wood used in building the original.

light, not an old tale at all but from the turn of this century; passing ships saw no light, night after night, and the eventual rescue party found the table laid ready for a meal, everything in perfect order—but no people were ever found. Gruesome tales also abound, none more so than that of the elderly keeper of Eddystone, a wooden light which caught fire (a common disease of early wooden lights); the poor old man of 94 who was employed there as keeper, in trying to put out the flames, had a stream of molten lead from the burning roof pour down his gullet and boil his innards horribly . . . despite this unbelievable ordeal he lived for several terrible days with half a pound of hot lead inside him, and those who wish can still see it, preserved in Edinburgh's medical museum. But there is no stranger story than the Smalls light, off the coast of Pembrokeshire.

The Smalls are a cluster of deadly rocks some twenty-two miles off the coast. They, and the Hats and Barrels, have been a scourge of shipping for centuries, and indeed still are, as the sorry affair of the *Christos Bitas* shows only too well! In the eighteenth century a passing Liverpool violin-maker, Henry Whiteside, was so appalled at the loss of life he heard about on the Smalls rocks that he settled in Solva, married the local publican's daughter and turned into a maker, no more of fiddles, but of lighthouses, an unlikely change of occupation for any man. But he could well have heard the ballad being sold and presumably sung in Solva, the *Phebe and Peggy*; this and its horrific toll of life may well have influenced him. In addition, he was a colleague of Liverpool merchants like John Phillips, who had Pembrokeshire connections too, and a year after the wrecking of the *Phebe and Peggy* obtained a lease of fifty years from the crown for the Smalls, to build a light there; Phillips and Whiteside, who was to become his engineer, sailed out to the little rock, standing only four feet above water at high tide, lashed by every sort of wild Atlantic weather, and conceived together a brave plan. Whiteside's light would not be the usual wooden or stone tower, solidly withstanding the elements by sheer bulk, but a flimsy looking dovecote of a building supported on wooden piles, moving with the waves, letting most of the force vanish between its spidery legs. This extraordinary structure was built, and stood for eighty years and more with its light nearly fifty feet above the water. Henry Whiteside had unbelievable experiences during the making of this light, including being marooned there in a storm:

> . . . in a most distressed and dangerous condition . . . our water near all gone, our fire quite gone, and our house in a most melancholy manner. I need say no more but remain
>
> Your distressed
> Humble Servant
>
> Henry Whitesides

This note, dated Feb 1 1777, was actually 'posted' in that traditional way of getting information through at sea, in a bottle—and it got there! Despite all this, the light was eventually finished, and became in its time the most lucrative light in the world—for it should be remembered that though some people, Whitesides included, might have had altruistic motives in their lightbuilding activities, for most Men of Business it was hard cash which made them hand out golden guineas for lighthouse building. So it was here. The Smalls is near what was the busiest shipping lane in the world, every ship wanting to reach Liverpool, on the America or Irish or Continental run in or out, had to pass within its light, and therefore pay dues when docking, and even at a farthing a ton, the light was 'earning' for its makers and their descendants anything up to £11,000 a year, the average being about £7000—as it cost about £300 in wages and supplies, it was a reasonable profit!

So by 1780 the light was burning, and paying its way. Four local men were employed on a 'month on, month off' basis to crew the light, which therefore only had two men on the light at any one time. And herein lay the way to tragedy and horror. Some time in August 1780, two men were on the Smalls together—not on very good terms, local gossip had it, but there they were, marooned for their month 'On'. They were Joseph Harry and Thomas Griffiths, both in their early thirties but opposite in character and health; Joe Harry was small, ill with consumption like all his numerous but very impoverished family, whose names fill the local church register for their often-repeated births and deaths, all the latter being premature. Tom Griffiths was a tradesman fallen on hard times, he had been a cooper, and probably felt the job of light keeper to be below him. But it was all he could get; unemployment was rife, the French war was on and off, inflation and our recent troubles with America . . . we were alone, at war simultaneously with Sweden, Russia, Denmark, France, Spain, Prussia, Holland and there were rumblings in India.

So Harry and Griffiths were lucky to have any sort of job, even one on the dreaded Smalls light. For even a hardened sailor would cringe at the thought of that tiny, delicate-looking wooden pigeon-house perched up on its spindly legs and having to brave the fury of the Atlantic for months at a time . . . because it often happened that your month ended when it was too stormy for a landing to be made, so there you stayed until you were fetched. You had enough water, enough coal, food and oil for the lamps, but the psychological effect of such incarceration must have been almost unendurable. And sickly Harry died there.

Now, Griffiths could simply have tipped his dead comrade's body out over the side, a burial at sea. But perhaps frightened about a murder charge, he sat with the mouldering corpse awaiting rescue, which was due at any minute . . . but it did not come. Day after day, week after week dragged by, and the storms went on battering the little light, it rocked at every thundrous wave, cringed at every

Stills from 'The Smalls Light Tragedy'—Two men are alone on the light, 20 miles out into the stormy Atlantic —Joseph Harry falls ill and dies . . . his colleague is left for two months alone with the rotting corpse . . . even when he manages to make a coffin and get it outside, its presence drives him mad by the time rescuers arrive . . .

Courtesy Nant Films Ltd (*Ffilmiau'r Nant*)

fierce blast from the westerlies; the glass was blown in by the force of the wind or by the bodies of gulls attracted by the light and then hurled against it. Griffiths built a makeshift coffin for the now distinctly decomposed and maggot-ridden body of Joseph Harry, and to avoid the overpowering stench, lashed this coffin outside the light, on a small balcony surrounding the lantern glass. Even there he was not free of his erstwhile colleague, as the coffin started to come to bits, and the wind blew against the glass (whose lantern had in it lamps which needed tending once an hour) the tap-tap-tapping fingers of bony, fleshless fingers. This and the solitude drove Griffiths mad, and so the eventual rescuers found one corpse and one lunatic. The burial register for Whitchurch parish sums it all up laconically in the Vicar's entry for October 28 1780:

'Joseph Harry, died and lay dead on the Smalls 2 mths'

Ever since, British lights have had three men 'on board' at any one time . . .

It should be said that in the other accounts of the Smalls light tragedy, the 'facts' are not as here given! You can find this story repeated again and again, in recent books about lighthouses of Britain, or books about Pembrokeshire. There the date is vague, but given as 'about 1800' and the names of the men are Howells and Griffiths—Joseph Harry not getting an honourable mention. It may well be thought arrogant in the extreme that this story is different in date and cast. The point may be that we are wrong! But there is another one, and it concerns how historians go about researching history: much depends upon written records, and there is a feeling about something written down that it *must*, somehow, *be right*.

Many accounts say such similar things, even using the same phrases, that it is tempting to ask who said it first—various newspapers printed both locally and nationally, repeat the same basic story —the tragic death, the marooning, the coffin, even the waving hand . . . but the names and dates are not ours. So the *West Wales Guardian* (17/11/33) reports a 'thrilling lecture' by Mr. Evans of Solva,

owner of a model of the first Smalls light made from bits of the original wood. *The Daily News* of 26/10/1923, has Howell and Griffiths in a 'romantic tale'. The *Western Mail* in 1912 tells of the tragedy but makes it '25 years after the French invasion (1797)'. 1823—bear in mind that Richard Fenton in his *History of Pembrokeshire* already knew about it, and treated it as an old story, in 1809! The *Pembroke County Guardian* wrote, in August 1906, of the story of Howell and Griffith and mentioned the 'crouching form of a dead man lashed to the balcony rails'. The *West Wales Guardian* of November 1899 gives a lot of space to the story and is most detailed as to facts, if that is what they are— but even this is, more or less word for word, a copy of a privately printed story of 1858, at about the time there was local interest in the Smalls and its light, as another, new rock-built light (the one that is still there) was about to be cut into blocks in Solva Harbour and transported, piece by numbered piece, out to that remote little rock twenty two miles away. Is this the 'original'?—it appears not. For even this, printed the year before the *Royal Charter* storm which so altered our coastline as well as sinking four hundred ships in a single night, no, even this is not the first time the story was told.

Ivor Emlyn of Solva wrote a pamphlet in 1851 called 'The Smalls, a Sketch of the old Light House, its projector and Builder'—and at last a source is quoted. Ivor Emlyn said his piece was taken from an article written, but not published, in 1825 by 'A local man much interested in the place and the event' but not giving the name—not unusual in the days when books were often written by 'Lady of Quality' or 'By a Gentleman'. This period, 1825, was a time when there was a lot of interest in the light, it was making big money, there were attempts by Trinity House to buy out the owner, by then the Rev. Buchanan, who was holding out for over £14,000, an enormous sum in those days. So all the other papers and books seem to stem from the 'original' anonymous author's story of 1825, and he, too, tells of Griffith and Howell. What happened? Who's wrong? Are we both?

Our main evidence is twofold—there is the vicar's burial of Joseph Harry who 'died and lay dead on the Smalls' in 1780, an event sufficiently striking for it to get written in the register; in an age of violent death only the goriest was noted. Then there is the death, in 1800 of one T. Griffith in an asylum record in the Poor Law Register. Was he the man who went mad at having to share his light with a mouldering corpse? How about this for a scenario:

1778: light opens; four men employed on a 'two on, two off' basis.

1780: Howell and another are 'off' Griffith and the unfortunate Harry are 'on'; Harry dies in August, is buried in October, local horror story, Griffiths, now mad, is carried off to the Poor Law Asylum. Everybody forgets it.

1800: Griffith eventually dies, temporary hum of activity, old people remember the story, but not the names of everybody; 'Griffiths' and 'Dead' enshrined in the folk law.

1809: Fenton in 'History of Pembrokeshire' (p.73) mentions the story with no names, but says 'I believe that at first in this light-house there were but two men employed, one of whom died, and the other afraid to make away with the corpse . . .' indicating in its phrasing that the event occurred some time before 1800

1825: half a century has now passed since it happened and a story is being written; the old people who might remember it are dead; there is talk of Griffith, dead in 1800, of a body lying dead on the Smalls 2 months . . .'; they must be the same. And Howell gets in on the act as one of the other keepers . . . poor Joseph Harry is now lost, except in the burial register, which nobody thinks to consult, and where he still is.

1850—1982: the 1825 story repeated, WITH AN EXCEPTION: Captain Mitchell in 'The Sea, Thine Enemy' gives the only report which suggests he had been to primary sources; in part his account reads 'four keepers, all from the village of Solva . . . engaged to tend the light of the lantern . . . had been in existence a short time only . . . on bad terms with each other . . .' and tells the rest without names, but mentions the waving arm and the rescue of a body and a 'near lunatic'

This detective work is what makes history such fun, of course. And we may not have got it right either . . .

Carew Castle started life as a sturdy medieval fortress and is still haunted (they say) by its original owner, the lovely Princess Nesta. It became in turn the HQ of Rhys ap Thomas (the real power behind Henry Tudor, and a lifelong friend) and luxurious and elegant country house of Queen Elizabeth's buccaneering, illegitimate half-brother Sir John Perrott.

God's Whiskers and White Boys

Travelling 'the long way' from Haverfordwest to Pembroke, you pass through Carew, and its fairy-tale castle reflected in a lake (made for the nearby medieval tidemill). It is one of the proudest possessions we now have from the age of the castle; home of a princess, scene of foul murder, and once belonging to a piratical, rumbustious Tudor bastard, proud Sir John Perrott. Many other parts of England and Wales were also in the hands of this unlikely man—his other favourite house lies in ruins by the edge of a sewage works, bypass and railway on the outskirts of Haverfordwest—Haroldston is a sad sight now but when he knew it it must have been magnificent, and from the air you can still make out the *parterres* of a glorious garden. For Sir John was a man of taste, of substance, of flexible conscience and very bad temper, inclined to speak his mind inconveniently . . . and his tongue was to be his undoing.

In 1527 young Mary Berkeley gave birth to a bonny son. Nominally the babe's father was her husband Sir Thomas Perrott—in fact he was one of the two acknowledged illegitimate sons of the Merry Monarch, Henry VIII. Sir Thomas Perrott died while John was still quite young, and never suspected his cuckolding by a king.

Carew Castle—Sir John Perrott's superb Long Gallery addition to the medieval castle, seen across the lake which powers the Tide-mill; the castle is now looked after by the National Park Department.

John Perrott grew up in amazing times; new worlds were being discovered, new faiths replaced or supplemented old ones; it was a time when few were your friends and many your enemies, when a word misplaced could find you in the Tower. Haverfordwest was a bustling seaport; the quay crowded with fine ships bringing amazing goods from all over the world; the streets and alleys were crowded with market women,

> '... theire basketts of egges, butter, poultry; the thoroughfares crowded with Squires from Tivyside and Labourers from Roose ...'

wrote a contemporary observer. Boys watched wide-eyed the sailors unload rich spices and scented woods, carved ivory and banded caskets of who-knows-what treasure, they smelled cinnamon and oranges, cloves and wine, heard tales of distant places and dreamed of being pirates. One of these boys was John Perrott. He was sent to the priests of St Davids for his education, then on to serve in the Marquess of Winchester's household—but he had been there only a year when his royal, real father died, Catholic Mary came to the throne, and there were hard times ahead for staunchly Protestant families like the Perrotts.

Once come into his inheritance, John Perrott could walk about the town he was making one of the richest in the land; he could ride home to Harold-ston House past the Augustinian Priory, which was to become his in time, earning him the hatred of other men who had coveted its lands as well. He could see (and probably smell also) the butchers parading their meat in a Shambles under the Guildhall attached to St Mary's Church, perched on that precipitous slope half way up High Street. Everyone knew Sir John, admired and feared him. He obviously looked a bit like his royal dad, an acquaintance said of him:—

> 'He is of the Kings's familiarity; if his sight, qualities, gesture and voice be compared with the King's, it pleads strongly that he was a surreptitious child of the blood Royal . . .'

There is a picture of Perrott in which he looks remarkably like the Holbein of Henry; and he had Henry's temper—nobody would have dared make such a remark as that above, anywhere near Sir John himself!

John Perrott's time was one of expanding trade and great riches from commerce with the rest of the world—and therefore of smuggling and of piracy. In 1566 a Commission was set up to investigate methods of suppressing piracy; Sir John was a member of this commission, which visited all the creeks and harbours around our deeply indented coastline, looking at places which might harbour ne'er-do-wells and no-good-boyos. But his enemies complained that this was really hunting with the hare and running with the hounds, for was not Perrott an intimate of

> '. . . the Infamous Pirate Callice . . .'?

Did he not know the Cornisham Hicks, and did not cases of spice, kegs of brandy, bolts of fine silk and lumps of ivory seem to arrive in the wrong hands via ships whose masters knew Perrott well? The clamour grew so great at one point that Sir John was invited, nay compelled, to go to London, and was lodged in the Tower while the Privy Council investigated this and other complaints about the bad tempered but humorous knight from Pembrokeshire, prone to shout, to flash his eye and swear

By God's Whiskers

'Good' Sir John Perrott—in his prime; grandson of Henry Tudor, '. . . a quarrellsome, coarse-minded bully, resembling his father in mind as well as body, loved well perhaps by a few, cordially detested by many . . .' His half-sister, Queen Elizabeth said mildly of her boisterous sibling 'Sir John doth SWEAR over-much'

in a day when such a phrase could lose you your head on the block for blasphemy. The Privy Council deliberated, and then let John Perrott go again, he came home to west Wales, planning great additions to his castle at Carew; he would build a long gallery for his fine collection of tapestries and pictures, great fireplaces to snug down by while he read books from his extenive library, or had the lute played to him. Sir John was a man of culture, and his castle needed not to be much of a defence, since

Pembroke was only a mile or so down river. As well as this gentler, more thoughtful Perrott, the 'Henry-Tudor' side came out too, and he had his accusers-of-piracy flung in the stinking town gaol. Was he not half brother to the new Queen, Elizabeth? Whichever side of the blanket, it was strongly influential, and it is unlikely he would have got away with his first brush with the Privy Council if he had not been so well connected. But now a Protestant queen needed friends and families by her who shared this view, to help counter the plotting and whispering—and Perrott was a good friend, if noisy; Sir John and Haverfordwest grew rapidly richer over the next few years. He was made Governor of Ireland. A rather scared eyewitness met him at this time:—

> John Perrott is a man in stature very tall . . . almost equal to the mightiest men who lived in his time . . . and as he exceeds most men in stature so he does in strength of body. His hair was auburn till it grew grey in these latter years—a countenance full of majesty, eye piercing marvellously, carrying a commanding aspect insomuch as, when he is angry, he hath a very terrible visage. But when pleased and willing to shew kindness he hath as amiable a countenance as any man. He hath a sharp wit, but cannot brook any crosses or dissemble the least injuries. He swears too much . . .

His half-sister, the Queen of England, agreed with this latter remark, saying to one of her ladies-in-waiting:—

> 'Sir John? A man of wealth, Madam, but he swears overmuch . . .'

And remember that his favourite swear was still

By God's Whiskers . . .

His former accusers must have heard it many a time as they rotted gently in the clink (of which he was the custodian) until their families and friends could find enough for the damages Sir John was claiming for defamation. He didn't need any extra, mind—by now he was the richest man in the county. But after his departure for Ireland his enemies could scheme and plot, and his downfall would be only a matter of time, especially given his unbridled tongue!

Carew: Entrance to Great Hall—Arms of Henry VII, his eldest son Arthur and Arthur's bride Katherine of Aragon, placed there by Henry's old friend Rhys ap Thomas when the young couple married in 1501—within a year Arthur was dead of TB, and Katherine was married off to Arthur's rumbustious young brother . . . thus becoming the first of the six wives of the future Henry VIII . . .

Queen Elizabeth I—Portrait on an iron fireback of Sir John Perrott's half-sister. He probably got away with as much as he did because of his royal connections, but in the end his violent tongue proved too much even for Elizabeth, and Sir John ended his days in the Tower . . .

Places close to Hell . . .
Top: Copper mine at St. Justinian's, opposite Ramsay Island, Pemb. Welsh Copper from North Wales was vital from Roman times onwards. (Parys, on Anglesey, controlled world copper prices in the 18th C from smaller mines than this).
Centre: Coal and iron dominate Wales's story as an industrial nation—they turn up together at Stepaside (detail of casting shed end wall).
Bottom Left: A visitor to Roman lead mines described them as "Places Close to Hell"; Roman remains still turn up in Carmarthen leadmines such as Llangunnor . . . with whiffs of devilish sulphur.

Bottom Right: This strange many-chimneyed building in Swansea was the workplace and laboratory of William Siemens when he pioneered the open-hearth steelmaking process in what was otherwise the "Copper Capital of the World", next to Henry Vivian's works. A building with a past, and a future if we've got any sense. It stands in the shadow of Landore railway viaduct.

Top: Carmarthen Ironworks tokens, unique records of vanished places and working techniques; a memory too of the Truck system where you were paid not in coin-of-the-realm but in tokens, minted by the ironmasters and worth only what the company store would give in the way of adulterated or second-rate goods.

Bottom: An ''industrial'' plant sprouting cheekily by the railway. Oxford Ragwort spread from its home in the Oxford Botanic Garden in the 1840s when its seeds stuck to the wet sides of I.K. Brunel's broad gauge express trains,—so everywhere the GWR spread its net you'll find *Senecio squalidus* (Carmarthen Station).

Came the threat from the Spaniards, the Armada and of War. Sir John was in the court of Dublin when his Queen sent him 'soothing and respectful letters' about the Spanish position and requesting him to join her coterie in London. Now, her favourites at court were pale young men ravishingly dressed, elegantly manicured and nothing, but nothing, like rough countryman John Perrott, who did not think much either of the Spaniard or the invitation to London:—

> 'Lo, now! She is ready to Damn herself for fear of the Spaniard, and I am again one of her White Boys . . .' *he roared. Someone told the Queen.*

And nobody, not even an illegitimate half-brother, could get away with remarks like this about Queen Elizabeth I; Sir John was summoned to London under arrest and thrown into the Tower to await

Carew and the Savage Ape. . .—By the time this engraving was made, the castle had been abandoned to its ghosts; one of the last owners, wicked Sir Roland Rhys, was found dead in a pool of blood after apparently having been attacked by his pet ape . . . but there was a curse upon him, and the castle was shortly afterwards found furiously burning . . .

trial for treason, which would lose him his head. But he was now an old man, the damp chill of the cell gave him pneumonia:—

> . . . where death in that tower put an end to his misery and troubles, and saved him from the ignominy of the scaffold . . .

wrote one of his many friends. So the man who had bought wine and horses from the pirates Marcroft and Hicks, whose houses included his beloved castle at Carew (his long gallery is still there with its fine windows, but it never got his priceless collection of works of art), lay dead in a London prison—his house at Haroldston fell into ruins, the elegant gardens were overgrown.

Go there now and you feel you might still meet his ghost, wandering in the one remaining cellar where once his wine from Callice had been stored, straight off the *Greyhound* from old Luke Ward, swapping rye for stolen Gascon wine, dried fish for silks and satins . . . or perhaps his shade may stalk the quayside of a night among the few remaining warehouses—unless he shares Carew with Princess Nesta and a murdered man and his pet monkey . . . but that's another story . . .

Drovers and Deathmongers

St Edrins—and its 'Corpse Road'—lanes seldom used except for funerals. The grass from the churchyard was a valued local remedy for mad dog bites . . .

A Few Roads . . .

This part of the world is catscradled with tiny lanes, deep banked and quiet, bits of history as well as sanctuaries for those of us now frightened by such noisy places as the M4, the bypass or super-highway. The lanes tell their own tales.

Our first roads seem to have been made during the latter part of the New Stone age, those times when man had just invented farming and was living in settled communities, making his pots, growing crops and tending animals—trade increased, people travelled quite extensively and through the heavy cover of oaks ran wide clear swathes cut and kept clear for travellers—our first attempt at civil engineering. The Golden Road past Foel Drygarn and Carn Meini is one such track, running from St David's across the spine of Wales to Gloucester, Hereford and the midlands, or by fording the Severn and travelling south, threading a land route to the rich prehistoric area of Salisbury Plain. By walking up the Golden Road towards Carn Meini from Croesfihangel you get a feeling of what these roads might have been like in their heyday—man had not yet tamed animals for transport, so anything carried, like the half-finished stone axes worked on Preseli, in North Wales or Northern

England, would have been in packs on mens' backs. The gold and copper from Ireland came across to Whitesands Bay, then was walked across land to its final destination on this five thousand year old track.

Roman roads do not seem to have invaded West Wales to any great extent, though a length can be seen near Y Pigwn Roman forts; another short stretch may lie alongside the tiny fortlet of Castle Flemish. Special roads had to wait until the medieval period, as the Saxons seem to have distrusted the whole idea of roads, and if they made anything at all it was a contorted series of lanes linking villages by the longest possible route! Roads tended to branch out into strands on hills. In winter a length of road soon became impassable. One of its parallel twins could be selected; constant tramping made the hollow-ways which occur in a number of places on the Preselau and around the hills east of Carmarthen. Pembrokeshire's deep lanes probably started out in this way, but their sides have been banked for centuries now, to increase the shelter. Roads ran from village to village, or to nearby industry, a well, or other sites needing regular visits. Sometimes this has left curiosities, like the Corpse Roads—in outlying areas a widespread parish might have its church a long way from the scattered farms—like the spokes of a wheel, roads would radiate from the church to the tiny communities; used only for odd occasions like funerals, these ways have become known as Corpse Roads, and sometimes the stones can be found on which the coffin was rested while the breathless bearers sang a wheezy hymn and got their breath back: St Edrins has good examples.

Drovers' roads are another special type of track, their origin lost in antiquity but probably at least Iron age in date. Many drovers' roads link like the bones of a herring to its backbone, their 'spine' being a large route like the Golden Road. Preseli abounds in them, so does the area around Bryn Mawr and Myddfai. Walking on them reminds us, again, of that time when everything that moved did so without mechanical aid. The drovers would be away for months at a time walking their flocks to the great market at Hereford. Even the geese had to walk, their feet protected from wear-and-tear on the journey by little leather boots. Less kindly drovers dipped the unfortunate creatures' feet in molten pitch to provide a cover for the journey. Drovers needed money to tide them over the year, and lending it to them (at a suitably extortionate

Mesur y Dorth—'Bread Measure Stone' by the roadside near Croesgoch.

rate of interest) became Big Business; many fine houses in Carmarthenshire bear witness to the money from Black Ox Bank . . .

Another very important track in early times, often dating from the Dark ages, was the Pilgrims' road. St David's was so important to early Christians that two visits to this shrine counted as one to Rome itself. So over the years millions of men and women walked the route—they needed somewhere to stay en route, so hospices were built while churches and holy wells all acquired a new significance because of the track by whose side they stood. Cottagers, however poor, would not cut a loaf without keeping the first slice to offer a passing pilgrim. At Nevern you will find the pilgrims' road up the hill from the church; over a clapper bridge, (the earliest form of bridge building,) through the beechwoods and past a cross, cut in the living cliffs and near which is a set of steps worn by the millions of feet which have scrambled up this holy way over the centuries. A very special place. When you get near St David's there is Mesur y Dorth, a stone with markings on it which seem to be a wheel cross of Dark age date. It is on the pilgrims' route, and its Welsh name, translated, means 'Bread Measure' stone; old tales say that a pilgrim, carrying his last loaf as he was at the end of his pilgrimage, could measure it against the markings and find if he had enough sustenance to get to the holy shrine of Wales' patron saint. What if it *is* just a legend? It shows the stone, and the place, to have had sufficient importance to have a story invented about them! And there is probably a kernel of truth in it—burial slabs and other ancient sacred stones were often used to mark such ways, or to give courage and hope to the traveller. This is possibly why the burial stone of some unknown Christian of the sixth or seventh century was taken, five hundred years later, and propped upright along the way William the Conqueror himself had walked, on the long haul to Salvation . . .

Pilgrims' Cross—standing proud from the living rock just above Nevern, a small niche cut below it that you might stop a moment, kneel and pray before continuing your journey to St Davids.

Pilgrims' Steps—a few yards up the hill from the Pilgrims' Cross, the rock worn smooth by the passage of pilgrims' feet over the centuries. Most of the steps have small crosses carved upon them.

"The Ears and Nostrils of the Dead . . ."

Porthclais Harbour—1898; the boat probably brought lime and culm (crushed anthracite for the limekilns).

Porthclais is one of the 53 ports of Pembrokeshire, just another inlet to us nowadays, but before the railway brought everywhere within reach of everywhere else in the 1850s, it was an artery for trade and a take-off point for many military adventures. Some limekilns grace its upper end, reconstructed but with their charging slopes and limeburners' cottage remains complete, giving an industrial air to what is now a place for owners of small boats, and the odd paddler, to enjoy themselves. A stream runs down the valley past a curious little brick shed which was the weighbridge for the gasworks . . . an even less likely thing to find on the edge of the sea near St David's!—

If you had come here in, say, 1385 you would have seen cargoes arriving by boat all the time, great purple, greenish and grey cut stones for the new cathedral the masons were busy building, loads of limestone and coal to power the kilns, the resulting slaked lime being used both on the fields and to make mortar and limewash for buildings. There was a certain amount of boat building which makes you wonder if the charming little scene on a misericord in the cathedral choir was something the artist had seen here at Porthclais. By 1566, when the Commissioners to Suppress Piracy visited it, Porthclais only had a 'fleet' of two vessels of its own, though there were plenty of visitors bringing anything from timber to saucepans, wine, salt or tallow for candles, spices and spirits, fruit and fine silk. In

Porthclais in 1871, with trading ketches. The breakwater is said by some authorities to be Roman (mainly because of the large regular stones at its base). Porthclais as it is now.

90

their turn the boats took our produce—corn, wheat barley, herrings salted or pickled, butter in great barrels, paper, cheese, leather or ale.

The Vikings came here time after time storming up the little valley to the spot where St David had his little monastic order quietly tending their animals, working in the fields, living simply on bread, 'roots of vegetables' and drinking only milk-and-water; poor David got his church burned ten times by the Danes before an even tougher brigand living on the hill above him lent his protection (Clegyr Boia).

This was by no means the only military action seen in this steep sided inlet; a D-day sized invasion fleet sailed from here in 1168 for Ireland, then as now the local trouble spot and excuse for violence from all sides. At that time the bother was caused by a rebellion, that of King Dermot MacMurrough, 'a consumate villain, unsurpassed even among his chieftains in cruelty, lawlessness and treachery' reported an eyewitness. Dermot sought the help of the English king, and so a lot of the Top People of Pembrokeshire took to their boats, loaded down with horses, arms, foot soldiers and soldiers 'half armed' (that is, not wearing complete suits of armour but chain mail weskits). 'Seventy heroes clad in mail' our reporter goes on, 'one Henry Fitz-Stephen brought with him knights of great renown nine or ten . . .' They were joined by King Henry I's grandson Meiler FitzHenry, Miles de Cogan, son of the Bishop of St David's, Maurice de Prendergast, a local landowner remembered in the name of an outskirt of Haverfordwest. The famous chronicler of the time, the priest Gerald de Barri ('Giraldus Cambrensis') saw his own brother Robert set off for the fray across the stormy sea to Ireland—and saw him back some weeks later, minus all his front teeth, knocked out by a ballista bolt . . .

Giraldus Cambrensis (de Barri 1146-1223)—born at Manorbier Castle in south Pembrokeshire, was for much of his life at St Davids, wrote vividly and entertainingly of his life and times—saw his brothers sail from Porthclais for the Irish wars in the 1160s . . .

So went thirty knights, sixty men-at-arms, hundreds of archers and foot soldiers, thousands of troops in *sixty ships*; it must have made a brave sight. But the fortunes of war are such that 'the Flower of the youth of Wales' had to throw most of their horses overboard as the poor beasts perished from lack of water on the voyage. There was a bloody battle with three thousand Irishmen supporting King O'Rouke (whose wife MacMurrough had stolen), and no prisoners were taken—anyone unfortunate enough to be left alive but injured had his head lopped off if he was lucky, something a lot more painful if he was not. After the battle a French reporter noted:

> Dermot with brutal glee turned over with his sword eleven score heads, he turned them over one by one, recognising many an old enemy . . . at last he recognised the King of Ossory, whom he hated above all others. He took the severed head and, holding it up to his mouth by the hair and ears he tore with his teeth the lips and nostrils of the dead . . .

If anything haunts me about Porthclais, it is the brutal memory of King Dermot MacMurrough, not a nice man to meet at all, at all.

More peacefully, local residents still alive remember another battle, with the gasworks, which often ran out of pressure during Sunday roasting. The custom in this emergency was to bike down with the manager Mr. Williams, and you both then heaved enough coal into the retorts to bring the lunchgiving gas back to life again!

The Mad German and the Mines Royal

A Story about Aberdulais

One of the loveliest spots in Wales has wandering through it the ghosts of some early industrial enterprise: not far from Aberdulais is a network of canals including the Neath and Tennant; Brunel's broad gauge railway ran nearby on the sturdy viaduct and impressive embankments; and there is the Neath river, over which a low but incredibly well designed aqueduct runs that was part of our earliest planned transport system—that of canals.

It was to a quay on this spot in 1584 that a ship arrived from Germany—she was one of many such traders, loaded with ore or coal or the other products of sixteenth century industry, which stopped here because they had to . . . they grounded and could get no further up river! Her owner, Ulrich Frosse, saw abundant timber for smelting, he saw collieries working busily and there was iron ore in the area; but what seems to have impressed him most was that copper ore could be brought up here to a secret site in the woods, ending its long journey from Parys Mountain on Anglesey, or from Cornwall or Pembrokeshire. The secrecy was vital to Ulrich Frosse, who was obsessed with the thought of spies (nowadays we insist on calling it industrial espionage); he had methods of purifying and smelting copper which he desperately wanted to keep to himself, so he set up his works in these woods, echoing to the soft splash of waterfalls (which also provided the secretive German with some of his motive power). Now the spies would have their foul designs frustrated. The locals all thought Frosse was potty.

Later, the Mines Royal Company worked with Frosse, and upon his death took over his works . . . but by the 1660s they were intent upon moving to Neath Abbey. Aberdulais ceased to be the place of guarded experiment, no more agents crouched behind trees spying out the mad German's secrets —if they ever had—and the place became an ordinary forge where iron, not copper, was worked from ore into saleable artifacts. It was so until the end of the eighteenth century, but by 1816 the

Aberdulais: 'The Bastion'—superbly intricate stonework painstakingly restored to perfection by the National Trust. Aberdulais has seen many industries come and go since Frosse's day—ironworking, tin-plating, it's been a corn and grist mill, and was painted by Turner . . .

'Before and After'—taking the old building to pieces to strengthen and restore it; around the 'bastion', excavation is revealing the waterwheel pit, rolling mill pits, furnaces, segments of tramway and much else . . .

lovely waterfall was driving a corn mill, which had two waterwheels on site. Then a local ironmaster, and coal owner, George Tennant tried to wreck the falls by blowing up some of the rocks for his canals in the valley below; the rock was too hard, but the mess he made is still clearly visible. Today the site is owned by the National Trust; some of Frosse's buildings, the mill and stamp houses were in a poor state and have been rebuilt; here, you will find the beauty which fascinated the famous artist Turner, the peace of falling water in your ears—and not a spy to be seen anywhere . . .

The Stack—few industrial sites can have such a romantic setting in woodland by running, falling water —industrial archaeology is now revealing Aberdulais as one of the most fascinating sites in Wales.

Canals in the Welsh Hills . . .

From about 1793 onwards, a canal was built and operated in the Gwendraeth Valley, linking the rich coalfields inland with the main transport of sea-going ships. At first it was the extension of the useful Kymer's canal, with networks of horsedrawn tramroads spiders-webbing off to individual collieries and little brickworks and quarries, limekilns and family foundries. Ideas were put forward to improve Cydweli harbour, to build a canal with 9 locks to Pontyberem, with a branch from Spuddersbridge to Llanelli. It was all very exciting, likely to make enough money to justify no fewer than three Lords meeting on site to talk it all over! They were the noble Lords Dynevor, Ashburnham and Cawdor; astronomical sums like £33,000 were splashed about as they talked of all that wealth waiting for them in the hills at Cwm y Glo, Cwm

Pembrey Station flooded easily as the railway had started life as a canal; the bridge carries marks left by the hawsers of horse-drawn barges.

98

Mawr and Cross Hands—of culm and hops and iron ore and limestone; bulky stuff for the appalling roads of the day. A canal was the answer. Kymer and Ashburnham had already shown the way. But the inland route presented a problem. Water doesn't go up hills.

By 1818 the lords' capital had grown to £60,000 with powers to raise £20,000 more if needed—the Pembrey canal was planned, and by 1825 Pembrey New Harbour Co. was incorporated to build what is now Burry Port . . . but none of this vast expense would be the slightest good unless they could get up the hills to Cwm Mawr. Now, to go uphill with a canal, everyone knows you have locks; but they are limited in height, slow and expensive in use—and they are vastly costly in water supply. The engineer of the canal was a man from the West Country, James Green and he suggested something not often used, and dramatic in form—an inclined plane.

Broadly speaking, the idea of an inclined plane is to bring the boats out onto dry land at the lower level, hitch them onto some haulage machinery, and pull them up a slope to the next level, where they are refloated and go on their way as boats again. There are fine examples in the industrial complexes now preserved as museums at Blist's Hill in Shropshire and Foxton, Leicestershire, where you get an idea of the ingenuity involved— Foxton had vast iron baths of water so the canal barges simply floated in, the door was shut and the whole shebang was lifted to the higher level on a railway of vast gauge, powered by steam engines

Top:
Iron Tub Boat—from the Kidwelly and Llanelly Canal, almost submerged in copper slag at the entrance to Burry Port old Harbour; nearby industrial buildings are partly built from this glassy slag . . .

Bottom:
Old Rails under Older Rails . . .—The old Ashburnham Canal, (later the Burry Port and Gwendraeth Valley Railway), dips under an 18th Century tramway which formerly took coal from Penllwyn and 'Bowser's Level' to its own jetty in Pembrey harbour. Now the collieries no longer need it, and even these rails are gone . . .

(Photo 1975)

Incline Inn—the label is plastic nowadays, but the memory stretches back to the canal age—Pont Henry.

winding wire ropes. The inclines our lordly trio had built were on a more mundane scale, but no less of an innovation for their time. A visitor to the first rise, that of 57 feet at Pont Henry, reported that 'the inclines are manipulated by pumps which are considered great discoveries . . .' So what Dic ap Huw may have seen were waterwheel-operated pumps filling iron containers which would counter-balance the weight of the tub-boats at the bottom of the incline and raise them bodily, on rails, to the new height beside what is still called the 'Incline Inn'; this seems more likely than the other method often used, which was moving the boats by the power of a tub of water descending an old mine shaft or well.

Imagine a line of four little iron boats in a chain, each carrying about six tons of coal or limestone— they are manhandled out onto the top of the incline, where tallow-greased iron rails on stone sleepers, like a giant railway, wait to minimise their friction on the downward journey—waiting at the bottom is another set of six boats, empty, also hitched to the rope. Then, kept under control by a wooden brake working on the edge of the counterbalance wheel, the full boats descend and the empty ones are drawn up. Then both continue, on water, horse-drawn, to their destination or to the next incline. The three inclines planned were Pont Henry, a rise of 57ft Capel Isaf, a rise of 56ft then a giant 84ft for the last

The Kidwelly and Llanelly Canal had a series of
inclined planes where lines of iron tub boats (p98) were
hauled up and down on dry land by hydraulic
machinery—in its day the Pont Henry incline was one
of the wonders of Wales . . . now it carries a colliery
railway, the 57′ rise being quite a climb even with
modern diesel haulage . . .

incline at Hirwaun Isaf, which was built but never
used. The whole of this canal system was fed from a
reservoir at Cwm y Glo, as were presumably the
pumps so admired by Dic ap Huw and other
visitors.

It's all gone now, and had a short enough life as it
was; because by the time it was built, the railway
was coming—ten years later we were in the Age of
the Train, the canal was converted to a track,
becoming the Burry Port & Gwendraeth Valley
Railway. But all along its now deserted trackbed,
you will find little clues as to its watery origin. Like
the canal bridge and 'maximum weight' notice at
Pont Newydd; like the deep scratches made on the
bridge at Ashburnham on the sides of the 'railway'
bridge by canal hawsers when it was a canal; and by
this incline, and the pub named after it, at Pont

BURRY PORT & GWENDRAETH VALLEY RAILWAY
TO DRIVERS AND OWNERS OF LOCOMOTIVES OR OTHER
PERSONS HAVING CHARGE OF THE SAME
IN PURSUANCE OF THE LOCOMOTIVE ACT OF 1861
NOTICE IS HEREBY GIVEN THAT THIS BRIDGE IS INSUFFICIENT
TO CARRY ANY WEIGHT BEYOND THE ORDINARY TRAFFIC OF THE
DISTRICT AND THE OWNER DRIVER OR OTHER PERSON HAVING CHARGE
OF ANY LOCOMOTIVE IS HEREBY WARNED NOT TO ATTEMPT TO DRIVE
THE SAME UPON OR OVER THIS BRIDGE WITHOUT HAVING PREVIOUSLY
OBTAINED THE CONSENT OF THE BURRY PORT & GWENDRAETH
VALLEY RAILWAY COMPANY
OFFICES   BURRY PORT
DATED THIS 1ST DAY OF AUGUST 1908

Henry, where a derelict cottage built over the incline when it was no longer in use, re-used a few of the stone sleeper blocks, which are still there, with the holes for the iron rails which carried this new marvel in the years immediately after the Napoleonic Wars, when the Gwendraeth cradled the infant anthracite industry.

Cast Iron Notices are becoming increasingly rare due to the activities of the careless motorist, the collector and the ever-present vandal. Sad, this, as they are so much a part of our history and deserve to be found, read and enjoyed on site rather than in a museum. This BP & GVR notice threatened Dire Consequences at Pembrey . . .

Mister Morris's Colliers' Castle . . .

Colliers' Castle—The colliers and their families had an amazing view over Swansea and its various industries (though whether they escaped the dangerous stench of the copper and arsenic works is debatable!) but was the situation worth the twice-daily climb from their work in the pits, or for their wives with all the drinking water? Mr Morris didn't ask—he'd wanted a castle and now he had it . . .

As you come into Swansea on the train you look out over the devastation of Landore and your eyes travel upwards through the houses and the streets to the skyline where there is a castle . . . or it *seems* like a castle. Gaunt windowless eyes stare sightlessly down to where a forest of grimy chimneys spumed forth poisons a century ago which prompted a traveller to the city, Mr. Baedeker, putting together his Guide to a Great Britain, to muse:

> About 20,000 tons of copper valued at £4 millions of Sterling are annually produced at its foundries. Two hundred and fifty coal pits lie around, and this abundance has led to the erection of numerous zinc, iron, lead and tinplate manufactories . . . in certain states of the wind Swansea is completely enveloped in the smoke of the copper works which, however, is said to be less unhealthy than one would suppose . . .

Herr Baedeker noted that the hotel to stay at was the Great Western Temperance as Swansea's Mackworth Arms had 'high charges'. 90,000 inhabitants lived in '. . . the most important copper smelting centre in the World . . .' But what has all this got to do with that castle up on the hill? It looks like a castle in the small watercolour in the Glynn Vivian but it was in fact one of Britain's earliest blocks of flats.

Mr. Morris built them—he owned a lot of those copper works and collieries which so boggled Baedeker . . . Mr. Morris gave his name to the

102

Swansea—A city of copper and steel; this was the view Morris's colliers would have had from their eyrie . . . Siemens' Steel works, blast furnaces, copper smelters, canals, tramroads, waste tips . . .

(from 'Great Industries of Great Britain', 1875)

entire area, Morriston. In about 1768 Mr. Morris decided his colliers and their families might need somewhere cleaner to live, up on the hill above the stench and grime of Landore and Lower Swansea . . . and one suspects John Morris, too, had a sparkle in his eye with regard to the Prospect. He duly got his castle, a block of flats with each floor separated from the others by patterns of copper slag, the local iron coloured sandstone providing the rest—if you go up there you can still make out the floors, stairways and approximate size of a few of the flats—half the place disappeared into later quarry works. So between 1768 and 1775 John Morris had homes for about 40 families 'all colliers excepting a tailor and a shoemaker who are considered as useful appendages . . .' he said at the time. Useful, especially the shoemaker, since the colliers all worked at the bottom of the valley and so

had the long climb home as well as anything else they might endure in the course of their work; worse, there was no water up there on the hill, so the wives and children (when not also down the pit) had to carry what was needed for washing and drinking up to the top of the hill, then up to their flat. Picturesque it may have been, thoughtful it was not. It failed, and by 1850 it was nearly empty, by 1880 deserted and partly quarried away. But outside are the little patches where the colliers grew their spuds, and you still get a whiff from the fennel which they used to make the lovely sauce for the mackerel brought into Swansea harbour . . .

Palmerston's Follies

It may sound like a music hall, but it's about a scared politician obsessed with xenophobic shivers which led to massive building and fortification around Milford Haven . . . the fears have long gone, only the buildings remain.

In the 1850s there were a few old people still alive in Pembrokeshire who could remember the awful shock of the Fishguard Invasion at Carregwastad in 1797. Napoleon could still scare people by his name alone. 1852 saw the death of the man who had defeated him; Wellington was a byword in Britain, its rulers now shaking as revolution seemed certain all over Europe. The events of 1848 were still fresh in peoples' minds—there had been a third revolution in France and its king had been forced to flee to England . . . the thrones of nearly every monarch in Europe tottered, including our own . . . there were revolts in Austria, Italy, Spain and Germany, anarchy was heard about in cellars, and there was Trouble in Ireland. A violent uprising was recommended by a newspaper called the *United Irishman*, whose editor was promptly transported. In England too, the elections saw some new names added to the list of candidates, some of whom were remarkably successful; the Chartists now hoisted their banner, chanted about the overthrow of Louis Phillippe in France, and threatened a gigantic march on London with a petition signed by five million people—a tremendous number when the population of Britain then was not much more than twice that.

Stack Rock—a fierce little fort built in a small islet in Milford Haven in 1852 and enlarged in 1870 . . .

Top:
Stack Rock—exploring the amazingly complete
interior; there has been talk of making it into a
museum—other Haven forts are in use as a hotel, a
field centre, and oil company offices.

Bottom:
Palliser Cannon—ultimate weapon of its day, lying by
an ammunition hoist which was intended to serve it in
the days when the French were our greatest worry; note
the rifle racks on the back wall.

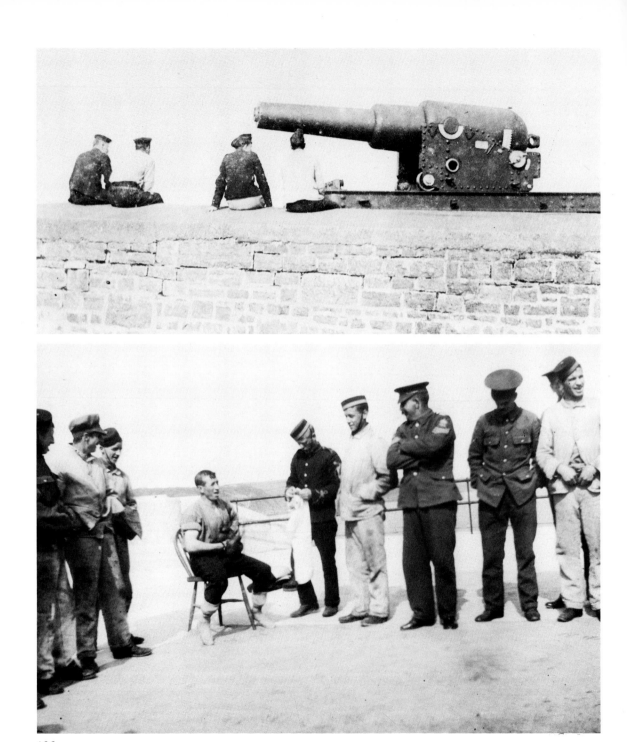

All this, then, was in the government's mind in 1852; all this trouble at home and on the Continent —we had been committing troops overseas to the Sikh War, which started with the murder of some British farmers and ended with the Queen of England acqiring the Koh-i-Noor diamond for the Crown Jewels. The uneasy coalition saw the greatest nation on earth—had we not just had the Great Exhibition?—menaced on all sides, particularly by the old enemy, France. While that country's leader was called *Prince* Louis, it sounded like more of the kind of government we could do business with, but when he sent troops into the streets of Paris, popped his political enemies in jug and declared himself *President* Napoleon III, we feared the worst.

A Palliser Cannon on its mountings and ready for action against the French or any other of the Queen's enemies. Stack 1898

Stack Fort in the '90s—livening up a thoroughly boring time with a boxing match on the roof . . .

Scoveston Fort—was built to defend the rear of the main garrisons from surprise attack—it is remarkably complete and of superb craftsmanship. Though built in the age of the gun, its main defence would be instantly recognisable to our Iron age warrior ancestors—it is a massive bank and ditch.

At that time Pembroke Dock was one of the biggest Royal Naval yards in the kingdom; it built and repaired Her Majesty's older Wooden Walls as well as the new Ironclads. The whole renowned British Navy could—and sometimes did—take shelter in Milford Haven, within easy sailing distance of the sea between us and Ireland, and worse—the Continent. Now here were the perfidious Froggies inciting the Irish, there were rumours of French help, even French troops to train the ragged band of Nationalists . . . Panic. Volunteer Dad's Armies were being raised all over the Kingdom, *Punch* carried violently anti-French cartoons, and Palmerston, smarting over his dismissal from office the previous year, scrambled back into the fray . . . the result was the forts around Milford Haven.

107

Thorn Island Fort—is now in use as an hotel for those
who REALLY want to get away from it all! West
Angle Bay and a Tudor blockhouse are in the
background.

Armies of convicts were drafted from their stony cells all over Britain, housed in stinking hell-holes of ancient hulks left over from the wars with the first Napoleon. They got cholera, but they were only convicts, weren't they? Contractors were called in, too, and from Tenby's St Catherine's Island to Norse-named Dale, Chapel Bay and South Hook, Hubberston, Stack and Popton, a chain of big, expensive limestone fortresses grew, casemated, with lifts for shells from underground magazines, intricate systems of passages, stores, barracks, for Britain's fine army to defend the realm, and this vital naval base, from the invading French.

The Frenchman showed his perfidy, his true colours, by not turning up. The immensely costly forts were never used, never heard a shot fired in anger. The Palliser, muzzle loading cannon stood silent, apart from the occasional practice, the garrisons arranged boxing matches or made mop-heads into stretcher cases. In 1870 the Franco-Prussian war frightened our politicians into action again, we sent fully trained pigeons into battle and photographers invented a cunning way of micro-filming *the Times* for the beleaguered foreigners. The balloon came into its own as a military option. It was the same bloke, of course, the Emperor Napoleon III who picked a quarrel with the King of Prussia; we again saw, or thought we saw, royalty tottering, and possible invasions of our sea-space, so a second set of unused defences was added to the first set around Milford; these extras are nicely dated, so the military archaeologist can trace the uneasy course of European politics in the nine-teenth century, the prelude to a united Europe and the fear of the Bear; because something else was happening, too—those men with snow on their boots. Another lot of untrustworthy foreigners happily tore up the 1856 Treaty of Paris one end of the Channel and the Ruskies the other! The only people we could now trust, it seemed to our dis-traught politicians, were our friends the Germans —after all, dammit, the Kaiser was nephew to our Beloved Queen . . .

So this is background to any visit you may pay to our ring of fine, if vandalised fortresses—to Hubberston or South Hook, Popton, Chapel Bay, Dale or to island-bound Thorn; one of the best, because it is well out to sea beyond the reach of most vandals, is Stack Rock, complete with a Palliser cannon, iron chimney pots and officers' quarters and galleys which you feel you could almost move into. The ammunition hoists look as if a touch of oil might get them going again, the wooden gun racks might again take the long barrelled rifles with their bayonets. Wrought iron casemates and heavy doors and rails for the cannon . . . all the panoply of a medieval castle translated into brick, iron and the era of the Gatling gun and the Ironclad. Though the last two world wars have left their mark on all these places, they still retain atmosphere from Victoria's Britain. Their kind will never be made again, if only because we have not got the power to call upon an army of sick convicts—the idea of forced labour having been passed on, like the concentration camp, to the Other Side in the years since Pam's Pembrokeshire Follies . . .

Porthgain

Porthgain—the port with everything—slate was worked from the pit (top of picture), from which also came a fine, brick-making clay—granite was quarried a mile along the cliffs and brought to the crushers by tramways. The hoppers in which the crushed granite was kept, the lines of railway, crusher, engine house, tunnel, leet and industrial housing all show up well from the air.

If you like history or archaeology, then this is a little heaven-on-earth for you; it's possible to potter among the ruins and rails and quarries and quays while your family can, if they wish, sun themselves or snooze, find sand, or tea, or a loo—there's room for the dog, and you can even push a pram. Little wonder so many people number Porthgain among their favourite industrial sites . . . for that is what it is. The snug harbour cradles grandeur on a conveniently small scale; even the redbrick cliffs (reminiscent of the Valley of the Kings more than west Wales) are not *too* towering. The gaunt, yet lived-in buildings tell you straight away you are in the presence of archaeology.

Porthgain had a fairly short—if dramatic—career in many ways, an intriguing tale of a set of unique natural assets near the sea exploited to the

Porthgain in 1910—the time of its greatest glory; one of its fleet of steamers leaves with a load of granite, bricks and slates, the haze of dust from the crusher is everywhere—a Peckett loco shunts a line of trams containing rough granite, at the clifftop.

full. Porthgain's development last century was an inevitable consequence of its three juxtaposed earthly riches; some shale had been pushed through by molten magma from deep in the earth's inner core, some 500 million years ago—the heat of the intrusion changed (or metamorphosed) the shale into slate, and the molten material cooled into granite. Around the edge of the intrusion, chemical action over the enormous time between then and now, decomposed some of the granite into a gritty clay rather like that on the edge of the granite *massif* of Dartmoor. So when man at last looked into the potential of this little inlet, he found slate for roofing, granite for building and that fine grey clay, which could be baked into excellent bricks. No Victorian industrialist could have resisted it, especially as it lay by the sea, so all the bulky products could be carried easily and cheaply to market.

VIEW OF PORTHGAIN HARBOUR & WORKS.

Porthgain—Detail of the harbour works (somewhat idealised!) from the Company's bill-head; the steam crane (c) was mounted on standard gauge track laid when there were rumours of an LNWR line to St Davids.

courtesy, Pembs Record Office

To begin with, exploitation was on a local scale— a couple of businessmen came to this straggly fishing village with its solitary limekiln, and lobster-pots drying in the sun. They did their best, but failed through undercapitalization; but a trio of men from far-off London saw its potential, saw the slate moving from nearby Abereiddi, and set to on Porthgain with *panache*. Their first enterprise was called St Bride's Quarries, hopeful advertisements appeared in local papers extolling the quality of their tombstones and kitchen floors and roof slates

'. . . at a price to compete with other quarries . . .' A chasm opened up where their quarrymen took out the slate, levering it from its 500 million year old bed with crowbars, then splitting it into Duchesses, Ladies, Countesses and all the strangely feminine sizes of roof slates. Railway systems snaked about the clifftops, and the place bristled with little sheerlegs to hoist lumps of rock onto trams—it got too deep for cranes and a Blondin was set up. This is a high-wire device (named after the Victorian showman who pushed wheelbarrows across Niagara) with two towers between which cables hung, their pulleys and hooks enabling trams and chains to be lowered to the working floors for the slate slabs to be hauled out for dressing. Eventually the hole got too deep to haul out all its riches that way, and a railway tunnel was dug from the harbour to the working base, with a 3'0" gauge tramway laid within it. Because not only slate was coming from the deepening hole.

Hoses splashed onto the sides of it to separate fine blue clay from the little bits of undecomposed granite. A leet had been built down the valley to supply water power to pugging and stamping machinery which turned the clay into bricks—an oval kiln was built next to the fine greenish granite building, its interior divided into four quadrants in which loading, firing, cooling and unloading were carried on in sequence continuously—it boasted a dramatic chimney, a landmark for the many little ships which now came here regularly. Another railway ran through cuttings down an incline to Pen Clegyr Point where the granite was being blasted out of the cliff, then trundled back to where the skilled masons turned it into the basis for fine architecture. Much of Dublin is built of Porthgain granite, as is the Tate Gallery in London.

Now three industries ran side by side; granite, slate, bricks—the harbour was always crowded, the company's own fleet of fifty-two ketches and eight steamships being supplemented by many more independently owned coasters of anything up to 350 tons burthen. The brisk trade in bricks was partly due to the company starting to advertise itself on each brick, proudly stamping 'Porthgain' on every frog; you can still pick them up right across the industrial belt of South Wales and the Midlands, into Ireland and even as far away as Bath, and along the Kennet & Avon canal in Wiltshire.

At the end of the century a new market for granite opened up—there was a newfangled machine, derided by nearly everyone as a noisy, smelly, here-today-and-gone-tomorrow contraption; it was the horseless carriage or Motor. It would never last of course. But in the meantime its rubber tyred wheels demanded a better road surface than our dusty hill-and-dale horrors or cobbled nightmares. Most country roads were dust-traps in summer and quagmires in winter, so from the 1800s on, Tarmac roads were being laid out, especially in the rapidly growing suburbs of the big cities with their red brick facades, clean blue slate roofs and granite gateposts—all of which could, and much of which *did*, come from Porthgain! So steam powered crushers started hammering and grinding

Steam and Sail—at the turn of the century; the jetty had to be altered to accommodate the larger steamships and the harbour regularly dredged to allow for their deeper draught.

away on the clifftop, fed by narrow gauge tramways and Peckett steam locomotives, and great brick hoppers were built to store the various grades of road metal while they awaited shipment to far away places to make our road system one of the finest in the world. Porthgain had reached its finest hours.

The harbour was altered and enlarged in 1902-4 as it was awkward for the larger generation of steamship; everyone still aimed for the dangerous inlet by using the tall brick stack and two white marker-cairns, and it must have been a nightmare for sailing ships, trying to get enough way on them to ease their hulls through a narrow, wave-torn gap in the cliffs once in their shadow and without motive power. Now ships took bricks and tiles and granite blocks to Cardiff, London, Dublin, the West Country, Kent, Rotterdam, France and Germany and the Baltic ports. The company had an imposing billhead to match its prosperity. There were rows of cottages by the harbour side, up on the cliffs and up the valley inland, and a little corrugated-iron

schoolhouse for the workmens' children. There were rumours of a connection with the railway system, and so a third gauge was added to the already complicated points system in the harbour— with 1'11½", 3'0" and 4'8½" it must have been an engineer's nightmare, especially where the lines met or crossed!

But troubled days lay ahead. Porthgain now had competitors on the main trunk railway lines— Blaenau Ffestiniog, Bethesda and Nantlle in North Wales, Corris and the others, all had links with the great railways; Porthgain had had hopes of this when the London and North Western Railway had planned to run a link from Fishguard to St David's —there are even plans of this odd scheme to be seen in libraries, but like many enthusiastic rail dreams, it faded, and all Porthgain's standard gauge track ever carried was a steam crane. After the peak year of 1909 the Company must have thought they were in the big time—four hundred shipments of over 40,000 tons of slate and granite chippings (bricks were no longer made and the kiln was being demolished), their proud little fleet of steamships constantly on the move with 4 smacks, 43 other steam ships as regular visitors, a permanent haze from the ground granite (which must have been a terrifying health hazard, but no-one knew about pollution then), mounds of road metal, waste from the old brick-clay washing, and loads being hauled about the place by traction engines . . .

The First World War killed Porthgain as it killed so many of her sons. The labour force vanished, some never to return. Some ships (including the flagship *Porthgain* herself) were sunk by U-boats; building was drastically cut as was new road building; the railway never came: Porthgain hoped for better days after the fighting, after the Boys Came Home. It wasn't to work that way. Other places could offer cheap road metal by rail, cheap slates

(which in any case were being supplemented by new materials like concrete or asbestos); by 1931 only one shipment a month was leaving the little port. It closed down, as these places often do, the labour force simply walking out and leaving the Peckett loco and its trucks, the railway lines, houses and workshops like some ghost town on the cliffs; though scrapmen and vandals have been through since. Although much ironwork went in the Second World War, there is still much to see of this extraordinary place, summing up how industries, like living organisms, grow and thrive and die. The horses are no longer in their smart, brick red stables alongside an engine repair shed and donkey engine stand at Pen Clegyr Point. The main brickmaking building stands in its magnificent granite glory as a centre piece to the now abandoned harbour, used by local lobster fishermen (who seem to leave a

Advertisement for Porthgain's wares, 1888, from a local paper. The granite was used to build much of Dublin and other fine city buildings including the Tate Gallery.

St. Bride's Quarries, Porthgain.

THE Manager of these Quarries wishes to draw the attention of Builders, Farmers, and others to the large quantity of Third Quality Slates which he has in stock and which will be sold cheap; also to the splendid Flooring Flags that are now ready. Floors are cut to order at the lowest price possible. There are also some excellent Trwyn Llwyd Slabs suitable for Tombstones and Trwyn Llwyd Sills which cannot be excelled in Wales; these will be sold at a price to compete with any other Quarries. For further particulars apply to the Manager, JOHN FRASER, St. Brides Quarries, *via* Letterston, R.S.O.

Early Days—a leet drives a waterwheel (bottom of picture) to crush and pug the clay for brickmaking, as well as cut the split slates to size. The 'Green' brick-drying sheds, kiln and office buildings, as well as the first stage of the harbour works, are clearly visible on this early photo (c. 1885); there are as yet no hoppers for crushed 'road-stone' granite (left).

morgue of carcases in the railway tunnel which means that the industrial archaeologist needs a strong nose or a clothespeg) or holidaymakers' boats. The leet still runs powerfully under it all to empty into the harbour below where the kiln once stood.

Now you can dream among the giant hoppers and walk past low lines of slate waste up on the cliffs which were, not more than a lifetime ago, kitchen gardens with runner beans and washing and prams and dogs barking . . . see the base of the Blondins . . . the Harbourmaster's Office next to the entrance . . . even the heap of rubbish dredged from the harbour by steam drags when this place was proud among the ports of the world for its trade and

commerce . . . and every now and again you may run up against a person with a furrowed brow, possibly talking to himself and scribbling on the backs of envelopes. He will be a railway buff trying to work out how in thunder you managed to do any shunting on a triple-gauge railway system . . .

Top right:
Brickmaking—The continuous kiln (l of centre) always had one quadrant firing another loading; the third cooling and the fourth unloading; the coal was powdered anthracite (from Pembrokeshire pits, brought around the coast by steamer) pumped in by compressed-air 'jiggers' whose descendants could still be seen at work at Goodwick brick works in 1969.

photo dated 1890

Lower right:
Three masted barque leaves the harbour into the teeth of the gale. Porthgain was a difficult port to enter in sailing days, the master having to 'aim' his ship at the small entrance while well out to sea, using as his beacons the main stack and a pair of white-painted obelisks on the cliff (one is visible, left)   photo 1895

The Little Giant and the Gorge

Railway Mania is not only something unique to the 1840s, when twenty new railways a week flooded Parliament with crazy little lines . . . no, Railway Mania is still with us. BBC engineers have formed a group who spend their off-time just walking along old railway lines . . . vicars stand at the end of station platforms, taking numbers, photographs or just dreaming . . . the cult of the steam engine makes preservationists of us all. No other industrial artifact has got such universal love, respect and affection, such a band of followers worthy of a religious cult. David Shepherd paints elephants to save wild-life—and steam engines. What *is* it about railways? Try this for a story—

The old lady did not know much about the railway in our valley, though she was old enough to remember its arrival, the sudden eruption of a navvy village on the hill between Treffgarne and Spittal; she and her sisters, and all the other children of Treffgarne village, were shepherded to school in Spittal each day by fierce parents or neighbours. They were not to look up from the ground at their feet, lest they be contaminated with whatever anarchic contagion the navvies brought. The navvies brought their own chapel, pub, shop, school—the navvy children were not permitted to speak to the locals (and we are not talking of the dark ages but as recently as 1905). Steam engines and the sound of blasting—one of the latter blew the head off James Spires and his mate, who were buried in Ford churchyard, their only known address being the railway workings; 'c/o G.W.R. Huts, Danbach' wrote the vicar in the burial register for these, only the latest in a long line of railway fatalities since Mr. Huskisson was run over by the Rocket. When the great embankment, the tunnel and cuttings were finished, the navvies vanished as if they had never been—it was always thus, and so the greatest engineering feats man ever accomplished are often remembered by the names of their engineers, the Brunels, the Stephensons, the Vignoles—never the navvy, ex-canal navigator, Irish hooligan though most thought him, superman of industry, able to move ten tons of stone or earth by his own muscle every day, known only by a nickname—'Cat's Meat', 'Mary-Ann', 'Wellington' or 'Joe-Socks'; heroes of the railways, without them there would *be* no trains.

Isambard Kingdom Brunel—photographed by the launching chains for the 'Great Eastern' in 1857; shoes and trousers as grimy as those of his navvies, cigar chomped firmly and many more in a vast box slung over his shoulder . . . our greatest engineer was no boardroom executive, but was out and about supervising every tiny detail, whether it be bridge or railway, ship or prefabricated hospital building or tunnel bore . . .

Haslemere Museum coll

Treffgarne Gorge—Brunel was here in the 1840s, when working on this section of the South Wales Railway to Fishguard, travelling, drawing and catching what little sleep he did in his famous black coach which his navvies knew as 'The Flying Hearse'. The modern railway, road and river all crowd together through the gap in the Rhyolite, topped by a fierce Iron-age fortress (one of nine in the valley). The old coaching road runs across, lower foreground . . . the farm on the other side of the river is where Owain Glyndwr was born. And the 'old Railway'?—that shadow, visible among the trees just above the modern line (right).

The old lady went on, almost as an afterthought '—you've seen the Old Railway, of course . . .' she said; I hadn't; nor had she, but she *knew* about it. And here the story really starts, as the Goon Show used to say! That bombshell of a remark, made in the rain of a Pembrokeshire afternoon with the smell of spring on it and the sound of lambs, set us off on a ten year investigation which led to The Railway That Never Was.

After the success of George Stephenson's Liverpool & Manchester, after the London & Birmingham, the Lancs and Yorks, all railways making a packet for their promoters, Britain went potty about railways; schemes great and small proliferated, there were plans to join absolutely everywhere with absolutely everywhere else—nowhere was left out. Scottish businessmen even built a railway with the cheapest source of motive power known to man—passengers were instructed to stand in the open carriages provided and open their umbrellas, the wind would do the rest. This, the Coatbridge Railway, did not remain open long, but has a memorial to an early suggested use of windpower in the centre of the town. Trevithick's use of a more solid and dependable form of motive power was first demonstrated in Wales, on the Pen y Darren tramroad, long before the railway age proper began—and of course we can claim one of the oldest railways in the world in Wales, that built for the silver mines at Penybont in Tudor times. So Welsh businessmen were thinking about rails, had been for a long time, and by the mid 1830s there a plan was drawn up for a rail link between Haverfordwest and Fishguard, to go through Treffgarne Gorge—it is still in Haverfordwest Library. Meanwhile the big boys were at work.

London and Bristol were joined at a staggering cost of 6½ million pounds, by 1835—the engineer was the indomitable Isambard Kingdom Brunel, Little Giant of the railways. He was already dreaming up thoughts of transatlantic steamships, and needed a port; he saw his friend and deadly business rival Robert Stephenson making plans to get to Liverpool, join it with north Wales and a harbour at Holyhead on Anglesey. His Directors instructed Brunel to proceed with plans for a rail link with Fishguard, in Pembrokeshire, to connect with 'the granary of England', which was what our pompous forbears called Ireland in the 1840s. Gloucester to Cardiff to Swansea, then around the coast to Carmarthen, west to Whitland and Clarbeston, north through Treffgarne Gorge to Fishguard—this was the plan; gangs of navvies were soon at work along the whole length of this proposed line, including Treffgarne, where a village or two, ancestors of the one so tutted at by Miss Lewis's parents, were

quickly thrown up on platforms carved out of the valley side, and soon liberally sprinkled with the square, brown shapes of discarded Kilmarnock Whiskey bottles! For the navvy lived on beef and booze; his monumental amounts of energy were derived from a half gallon of the hard stuff and ten pounds or so of good Welsh beef. He was marvellous while he lasted but usually dead by the time he was 25.

Brunel did not work on precedent, like his colleagues and rivals in the railway game. Not for him the mean little 'colliery gauge' of 4'8½", the width of track favoured by Stephenson because it had worked alright for the waggonways of Durham, or Roman chariots. Brunel made his railways with a generous seven feet between the rails—the battle of the Gauges was joined, and would rumble on expensively until 1892 when the last chunk of Great Western broad gauge line was ripped up by the grandsons of the navvies who built it. As well as this innovation, Brunel did not like transverse sleepers as we have them still, across the track at fixed intervals; his sleepers lay longitudinally under the rails with a band of leather enabling a bit of 'give' and a more comfortable ride; way before its time, this too was doomed, though it is interesting that the current experiments concerning high speed railways have been very successful using concrete longitudinal sleepers with plastic where Brunel's leather would have been!

Work was well advanced, and there were several cuttings and embankments finished in Treffgarne when dread news flashed along the line, from mouth to mouth, men crossed themselves and thought of conditions back home in Ireland—for the potato crop, on which Ireland depended, failed in 1846; a lot of the potatoes the people had hoped to eat, had to be planted for the next year's crop, and they went hungry . . . and that crop failed too. Half of Ireland died; no longer was it the Granary of England (typically we had eaten the grain, leaving the peasants the spud; now they had neither). Hard headed businessmen in Bristol and London did not see why they should continue a line to Fishguard merely to get to a starving country, and tried to abandon the whole thing—Brunel fought to keep it going, aided by a clause that the South Wales

Top: inset
A section of Brunel's broad gauge line as it is today, sleeping quietly in the leaf litter, and . . .

Bottom:
. . . ringing to the pick and shovel for the first time in 140 years, as modern navvies from a local historical society dig sections across the works, during a survey to record this unique length of line. Here the 30′ width has been ballasted to only half its width for a single line of 7′ 0″ gauge track . . .

Friends of Pembrokeshire Museums

Railway Co would not get its pay from the parent G.W.R. unless they reached Fishguard (the Railway Mania had taught us a few things about rash railway promises . . .) The line dawdled on till March 1851, when Paxton's great greenhouse, the Crystal Palace, was just going up in Hyde Park for the Great Exhibition. That spring the line was finally abandoned, grew green and was forgotten— or nearly so . . . for villagers still talked about the rumpus of the New Railway and eventually Miss Lewis told me.

In the meantime other schemes had been put forward; Brunel's railway had gone to Neyland via Haverfordwest in 1853-5, so Pembrokeshire at last did *have* a train service. He had been told he must

not go to Fishguard anyway now, as his brother in law, the Minister of War Sir Benjamin Hawes, was getting ready for more trouble from the French, trouble which in this area was going to lead to the building of the great 'Palmerston's Follies', forts around the Haven. Instead Brunel submitted plans, and even built some of the line, to go around the corner from Fishguard, to Aber Mawr, a bay still with its little lengths of embankment, cutting, station and incline, abutments for jetties and inclus-

Success to the Railway say the banners, in Welsh and English, as the first train runs through towards Haverfordwest in December 1853—the Fishguard section had been abandoned two years before, and the line now met the sea at Neyland . . .

ion in a Welsh school textbook map for 1860. Brunel died in 1859, broken hearted at the catastrophic explosion aboard his liner *Great Eastern* on her maiden voyage, a ship six times bigger than anything else afloat, and destined to spend much of her life here in Milford. Brunel's pupil Brereton was engineer of a mad-sounding railway scheme of the 1870s called the Manchester and Milford Railway, some of which got built and gave many rail links in mid Wales, though it reached neither destination. It would have used Brunel's workings through Treffgarne. It didn't. Others came and went, but it was the Great Western which finally came here, to the Lewis family's discomfort, in 1905, when James Spires got himself decapitated with explosive. But the new railway did not seek to take the old line; instead they came up the middle of the valley on a massive embankment which is still one of the western region's engineering masterpieces. The old railway slept on. So came the era of the Ocean Mails trains to Fishguard, double headed express trains thundering down the gorge to meet the new giants. For we had now outgrown the *Great Eastern*—*Mauretania* called, so did illfated *Lusitania*, in the years before World War One killed off not only a whole generation of young men but any dreams the rail and shipping companies might have had of Fishguard as a transatlantic port.

So when a survey of the old railway of Treffgarne was undertaken, it was found we had something unique on our hands—a length of broad gauge trackbed just as Brunel's navvies and engineers had left it in 1851; and as it was incomplete, we could see how his thinking went, how he divided up his gangs of men when sinking a cutting (first, a 6′ wide trench on the line, then a second, half way down to datum, of full 30′ width, then the third down to trackbed level and ballasted, the men following each other, making for easier removal of earth by hand barrowing); we could see a crossing, with its keeper's hut and garden. We could see the reinforcement of drystone walling to take the sideways pressure of high speed trains on Brunel's broad gauge. And we got a glimpse of Brunel's final genius in the 'atmospheric caper', for which this line was apparently designed—Not another mad scheme, we hear you cry! Oh yes it was . . .

The Mayor's Present—a silver candelabra presented by the South Wales Railway to the Mayor of Haverfordwest, the day the line opened; there was a huge 'do', dancing, a feast in a red-and-white striped marquee in what is now Haverfordwest goods Yard, and fireworks in the evening . . .

Pembrokeshire Museum collection

SOUTH WALES & VALE OF NEATH RAILWAYS.

CHEAP
EXCURSION TO LONDON.

On MONDAY, AUGUST 7th, 1854,

A

SPECIAL TRAIN

WILL LEAVE

HAVERFORDWEST FOR LONDON,

Calling at the undermentioned Stations; and will return from the Paddington Station on Saturday, August 12th, at 8.0 a.m.

A TRAIN will also leave **MERTHYR** and **ABERDARE** for **NEATH, in** connexion with the South Wales Train.

On the Return Journey, passengers will be forwarded up the Vale of Neath by the next succeeding Train after the arrival of the Train from London.

TIME AND FARE TABLE.

	A.M.	FIRST CLASS.	COVERED CARR'GES		A.M.	FIRST CLASS.	COVERED CARR'GES
Haverfordwest	7. 0	33s.	23s.	Aberdare	9. 5	30s.	20s.
Narberth Road	7.30	30s.	20s.	Neath	10.15	27s.	18s.
St. Clears	7.50	30s.	20s.	Port Talbot	10.30	25s.	17s.
Carmarthen	8.15	30s.	20s.	Bridgend	10.55	24s.	16s.
Llanelly	9.15	30s.	20s.	Cardiff	11.55	22s.	15s.
Swansea	9.50	28s.	19s.	Newport	12.10	22s.	15s.
Merthyr	9. 0	30s.	20s.	Chepstow	1.15	20s.	13s.

THE

CRYSTAL PALACE AT SYDENHAM

Is now open at 1s. each, and parties therefore will have ample opportunity of visiting it by these arrangements.

TICKETS will not be transferable, and are only available for the Return Journey by the Special Train. One single Package of Luggage will be allowed to each Passenger; all other articles will be charged as parcels.

SWANSEA, JULY 19th, 1854.   FREDERICK CLARKE.

E. PEARSE, MACHINE-PRINTER, "RAILWAY GUIDE" OFFICE, SWANSEA.

Train in a Welsh Landscape—as seen in a detail on the amazing candelabra (p.123); such a scene was intended for Treffgarne Gorge with viaducts to span the Cleddau and its tributaries—the remains of this work still lies in the woodland . . .

Pembrokeshire Museum collection

A Revolution in Travel . . .—For the first time, you could now reach London from West Wales in less than a day—to people used to journey times of a week or more, this was a far more dramatic leap in speeds than, say, the arrival of the car or the airliner this century. Travelling so fast was frightening (the papers produced Experts who said your head would come off and your wife would miscarry). Rail travel was very expensive . . . hence these 'Specials', to get us used to the Age of the Train . . .

Briefly, in its early days the railway was handicapped by rotten engines—this may be thought to be heresy, but Brunel would have been the first to agree; underpowered, underbraked, and prone to die at inconvenient moments or come off the rails . . . well, as if these were not enough drawbacks, any locomotive, even a modern one, is an expensive luxury. It is heavy, it has to drag all its fuel (plus water for a steam loco) along with it; much of the weight of a train is the loco pulling it. So a pair of inventors, Samuda and Clegg, came up with an interesting idea to overcome this, especially on the crowded commutor lines in inner cities—just the lines where today we *do* have locomotiveless trains, the Underground and Southern region e.m.u's, who pick up their power from the track. Brunel was

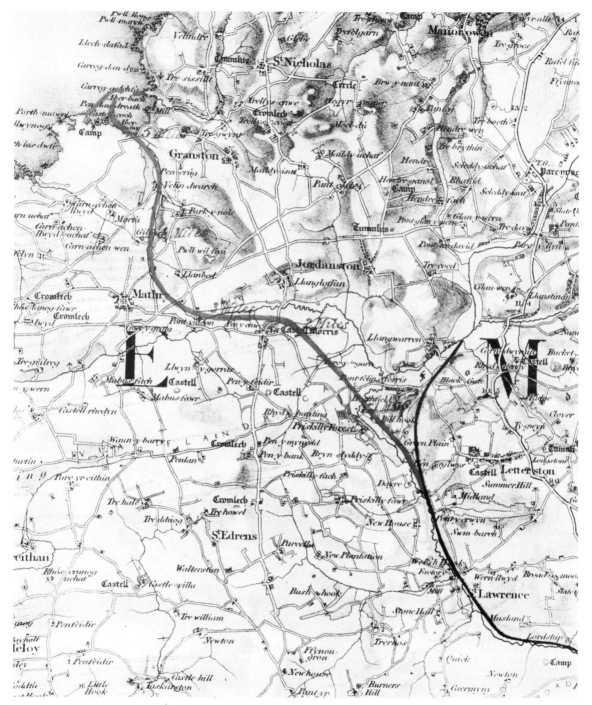

126

Down Trains.		Week Days only.					Up Trains.		Week Days only.				
		a.m.		p.m.		p.m.				a.m.		p.m.			p.m.	
Clynderwen	... ... dep	10 43		2 25	...	5 50	...	Goodwick	... ... dep	9 5		12 15	...	...	5 20	...
Llanycefn	... ... "	10 50		2 35	...	6 0	...	Letterston	... ... "	9 25		12 32	...	...	5 37	...
Maenclochog	... ... "	11 3	Mixed.	2 48	...	6 13	Mixed. ...	Puncheston	... ... "	9 42	Mixed.	12 48	...	...	5 53	...
Rosebush	... ... "	11 13		2 55	...	6 23	...	Rosebush	... ... "	9 58		1 4	...	...	6 8	...
Puncheston	... ... "	11 20		3 11	...	6 39	...	Maenclochog	... ... "	10 5		1 11	...	...	6 14	...
Letterston	... ... "	11 43		3 25	...	6 53	...	Llanycefn	... ... "	10 17		1 23	...	...	6 25	...
Goodwick	... ... arr	12 0		3 45	...	7 10	...	Clynderwen	... ... arr	10 30		1 35	...	...	6 35	...

Section of the Great Western Railway's timetable for 1903 (top) showing times for the Fishguard and North Pembrokeshire Railway's run to the north Pembrokeshire port—the GWR was forced to buy out their tiny rival, though they continued to use the smaller company's station at Goodwick (centre) until they had completed their own terminus at Fishguard Harbour. The loco in this picture is 'Ringing Rock', sister to 'Margaret' (now preserved at Scolton Manor Museum near Haverfordwest).

Near miss for Aber Mawr—Brunel's red-inked scrawl on an early map of North Pembrokeshire shows where the railway was to have gone after the Napoleonic scare and European revolutions of 1848; his original line to Fishguard is abandoned, and the line now runs via Castle Morris and Mathry to Aber Mawr Bay, where he has sketched in jetties and landing stage.

Pembrokeshire Record Office

thinking in the days when steep inclines on some railways still had rope haulage, a stationary engine alongside the track winding the carriages up the hill. Clegg and Samuda proposed a pipe along the centre of each track, split along the top with a valve which could be re-sealed; each set of coaches would have a piston on one of them, which fitted into this pipe. Then vast beam engines alongside the track would suck the air out of the pipe, and the train would be pushed along by atmospheric pressure— they were called Atmospheric railways.

And they actually worked. Speeds of sixty miles an hour, amazing acceleration, silent working (which killed a lot of people who had got accustomed to walking along the tracks—you could always hear a train coming, couldn't you? Well, you could

127

The 1905-7 works in Treffgarne Gorge
were serviced by a number of ancient
and battered locos like this 0-6-0 Manning Wardle
while the Spittal tunnel and giant embankment were
under construction.

not hear a Clegg & Samuda . . .); again, the railway could be operated with very close train running times of two minutes (or even less) between trains— they could not collide, for if one started to catch up another, its vacuum ran out and it stopped. Brunel was thrilled by this idea, and steamrollered his Directors into adopting it—had they not got ample room between his seven foot metals to put bigger and better pipes than anyone else? Could it not be used in places like Ireland where there was no coal but abundant, if heavy, peat? Was it not the highest of high technology? It was, the Directors agreed, several lines were built with amazing gradients which have been a curse to enginemen ever since (like the North Devon, one of the few lines still to

have a brace of engine houses in situ from this ill-starred experiment). Treffgarne would have had one of these too, had it not been for the potato famine which gave rise not only to a lot of rethinking in railway and shipping terms, but indirectly contributed to the terrible carnage of modern times in that beautiful but unhappy land.

Today, then, you can explore a length of line actually walked by Isambard Brunel. You can imagine the ghost of his horsedrawn black Britska, a coach of his own design which contained his

128

drawing and survey gear, a rudimentary bed, and an everlasting supply of cigars—his navvies affectionately referred to this conveyance as 'The Flying Hearse'. You can muse upon the life of a man so varied in his interests and skills that he built bridges, steamships unsinkable by *Titanic* standards half a century in advance of their time; caught murderers by electric telegraph; was a friend of one of the earliest railway nuts, Felix Mendelssohn the composer; could paint a fine oil; a man who, when he inadvertently swallowed a half-sovereign during an ill-advised conjuring session for his children and started to choke, calmly sat down and designed a medical innovation still in use (albeit for obstetrics and called 'Brodie's forceps').

And the man who, when told by his brother-in-law about 'that fierce little Nightingale woman'—Florence Nightingale, who had seen the enormous toll of our men in the Crimea, as much from cholera and poor medicine as from battle wounds—produced in six short weeks the world's first prefabricated building, still a model for army field hospitals, shipped it out to Russia with some of his navvies to erect it, as he (rightly) didn't trust the War Office to get anything right . . . and is it a coincidence that because Brunel got there first, Russia's railways are still on The Broad Gauge?

'Cardi Bach' and Sophie the Tanner

Cardigan Station at the turn of the century, a piece of pure Betjeman with iron adverts and lovely flower beds —local people still speak with great affection of the 'Cardi Bach' (from an old post card).

The Railway which inspired an Eisteddfod poet ...

People get in to industrial archaeology for lots of reasons—it is a more accessible period to imagine yourself into, as most of it is fairly modern; the remains are usually reasonably dramatic (the humps and hollows of classical archaeology are often worryingly slight); they can be found almost anywhere from the densely populated town centre to the bleakest countryside, the top of a mountain or the edge of the sea . . . There is a lure of greed—to look for treasure. There is a history of technologies we use today and therefore can readily discern and understand. And there are the heroic, tragic, spooky and often comic stories which any who delve into history can dig up wholesale. A lot of industrial history is very, very funny.

Pembrokeshire is crisscrossed with mad little railways—or at least the remains of them, since it was well and truly Beechinged, and is still under threat. They started very early, as has been seen in Treffgarne—they could be big, like the Great Western; they could be tiny, like the Eglwyswrw Tramroad—they could have earthworks so massive they dominate like the great wall of China or so whispy you need all the skills of classical archaeology plus the nose of a Sherlock Holmes to dig them out. And nearly all of them are within living memory. The Pembroke and Tenby, the Rosebush line, the Whitland and Cardigan—beloved 'Cardi Bach', still remembered with affection by railwaymen and enthusiasts alike, with its lazy schedules and busy looking stations like Cardigan; its cargoes of thousands of rabbits for the East End of London; it is the railway to Glogue and Llanfyrnach, of steep hills and tortuous curves, dreamed up by a man in a Brunel First-class railway carriage.

John Owen was a prosperous Victorian land-owner whose interests included the slate quarries at Glogue; as he was whisked to business meetings in Cardiff and London by the newly completed South Wales Railway on its imposing broad gauge, he decided Glogue must have a rail link with Whitland, a line running up the Taf valley through the silver lead mine at Llanfyrnach and the farming area around Crymych; why, it might even go down to Cardigan and meet the sea . . .

Owen commissioned a survey by the engineer of the Pembroke and Tenby line, then under construction—this was John Szlumper, and he was asked to design for Owen 'a cheap railway' from Whitland to Crymmych Arms. This was in 1868, and the line slowly grew—it was always poor, directors were wont to pay for individual rails from the small change in their pockets! The staff was acquired in odd ways. A Narberth stationmaster defected from Brunel's broad gauge empire and became master of Llanfyrnach, next to the great engine house of the lead mine. In 1873 their first loco arrived and was named, not surprisingly, 'John Owen'; she was driven in by one of the infant company's more maverick characters, Driver Pugh. The company's books are thereafter periodically peppered with references to

Driver Pugh, intoxicated in duty.
Driver Pugh, speeding
Driver Pugh, Refusing to obey orders
                    and, raising a boggling picture
Driver Pugh, shunting Furiously.

Nothing seems to have been done about Driver Pugh, and he continued on his alcoholic way until he left a whole train at Taf Vale Junction one day, clogging the main line, while he roared off up the valley towards Llanfallteg 'with beer on his breath',

light-engine and light-headed. There was a monumental row—we hear no more of Driver Pugh.

He had, however, contributed to railway mythology—it was a somewhat disaster prone concern, was the early Cardi Bach, and on 25 August 1885 two trains collided after a runaway, both drivers were killed, and a poem written about it was entered for the Eisteddfod, In part it said (trans.)

> It ran like a grey hound through Dolau Mawr, out of control crashing most dreadfully, and that Sophie the Tanner was to her great grief Buried alive in dusty coal . . .

Another railway poem about Cardi Bach was entered in an Eisteddfod in 1911; it was called 'How to Secure a late Train' and it won. Cardi Bach trains were often late. Passengers, when there were any, complained about this, muttering rebelliously about the wet goods, the damp seats; for years the line couldn't afford tarpaulins, and your stuff often arrived drenched—but pity the poor guard, he wasn't covered-in either and got wet almost every day.

In 1875 the line started to consider passenger traffic and optimistically ordered a second engine, imaginatively named 'no 2'. But the Board of Trade's inspector took one look at the railway and flatly refused a certificate; signalling was poor or nonexistent, rails needed attention, points were rickety; his catalogue of defects makes it a wonder any train ever got anywhere except down the embankment, but the line soldiered on, politely accepting, then filing and forgetting, the many refusal notices which fluttered in like bureaucratic snowflakes for years. Szlumper the engineer, saw a great heap of forbidding buff paper one day and asked Owen what it all was. Nothing of importance he was told. What is to be done? he asked. Tell 'em to mind their own business, the owner snarled—he had a healthy dislike of officialdom in any form.

But the little line prospered in its way, selling ballast to the GWR, its giant neighbour, several thousand tons of slates went out every year, the rabbit trade picked up nicely, as did passenger

WHITLAND, TENBY AND PEMBROKE DOCK.

Down Trains.		Week Days only.								Up Trains.		Week Days only.							
		a.m.	a.m.	a.m.	a.m.	p.m.		p.m.	p.m.			a.m.		a.m.	p.m.		p m	p.m.	p.m.	p.m.
Whitland	dep	5 55	...	10 35	...	11 50	2 10	...	5 20	7 40	...	Pembroke D'k dep	7 45	...	10 20	12 30	...	2 50	4 20	6 0	7 30	...
Narberth	"	6 5	...	10 45	...	12 2	2 22	...	5 30	7 50	...	Pembroke "	7 49	...	10 25	12 35	...	2 55	4 25	6 5	7 35	...
Kilgetty	"	6 22	...	11 1	...	12 16	2 36	...	5 43	8 4	...	Lamphey "	7 54	...	10 30	12 40	...	3 0	4 30	6 10	7 41	...
Saundersfoot	"	6 24	...	11 4	...	12 19	2 39	...	5 46	8 7	...	Manorbier "	8 2	...	10 38	12 48	...	3 8	4 38	6 18	7 48	...
Tenby	{arr	6 35	...	11 15	...	12 30	2 50	...	6 0	8 20	...	Penally "	8 9	...	10 45	12 56	...	3 15	4 45	6 25	7 55	...
Tenby	{dep	6 40	9 15	11 20	...	12 35	2 55	...	6 5	8 25	...	Tenby {arr	8 15	...	10 50	1 0	...	3 20	4 50	6 30	8 0	...
Penally	"	6 45	9 18	11 26	...	12 40	3 0	...	6 9	8 28	...	Tenby {dep	8 20	...	10 55	1 5	...	3 25	4 55	6 35	—	
Manorbier	"	6 52	9 25	11 34	...	12 47	3 7	...	6 17	8 36	...	Saundersfoot "	8 30	...	11 6	1 15	...	3 35	5 7	6 45	...	
Lamphey	"	6 59	9 32	11 41	...	12 57	3 17	...	6 27	8 43	...	Kilgetty "	8 35	...	11 11	1 20	...	3 40	5 12	6 50	...	
Pembroke	"	7 3	9 35	11 45	...	1 1	3 20	...	6 31	8 47	...	Narberth "	8 48	...	11 24	1 33	...	3 53	5 25	7 3	...	
Pembroke D'k	arr	7 10	9 40	11 55	...	1 8	3 28	...	6 40	8 55	...	Whitland arr	9 0	...	11 35	1 45	...	4 4	5 40	7 15	...	

TEMPLETON PLATFORM.—The 5.55 a.m. Train from Whitland calls at Templeton Platform on Fridays, when Market Tickets are issued to Pembroke Dock. Also the same Train calls on Saturdays, when Market Tickets are issued to Tenby and to Pembroke. For Fares and Return arrangements see Market Ticket Bills. Ordinary Tickets are also issued by the Trains which call.

WHITLAND AND CARDIGAN.

Down Trains.		Week Days only.					Up Trains.		Week Days only.				
		a.m.	Mxd a.m.	Mxd p.m.		p.m.			Mxd a.m.	Mxd a.m.		p.m.	p.m.
Whitland	dep	5 50	10 30	2 15	...	6 15	...	Cardigan dep	7 30	9 50	...	4 0	5 35	...
Llanfalteg	"	6 0	10 39	2 25	...	6 25	...	Kilgerran "	7 40	9 59	...	4 10	5 45	...
Login	"	6 9	10 48	2 34	...	6 34	...	Boncath "	7 52	10 12	...	4 22	5 57	...
Llanglydwen	"	6 17	10 57	2 42	...	6 42	...	Crymmych Arms "	8 5	10 26	...	4 35	6 10	...
Rhydowen	"	6 22	11 5	2 47	...	6 47	...	Glogue "	8 14	10 35	...	4 44	6 19	...
Llanfyrnach	"	6 30	11 13	2 55	...	6 55	...	Llanfyrnach "	8 19	10 42	...	4 51	6 26	...
Glogue	"	6 35	11 18	3 0	...	7 0	...	Rhydowen "	8 27	10 50	...	4 59	6 34	...
Crymmych Arms	"	6 47	11 30	3 12	...	7 12	...	Llanglydwen "	8 32	10 55	...	5 4	6 40	...
Boncath	"	6 59	11 43	3 24	...	7 24	...	Login "	8 40	11 7	...	5 12	6 51	...
Kilgerran	"	7 11	11 55	3 35	...	7 35	...	Llanfalteg "	8 48	11 15	...	5 20	6 59	...
Cardigan	arr	7 20	12 5	3 45	...	7 45	...	Whitland arr	8 58	11 25	...	5 30	7 10	...

Section of timetable for 1903 showing the old 'P & T' (or Pembroke and Tenby Railway) and 'Cardi Bach's leisurely services in the great days of the branch line.

traffic once Whitland opened its Mart in 1884. A few lazy trains each day, pigeons, parcels, geese, machinery, lead ore and slates . . . the line was taken over by the GWR in 1890. A timetable from those years gives a flavour of life on the Whitland and Cardigan, four up and four down each day, extra on mart days, occasional school outings or choirs for Eisteddfodau. During the Great War the even smaller line to Eglwyswrw and Pengelli brought its loads of pitprops to Crymmych Arms, hauled by its one engine driven by almost the only member of the concern that wasn't a refugee from middle Europe. After this one bit of excitement it settled back to peaceful obscurity, loved by the locals as part of the landscape, even if they *were* still slightly annoyed by Paddington's insistence on spelling Cilgerran station with a 'K'—it was never a speedy service, the 28 miles being covered, on average, in an hour and a half, everything stopping everywhere. Then Beeching; passenger services stopped in 1962, and a year later goods also. Now only trackbed remains, old photos and the ghosts of

Driver Pugh, shunting furiously with beer on his breath, of the sad fate of Sophie the Tanner, two drunken sailors assaulting Guard Evans at Crymych in 1882 (we don't hear much more, but Guard Evans might well have had a couple too, since he was hauled up before the top brass later for shouting insults at the Manager).

One disappointed ghost might have been an enterprising slate quarry which used the line regularly for one of their products, too hefty to go conveniently by other transport—to their slates and kitchen floors and milk and butter tabletops and sinks, they added slate billiard tables and—oh eternity—slate Coffins.

WARNING

Nervous and Easily Upset Readers Might Do Well to Turn the Next Few Pages as we are about to visit . . .

Oystermouth and the Grave of Dr Thomas Bowdler Inventor of Bowdlerization . . .

Curious how we cannot, as the Thinking animal (self-styled 'Man-the-Wise'), ever do things by halves; we veer from extreme to extreme like a mad pendulum. One minute we have social systems where workers are held tight and subservient under tyrannical masters where to speak out, or even to look up and face your boss's gaze, is as bad as murder and treated as such. Next we have formed trades unions to deal with this unfair and unjust system, and what happens? The closed shop, the demarcation dispute, strikes over this, that and the other—and the boss dare not look his shop steward in the eye lest there be Action—which word in these circles means total *in*action. One moment we have total repression—as with the Puritans and Cromwell and their 'Committees for Detection of Scandalous Ministers', their burnings of books, closings of theatres . . . the next you have the Restoration when, suddenly, anything goes and to write a play without at least fifteen seductions is showing yourself to be terribly old hat. The Victorians covered their pianos' legs for fear of exciting lascivious thoughts; we uncover everything for fear of leaving psychological scars. There is no middle way, it seems, the pendulum never stops dead centre.

These thoughts are bound to wander through our heads as we visit the solid, be-gargoyled, echoing parish church at Oystermouth on the outskirts of Swansea. It has much to see including a window of stained glass commemorating, of all things, the oldest passenger railway in the world, the Mumbles Tramway, running before the Napoleonic wars and officially strangled in our own time. But in the south east corner of the churchyard a solid, plain stone box marks the grave of a man some might think of as father of the Festival of Light—Dr. Thomas Bowdler. Mr. Hoover soon ceased being the man who invented the suction cleaner and became a verb, to hoover, so Dr. Bowdler has given us, posthumously, to bowdlerize—to clean up literature, especially salacious and overt sexual ref-

Oystermouth Church—and the grave of Thomas Bowdler, the Victorian "Whitehouse".

erence. Until you stand before his grave you think surely he must be Victorian along with the piano legs in their Directoires, and the hint of an ankle an incitement to lust. But no; Bowdler was born in the reign of George II and died the year the Stockton and Darlington Railway first ran, twelve years before young Victoria came to the throne.

133

Young Thomas Bowdler trained and became qualified in medicine (a profession which should have got him used to the seamier side of life); but he caught TB from a dying friend he was nursing, and though Bowdler recovered, he was forbidden to practise for his health's sake; for the rest of his long life he travelled, wrote and researched whatever interested him, helped by a comfortable private income—he became a Fellow of the Royal Society, of the Society of Antiquaries and was elected to the College of Physicians. He was a man concerned about social reform, and helped John Howard look into the truly horrific condition of our gaols. He entered the church, and came to settle at Rhyddings in Oystermouth, where he sat in his study overlooking the sea, writing many books, biographies and his 'edited works' which have made his name a household word. He lived in Oystermouth from 1810 until his death fifteen years later.

In 1818 the first books appeared which coined the new word for the English language. 'The Family Shakespeare' was in 10 volumes *'In which nothing is added to the original text but those words and expressions are omitted which cannot with propriety be read aloud in a family'*. Dr. Bowdler knew his audience would share his distaste for the bawdier Bard; there

Oystermouth Church—windows commemorating the Mumbles Railway, first passenger line in the world, from horse to steam to electric tram . . . and now its track is reduced to a way for the humble bike . . .

was a reaction at the end of the Georgian period to the goings-on at Brighton with 'Prinny' and Mrs. Fitzherbert. There was retrenchment after the victory over Napoleon; inflation was a galloping 400%; soldiers returned from keeping the world free of Froggies and found themselves unemployed and starving. Had not the windows of the Prince Regent's carriage been smashed as he drove to the House? Were there not myriads of secret societies and dangerous talk of Socialism? Of treacherous nonsense about Parliamentary Reform? Riots and mayhem in our towns and cities? Of what the *Times* thundered as

Stirring up the People with disaffection and contempt for law, religion and morality.

The government noted with worry a march of the unemployed from Manchester to tell the future George IV their troubles; in those less heedful days the working classes were dispersed by the army, with bayonets.

The year after Bowdler's 'Shakespeare' would see the Peterloo Massacre, the deaths of unemployed and starving workers and savage repressive measures advocated in Parliament. This is the backcloth against which Bowdler was attempting to protect us from jaunty Tudor smut.

'*Many Expressions and words occur which are of so indecent a nature as to render it highly desirable that they should be Erased . . .*' it says in the introduction to his monumental work; but it wasn't just the book left in every hotel bedroom and on every desert island—the other one we will find under our palm tree, if Roy Plomley was to be believed, fell under Dr. Bowdler's scrutiny, and was found wanting; '*there are allusions in Scripture*' he thundered '*which call expressly for their Erasement . . .*' Eventually, after Shakespeare and the Bible had been cleaned up, he turned for the last years of his life to Gibbon's 'Decline and Fall of the Roman Empire'. He liked to keep busy, did the good Doctor. He was Chairman of the Society for the Suppression of Vice until his death. What sort of things caused the doctorial eyebrow to raise, the quill to Erase?

Shakespeare was, of course, a man of his time, he was writing to amuse as well as to educate, and his audience liked a bit of naughtiness now and again; in history or tragedy, the strain is relieved every now and again by a comic character like the Nurse in 'Romeo and Juliet', the rustics in 'Dream' or that inevitable buffoon, Falstaff. The texts abound with Elizabethan double-entendre, some of which even Dr. Bowdler missed. Falstaff itself is one, as is one of the soldiers in Henry V's '*Pistol's cock is up*'; the nurse in 'Romeo and Juliet comes in slyly to wake the 'friar-drugged Juliet': Shakespeare has her say:

A puritan's grave—Thomas Bowdler cleaned up
Shakespeare and the Bible but died before he could do
the same for Gibbon's 'Decline and Fall' . . .

. . . fie you slugabed!
Why, love—I say—Madam Sweetheart! Why—
  Bride . . .
What, not a word? You take your pennyworths now
Sleep for a week; for the next night, I warrant
The county Paris hath set up his rest
That you shall rest but little . . .

Dr. Bowdler did not like this. It becomes

You take your pennyworths now, sleep for a week
  exit 4 lines
How sound is she asleep! I needs must wake her—

                              and on with the plot.
It's bad enough in the tragedies, the histories
contain fact not easily covered up. Thus Henry V
outside the gates of Harfleur reminds the defending
French of the consequences if they do not sur-
render:—

I will not leave the half-achieved Harfleur
Till in her ashes she lie buried;
The gates of mercy shall be all shut up
And the flesh'd soldier, rough and hard of heart
In liberty of bloody hand shall range
With conscience wide as hell, mowing like grass
Your fresh fair virgins and your flowering infants . . .
What is't to me, when you yourselves are cause,
If your pure maidens fall into the hand
of hot and forcing violation?—

Bowdler gulps hard here, and does a quick rewrite

. . . and the flesh'd soldier rough and hard of heart
In liberty and bloody hand shall range,
What is it then to me if impious war,
What is it then to me when you yourselves are cause
  CUT pure maidens
What rein shall hold licentious wickedness

                              and back to the Bard.
Once we get to the Comedies, of course, they are
mostly smut and Dr. Bowdler has a hard task. What
is he to do with an exchange like:—

Yonder man is carried to prison
What hath he done
A woman
But his offence?
Groping for trouts in a peculiar river . . .

Easy. He swipes out the whole thing, Pompey and all, and inserts 'Enter a Clown' and mumbles on about all the houses in Vienna due to be pulled down. This is '*Measure for Measure*', a difficult play to Bowdlerize even for Bowdler since it is *all* about licentiousness and its syphilitic consequences. Even the good Doctor had to preface it 'This comedy contains scenes which are truly worthy of the first of dramatic poets . . . but the indecent expressions with which many of the scenes abound are so interwoven with the story that it is extremely difficult to separate the one from the other'. Indeed, after the above exchange has been clowned, five solid minutes of bawdy dialogue go in one slash, making a complete nonsense of the plot, and we haste to Scene III, breathless but pure-hearted. The '*Merry Wives*', of course, is all about sex too, and needs similar treatment. Bowdler's books ran to millions; all editions were a sell-out in 1818, 1824, 1831, 1851, and 1861 he wrote that 'Nothing is added to the original text'; maybe not, but it often does not make much sense either. My copy has on its flyleaf 'To Percy from his affecte Great Aunt' and was for Christmas just a century ago. Percy, I fear, didn't even cut the pages—the books were—if you will forgive—virgin when I bought them. But Bowdler had a point to make; his society *did* need change, it *did* need cleaning up; it still does. But his way, and maybe ours too, is not the right one; it did not work . . ..

THE

FAMILY SHAKSPEARE:

IN WHICH

NOTHING IS ADDED TO THE ORIGINAL TEXT,

BUT THOSE WORDS AND EXPRESSIONS ARE OMITTED WHICH CANNOT

WITH PROPRIETY BE READ IN A FAMILY.

BY

THOMAS BOWDLER, ESQ., F.R.S. & S.A.

Title Page—from Bowdler's cleaned-up Shakespeare, whose preparation has given us a new word . . .

Three Times Widdershins or

How to Become a Toadman in Pembrokeshire

Trellyffaint means 'Toad's Town'—an odd name for a New Stone age burial chamber if ever there was one. Nearby is a farm which used to have a toad carved over its fireplace; Richard Fenton visited it in 1809:—

'. . . alight to see the figure of a toad, well sculptured in black marble, which is introduced into a chimney-piece . . . said to have been brought from Italy . . . it had filled its present station for centuries . . .'

The family then living there had a toad as part of their crest; but he was by no means the first visitor. At the end of the 12th Century Giraldus Cambrensis also went to see the little tomb, and tells us a tall story about it:—

'In our time'

He says

A young man, native of this county, during a severe illness, suffered as violent a persecution by Toads as if the reptiles of the whole province had come to him by agreement; and though destroyed by his nurses and friends, they increased again on all sides like hydras'

heads. His attendants, both friends and strangers, being wearied out, he was drawn up in a kind of bag, into a high tree, stripped of its leaves and shred; nor was he there secure from his venomous enemies, for they crept up the tree in great numbers, and consumed him even to the very bones . . .'

Quite why toads are thought to be poisonous, or magical, or the witch's friend, or to give a deadly bite when guarding treasure, is not clear:—

Round about the cauldron go
In the poison'd entrails throw—
Toad, that under coldest stone
Days and nights hast thirty one
Sweltered venom sleeping got . . .

mumble Macbeth's witches; they go on to mix in adder, newt frog, 'fenny snake' (a dirty or mouldy one)—obviously amphibian or reptile is good enough for magic.

An old man living near Trellyffaint told a strange tale, especially if we bear in mind the connections with toads and witchcraft (often a corruption of pre-christian religious rituals); when asked if he knew

why the little tomb was called 'Toads' town' he did not know, but he knew how you became a Toad Man, because his father had gone through this grim ritual, in order to gain power over animals, especially cattle. You caught and killed a toad, the old man said—then you pinned the body over an ants' nest until the flesh had all gone, leaving only the bones. These you took to the Caman brook, the little stream which flows through Nevern, and threw them in one by one. Eventually, he said, his eyes twinkling, one bone would turn and swim up against the stream, screaming as it went—this bone you caught and carried about in your pocket for three days and nights, returning to Trellyffaint tomb each night to walk round it three times, widdershins (against the going of the sun, anticlockwise). At the third time, the Devil would try to get the bone from you—but if you survived that ordeal, you were then a Toad Man, and had power over animals. *He* did not believe it, he said, like most people do when they tell you they aren't at all superstitious, but touch wood just to make sure. But his father had done it, about 1890 it would have been.

Now, what are we to make of this? Mumbojumbo it most certainly is, but like most folk tales, what does it tell us about how earlier men and women *thought*? The two stories together, ours and Giraldus's, have remarkable similarities, separated though they are by eight centuries in the telling. Toads . . . bones . . . the cromlech . . . how does *that* fit in? It is an oddity, the cromlech, two small chambers side by side but pointing in opposite directions,

Toad's Town—Trellyffaint Neolithic burial chamber, its capstone's surface covered with mysterious cup marks . . . folk memory gave it such powers that five thousand years after it was built, the strange 'Toad Man' ceremony was still being celebrated here, and 'Dumb Cakes' were left on the capstone by girls needing its magic to find them a husband—the tomb is on a magnificent site overlooking Nevern and the Preseli Hills.

Toad in the Hole . . .—emerging sleepily from his hibernation . . . many odd legends cling to this amphibian, such as his poison, his guarding treasure, the use of his insides in Witches' brews . . . but surely none is odder than the Toad man story? . . .

like those Victorian kissing seats. The capstone of one chamber is gone, the other is collapsed but has the remains of drystone walling about it—both lie in the same pear-shaped mound. On the surviving capstone are some cupmarks, which some authorities think may have been an attempt to make star maps, the magnitudes given by the size of the cup. Now, the people who built this tomb and its neighbours were the first farmers—up to that time Man had been a hunter, chasing and killing animals he needed for food and clothing. In this new order he kept animals in fields, grew cereals, could settle in one place and own property, clear forest for his farm . . . but he needed some courage to start coming to terms with domesticating the wild ox, the wild boar—large fierce animals both, with damaging tusks or horns and a lot of weight behind them. Was *this* when we needed power over animals so much we gave ourselves confidence with this odd ritual of the toads' bones?—because this strange ceremony can be found to have been practised right across Europe—and *always* in the same area as you find Neolithic Burial chambers . . .

A cure for Arthritis?

Cucumber Tea . . .

Nobody who hasn't got arthritis, even slightly, can measure the agony and discomfort of this universal disease; you don't even have to have one foot in the grave . . . patients in a rheumatology unit can be as young as six months old. It is a goldmine for the pharmaceutical industry, and a host of new drugs comes out constantly, some with unpleasant or even dangerous side-effects. Plain painkillers aren't much better, and if you have a 'delicate stomach' too, then aspirin, the one good old standby for pain relief, will give trouble and may even cause internal bleeding. So what to do?

The first thing is, of course, that it isn't a new disease, like the endemic heart trouble in Western Man due, it is said, to our fatty diet; or lung cancer, linked with cigarette smoking. Either, of course, may be due to the simple statistic that until the start of last century, few lived beyond thirty five or forty; then diseases like TB and cholera and typhus kept the adult population down, while infant mortality, even among the rich, was high, due to diseases now almost as historic as Stonehenge . . . measles, whooping cough, scarlet fever, diptheria . . . now we live long enough to *get* the illnesses of people who are elderly. Heart trouble, cancer, arthritis, back-ache, strokes and so on. These words, from a total non-medic, will probably give some Doctors a stroke, and in which case I'm sorry! But as a chronic patient for so long I don't even like to think about it, my feeling about medicine is that a lot of it is you; you may have a disease, but whether or not the cure works is often due to you, your attitude, your deciding 'I'm going to beat this . . .' and this is when the Doctor's 'Bedside Manner' his person-ality, helps you. Faith healing may be helped by this personality effect too; and how much stronger it must have been in the days before modern drugs, when a lot of medicine *was* faith of one sort or an-other, when a taste of something really nasty (so it *must* be doing you good), a kindly word from the grave and sober specialist that you must mend your

Meadowsweet—*(Filipendula ulmaria)* likes growing in damp situations, and so its froth of creamy flowers, dark green elm-shaped leaves and red stem are features of our ditches, streams and river banks. Old Wives numbered it as one of their most powerful medicines . . .

ways, Take The Mixture, sleep a lot and Get Some Exercise.

What was that mixture, to be taken (after shaking) three times a day? For centuries, medicine relied upon an ancient piece of wisdom called the Doctrine of Signatures. Briefly, this said that the gods (or once Christianity had arrived, God) had decreed that various plants had built into them a Sign which the Doctor or Physician or Barber-Surgeon could spot, when collecting his herbs for the dispensary. A plant which would cure lung dis-eases was marked with spots on its lung-shaped

140

leaves . . . thus Lungwort entered our pharmacopaia, and is known to science still as *Pulmonaria officinalis*, the first name from the latin for 'Lung', and the second from the apothecary's shop. An upset liver would respond to treatment with Liverwort, which had livery looking leaves, spleenwort . . . well, you get the picture. The ancient herbalists had an armoury of plants to help cure our ills, many of which didn't do a lot from the physical point of view, but which were good psychologically, helping with that vital function of a medicine (or a Doctor) —they made us *believe* we were going to get better . . . and that is half the battle! The Doctrine of Signatures was used in other ways; for example, the little Speedwell plant was known for centuries as something any traveller would tuck in his socks before a journey, as it was known to ease tired feet. Another name for it is Traveller's Joy. But Speedwell doesn't do much for the bunnions and aches of walking . . . what it HAS got is stamens which look like a pair of boots and stockings on walking legs . . . the Doctrine of Signatures, and our belief, did the rest. Walking along a hedgerow nowadays is like taking a stroll through an old chemist's shop—you spot remedy after remedy, some of which worked, and most of which helped. For years, after all, old Wives plastered deep wounds with mouldy cheese; they knew it worked, they just hadn't given the name to Penicillin. People with heart trouble were given infusions of Foxglove; then it was mumbo-jumbo, now, it is respectable because we call it Digitalin.

A riverside plant which smells and tastes of cucumber was used to ease the pain and stiffness of arthritis; it was—and is—called Meadowsweet. Sufferers were given a 'tea' made from the roots, stem or leaves, or a sandwich in bread. And it works, to this day—because Meadowsweet is chock full of Salicylic Acid . . . Aspirin. The one difference between Aspirin on Boots' shelves and the natural product is that Meadowsweet has in it a mucilaginous jelly which seems to coat the inside of your tum when you swallow your mixture, and this has

Woodcut from Gerarde's 'Herball' of 1597, one of the first books to treat medical herbalism and botany scientifically.

the right effect on the arthritic joints while protecting your innards from the Salicylic acid's rather drastic irritation. Natural, and cheap (the price of a walk to the riverside) and safe; could you ask any more of any medicine?

Alternative medicine has bloomed in the last few years as some people have thought 'Traditional' high-tech treatment might be doing harm, or at least not doing much good. Acupuncture, hypnosis, herbalism . . . accepted for centuries and now making a comeback. But with a bit of searching, you can find amazing uses for all sorts of commonly occurring roadside plants—indeed, it has been suggested that this was the reason for some of them to be introduced by Man in the first place. Looking through the work of the ancient Herbalists it is easy to laugh, not so easy to see why these methods were relied on for so many centuries. You were told to go out on moors like that near Foel Drygarn to pick Sphagnum moss, then to dry it and keep it in case you got a bad cut, then it would be useful as dressing. So useful was it, in fact, that in both World Wars it was used as an emergency dressing to such an extent that a major industry grew up to pick, dry and pack the moss to send to the Front. It was even recommended as an emergency treatment during the Falklands campaign; not bad for an idea which goes back to the Bronze age! Yet modern investigation has shown that Sphagnum not only absorbs a vast amount of liquid, and will therefore staunch bad wounds and soak up discharge, but that it contains a powerful antibiotic—like the mouldy cheese, the wise men and women who prescribed it in the middle ages didn't have fancy names to put to what it did, they only knew it *worked*.

Arsenic and Old Bishops

The Mad Hatter is a reality. Hatters went mad, in past times, as they were poisoned by the preservative they used to prepare Beaver hats—the skins were washed with soap containing arsenic. And everybody knows about arsenic as being poisonous, it was used extensively by the Victorians themselves as a rat poison, weedkiller . . . and an occasional draug'it given to inconvenient or rich relatives.

Arsenic was much used for paint colouring (its salts produced a beautiful dark green much liked by the Victorians)—it was mixed with equally poisonous lead to make the resulting shot harder, it was used in the manufacture of high quality glassware . . . and every chemist had some on his shelves for medicinal purposes, as indeed some still do. So there were arsenic works near every town in which nonferrous metals like copper or lead were smelted, as arsenic, tin, antimony and bismuth were valuable, much needed byproducts of the chemical industry—and in Clyne Wood there is an old arsenic works.

The production of lead, arsenic and antimony killed a lot of people. It did not worry the industrialists of the day—they were there, after all, to make money for themseves and their share holders, and anybody who suggested that there were safer ways of extracting poisons than those used were given Company balance-sheets to read; we have not changed, of course, as the current debates about pollution show! But one man was concerned, and he was a cleric—Bishop Watson, worried about his flock and their premature deaths, realised the poisoning to be due to fumes from the furnaces and smelting, and designed a special chimney known ever since as Watson's Flue. The poisonous fumes were carried up the hillslope to a tall chimney, where, it was hoped, the wind would do the rest. The only trouble was that the industrialists didn't want to know about the good bishop's invention. Where's the profit, they asked, in a chimney of immense length and cost whose only virtue is preserving life? There are plenty of cheap workers.

But the bishop was a cunning man, and his next design did not simply disappear up the hill to dis-

Watson's Flue, Clyne—poking out of the vegetation near the arsenic ovens in the woods west of Swansea; there is still a whiff of garlic in both . . .

sipate the noxious fumes, but steered a zigzag course to give it immense length, and its cool sides condensed the lead, antimony, arsenic and a lot more besides—now, said Bishop Watson to the industrialists, you can scrape out sheer profit from my flue, you were *wasting* all that lovely arsenic and so on, now you can catch it and sell it to hatters, shotmakers and men with inconvenient mothers-in-law. The industrialists gave a concerted cheer and the Watson's flue has been with us ever since. There is one here in the wood at Clyne, sneaking its way up to an old stack on the hilltop, still with the occasional whiff of garlic which tells you arsenic was once distilled in it.

Its companion antimony was also much in demand, and in medieval times the monks of the Cistercian order, whom we have met several times (Talley, Neath, Margam), extracted it along with the bismuth, lead and silver they were getting from their mines like those near Strata Florida or

143

Talley. And in doing so they died in such numbers they asked themselves if this new element had 'got it in' for monks generally—was it Anti-monk or, in Latin, Antimonas?

We have never taken too much notice of poisonous chemicals—we breathe lead and asbestos from cars now, and seem quite unconcerned about nuclear waste or plastics byproducts like polychlorinated biphenyls (PCB's) so it's hardly surprising that earlier generations should have laughed at Bishop Watson's concern for his flock. Were not ladies plastering their faces with arsenical, mercurial and lead preparations to make themselves interestingly pale? (they did—it often killed them, and you can't get paler than that . . .); were not sufferers from epilepsy, nervous disorders and tuberculosis actually helped by arsenic? You couldn't argue with that. Did not the arsenic eaters of Styria have fine complexions and outlive their non-arsenic-eating neighbours? Right again.

But some doctors noticed odd happenings; there were unexplained deaths in houses papered with that nice green wallpaper . . . even Napoleon died of arsenical poisoning—he accused his British captors, but the probable culprit was the wallpaper, as it was thought to have been in the *Cause Celebre* at Cydweli in 1920, when Harold Greenwood was accused of killing his wife with . . . Arsenic—

Sulphurous Stalactites hang from the arch of the Watson Flue in Clyne Woods, Swansea, reminder of how the cunning cleric conned local businessmen into spending a lot of money on his sinuous tunnels, a very early example of practical pollution control—those now campaigning to reduce the ravages of acid rain could take a leaf from Bishop Watson's book, as industry has not changed its fairly short-term attitudes since Clyne was a reeking arsenical hell hole.

Hooray, Hooray, St. Lubbock's Day . . .

Parc le Breos Cwm neolithic tomb seen across the wooded valley from the nearby limekiln.

A visit to Parc le Breos Cwm, a neolithic burial chamber near Swansea, is not just a pilgrimage to an ancient site with a lot of intriguing archaeology to it, (though it is that as well), because the excavator of Parc le Breos Cwm was the son of a copper smelter who made good in true Victorian fashion and became Lord Swansea as well as its M.P., and whose name is attached to the art gallery there—he was born Henry Vivian.

'Under his influence Swansea became the metallurgical centre of the world' eulogised a contemporary; Henry Vivian had got there the hard way; he had travelled extensively, got to know all he could about copper and all other nonferrous metals, then improved on the techniques he had seen. He patented methods for zinc, nickel and cobalt extraction; his knowledge of chemistry enabled him to remove and *sell* the sulphuric acid which had previously run to waste in his chimneys (something to ponder on in the current arguments about acid rain) writing that:—

> '. . . buildings and persons alike seem much improved by it . . .'

He got gold and silver from his copper deposits by a new process, he promoted the Rhondda and Swansea Bay Railway, he was M.P. for the City, the first Chairman of Glamorgan County Council, a typical Victorian man of affairs. And in his spare time (one boggles at where he found any) he liked photography and—archaeology.

145

He would survey and excavate sites on his estates at Singleton and the Gower, one of which was to be Parc le Breos Cwm. His friend and companion on many of these jaunts was another typically versatile Victorian, John Lubbock. Together they not only made progress in archaeology and history, but influenced profoundly the social development of Britain—they doubtless talked about it while drawing, measuring and digging this little tomb of Stone Age Gower farmers of five thousand years ago.

John Lubbock was a man bubbling over with ideas, and the energy to talk and urge and write and exert influence until people—even M.P.s—listened! He was the son of an astronomer, eminent natural historian and banker—the family had known Darwin since his earliest days; John Lubbock went into banking at the bottom, was an able mathematician, Treasurer of the Royal Society, and was a man very concerned about social evils which accompanied the industrial revolution; these, too, he discussed with Henry Vivian in that quiet little valley with its mysterious stone cairn overshadowed by ancient oaks, near a tinkling little stream.

Vivian and Lubbock were excavating the New Stone Age tomb within a few yards of this fine kiln (also owned by Henry Vivian) which would have been working continuously then to produce lime for agriculture, mortar, disinfectant and household paint. Like the tomb, it is now preserved as an ancient monument, which might well have surprised both Henry Vivian and John Lubbock—none of us like to think of ourselves as potential archaeology!

Parc Le Breos—Five thousand years ago this was a
place of burial for Wales's first farming families of the
New Stone Age. Burial was communal and the remains
of 24 people (and some of their pottery) were found
when Lubbock and Vivian dug here in 1869. Detail of
the entrance gallery.

John Lubbock, by now a Liberal M.P., was
worried about the working conditions in mines and
factories, had forced a lot of early legislation on
safety and talked the House of Commons into the
laws concerning Early Closing (which gave the unfortunate shop assistants a bit of time off). He was
convinced that only an educated working class
could save this country as the industrial revolution
continued, and for years he was the Principal of the
Working Mens' College and a Trustee of the
British Museum—this may well stem from his

memories of having to leave school for the high stool
of a bank at 15 when his father's fortunes crashed.
He became Vice-Chancellor of London University
and founded the Society for the Extension of University Teaching, a direct ancestor of the W.E.A.
and of the Open University.

He and Vivian were appalled at the treatment of
our legacy of ancient monuments; they were at the
mercy of local landlords and farmers who could—
and did—plough up and destroy, dig and overturn
unique memories of our long past with little or no
attempt at recording what had been lost. Local
vicars were wont to turn over the odd cromlech (to
which local people had resorted, they knew not
why, for centuries) as AntiChrist; the upper crust
would turn out for an afternoon's entertainment,
picnicking *al fresco* while teams of workmen dug up a

Parc Le Breos—Detail of one of the side chambers in which the burials were made.

handful of Bronze Age barrows—pots would be dug up complete . . . and smashed by the party so every member could have a 'keepsake'. Such wanton vandalism astonished and angered Lubbock, and in 1882 he pushed the Ancient Monuments Bill through Parliament, despite much ridicule. Who was interested in old ruins anyway? What was their value? What did it matter if there *was* a little man hiring out a hammer at Stonehenge so visitors could chip off a bit for themselves (crushed chunks of this monument were taken as medicine . . .)? The largely landowning House of Commons obviously thought the whole idea either laughable, or disgraceful—one said during the debate:—

> . . . a monument on any part of the land of any private owner is as much his property as if it were his park, garden or pleasure ground; you might as well deal in

this way with an old picture which has come down to the owner with the family estate . . .

(enraged, Earl de la Warr, 1882)

This bill had powerful supporters too, including William Morris and the newly formed Society for the Protection of Ancient Buildings, so it went through. It seems a pitiful amount of protection now, a mere 50 monuments protected, with one Inspector appointed—this was General Pitt-Rivers, who could at least talk to landowners as a fellow owner since he had twenty-five thousand acres of Wilts and Dorset as part of his estate. He formed his own museum (still an excellent collection), and Sir John Lubbock became his son-in-law!

So this tomb has historic importance outside its place as a Neolithic communal tomb, which Lubbock and Vivian recorded as containing:—

> Men, women and children at all stages of life had their remains mingled together; twenty four in all, including 3 children between 8 and 11 years old, 2 very old persons (over 70 years), the rest between 25 and 45 years. Charcoal, fragments or shards of pot . . .

It is a typical tomb of a group found across south Wales and Gloucester, known as the Severn-Cotswold type, a pear shaped mound with an entrance, then a gallery with transepts in which the communal burials were placed; originally a family tomb, as each member of the family died they were buried in this 'womb of the earth mother-goddess' ready for rebirth into the next world; only the last person buried was complete and undisturbed, leading excavators to think that once decomposition had taken place, and Auntie Flo no longer looked like Auntie Flo, her skeleton was unceremoniously scattered to accommodate the newly deceased member of the clan. Parc le Breos Cwm is 90' by 55', orientated north/south with a V-shaped forecourt where the funeral dancing and ritual took place five thousand years ago. It is now one of the twelve thousand five hundred sites protected by Lubbock's bill, joined by a quarter of a million listed buildings (William Morris would have been pleased).

And the fact that we can, on a bank holiday, go to these sites and muse about the people who built them is also a tribute to Lubbock. For another of his bills forced through an unwilling and apathetic Parliament was the Bank Holiday Act; the Glamorgan miners used to troop for a legally enforced day in light and air, chanting 'Hooray, Hooray, St Lubbock's Day'—so these two men, Lubbock and Vivian, did a lot for us all in their different ways. This tomb, and the freedom to view it intact, while on holiday, is their legacy—a lot of history concealed in this quiet corner of south Wales.

A Faithful Hound Remembered

Scourfield Memorial, New Moat—Some are finely carved in marble, some bear remains of brightly coloured paint and gilding—but all have their pack of lithe greyhounds . . .

New Moat and Old Moat stand a mile or two from each other in the Preseli Hills of North Pembrokeshire; originally two motte and bailey fortresses were thrown up by the Norman invaders of this area in the 1080s, but the old motte (still just visible in the grounds of the ruined mansion just south of the church) was soon replaced by a larger and more imposing 'new' motte in the field behind where the council houses now stand. This was the tump of earth which gave its name to the village, while up the lane to the west Castell Hen Dre (old castle) became Henry's Moat.

These and other small fortresses supplemented the line of great castles which separated the French-speaking half of Pembrokeshire, in the fertile south of the county, from the Welshmen and women, driven back into the hills by their conquerors in the eleventh century. The 'Landsker' line is so fiercely drawn that you still find a Welshness north of it and an Englishness south of it after eight hundred years and more. New Moat seems tiny enough now, but the size of its church, dedicated to St Nicholas, shows it was not always so insignificant—indeed, it was an important manor of the Bishops of St David's, Bishop Adam de Rupe noted in 1200 A.D. that

> *In villa de Nova Mota quoddam burgagium proximum portae orientali*
> In the township of New Moat a burgage by the East Gate and one burgage by the North Side

The gate mentioned presumably implies a fortified small town, and from the air the lines of garden walls and collapsed houses indicates a far bigger place than nowadays. A manor, 'the Mote' formerly lay in the woods to the south of the present village, and there was a twice-yearly fair by 1291— New Moat was an important place. The historian Richard Fenton rode out here in 1809 and recorded:—

> ... with regret the shell of one of the most ancient houses in the mountain district, now unroofed, where, till within these forty years, the family of Scourfield from the time of Edward the First, had continued to reside in the midst of a large and contiguous property, and a wealthy, respectable tenantry. The house of its sort ranked among the very first surrounded by spacious and majestic woods abounding with Sweet Chestnut of large growth, near a handsome church ...

Fenton didn't like the Scourfields' new mansion at Robeston Wathen, which he thought 'unpleasantly circumscribed'; a later mansion at New Moat is also now a ruin. But its church is undoubtedly a sturdy, fine specimen and absolutely enormous for what is now a fairly small community. Its great battlemented tower (which is accessible, with the Rector's permission and a key) gives views across the whole of south Pembrokeshire; from its lordly height you can still see humps and hollows that are all remaining of the houses and gardens of that

'wealthy and respectable tenantry', and can muse upon the fortune of the local family, the Scourfields, many of whom lie buried beneath you in the church, the yard, or in their own vault.

New Moat Pembs—The church tower, one of the tall types which were used to keep a lookout in early medieval times.

Curled up under his master's coffin? The greyhound's
skeleton in the crypt of New Moat Church.

Set about the interior of the church are monuments to various Scourfields, some bearing the
faintest traces of what must once have been
elaborately coloured paintwork and gilding. And
each one bears the family crest—this is what needs a
close look, since it is dominated by lithe dogs . . .
lean, smooth, speedy whippets or greyhounds.
They seem unusual beasts for coats-of-arms. Lions
passant, yes, the odd griffon or fabulous beast—
but the Scourfields' shield looks far less something
from the Field of the Cloth of Gold, far more like an
advertisement for White City Stadium. And herein
lies a curious tale.

Local legend has it that the riches of the medieval
Scourfields were founded upon the proceeds of a

dog race, and in gratitude for this *largesse* the newly
rich family included the speedy little dog in its crest
and arms. A likely story, I hear you cry . . . but
there they are, all the same. And a visit to the vaults
provides a very odd sequel, which in my work as a
photographer for museums I came upon in my
earliest days here in Pembrokeshire. In the course
of the recording of this church's secrets I was
allowed into the vaults to see and photograph the
magnificent, if gloomy lead coffins containing early
Scourfields. Such was the atmosphere of preservation, the lack of visitors at that time, that the
funeral hangings were still in place on some coffins,
rich velvets on wooden frames, chased metalwork
and brass name plates . . . it was the patterned cloth
which somehow had the scruff of the neck raising its
hackles. The musty air down there was only occas-

ionally distributed slightly by the passage of the present living inhabitants, the rare Greater Horseshoe bats, hanging from the vaulted roof like something out of a Dracula movie.

While photographing the funeral arrangements for vanished Scourfields there appeared suddenly a pathetic little detail which all but took my breath away. At once all those folk tales of the dog race, the new riches, and the undoubted fondness of Scourfield for dog and *vice versa*, came to brief life. The wagging tails, the excited barks, chasing of hares across those fields, the barking joined in by others in those now long-gone gardens—all the joys and amusements that go with owning or rather of being owned *by*, a dog. Elsewhere in this book you will find reference to the dog as being our oldest ally in the animal kingdom, taking us over some time in the middle Stone age, six or seven thousand years ago and more. Later Welsh tales of a dog's faithfulness sprang to mind, some of them less than the truth . . . such as Beddgelert's famous hound, the grave invented by a local inkeeper to increase flagging trade. But this was something quite different.

These lead coffins are supported on blocks to allow circulation of air, and perhaps because the place became flooded from time to time. Labelled with the name of the occupant, they gloom away for ever, their once-important people now as unimportant as we all become sooner or later, be he king or peasant. Under one of the earliest was a pathetic little pile of bones which closer inspection revealed to be those of a whippet, curled up as if asleep by his master's feet. It seems to have entered the vault voluntarily, to die by its master's remains rather than live on out in the air, without him. Here it lies still, the other side of a story of impressive coats-of-arms decorated with fleet, speedy greyhounds . . .

Limekilns

More confusion seems to arise over Pembroke-shire's limekilns than almost any other of our industrial remains—they have been described as pigsties, cells for hermits (would a female version be a hismit? We don't know, or wish to . . .), and the position is further confused by the presence in several places (Newgale, Abereiddi) of round stone structures which look like limekilns but are in fact gunpowder houses (in Welsh Tŷ powdwr) where the quarrymen kept the powder used in blasting. So every time you go to one of our dozens of small inlets, big or small, you are likely to meet a limekiln, either singly or in a cluster (Porthclais, Solva, Dale).

Lime has been important since the earliest times, both as the first chemical fertilizer and as a constit-uent of paint and mortar—our cottages were lime-washed, our castles and churches held together with lime mortar. And all the ingredients occur locally. Limestone from places like Williamston or Penally quarry, coal from any of the anthracite pits of New-gale through Johnston to Saundersfoot and Amroth. A kiln is a funnel-shaped stone hollow with one or two small openings at its base. A pile of

Newgale Limekiln—among the debris and waste from the twenty six collieries which flourished there last century—drawing by Piet Brinton.

Superbly built line of seven limekilns at Mynydd y Garreg, Carms.

furze was put in the bottom, followed by alternate layers of coal and limestone. This was then lighted, and the coal soon took over, burning silently, hotly, turning the calcium carbonate of the limestone into calcium oxide, quicklime. It was a continuous process, and limeburners tended to live on the job, barrowing the lime and coal to the charging platform at the kiln's top, and raking out the highly dangerous quicklime from the openings at the base. 'Quick' here means living, lively—think of the Quick and the Dead, or cutting to the quick; calcium oxide is highly unstable, the moment it gets wet it explodes into life, steaming and smashing itself to powder, becoming slaked lime, calcium hydroxide, in the process. This fierce reaction took place on the flat floor in front of the kiln, another reason for its being near water. Towns like Haverfordwest and Fishguard had their kilns, whose slaked lime was used for building and limewashing; country districts like Porthclais had limekilns for agriculture, especially important during the Napoleonic wars, when this country was blockaded by the French and our burgeoning industrial population needed feeding; so improving productivity of the land needed drastic measures—and this the limekilns did with a vengeance.

Carew Castle by Gastineau, drawn about 1820; there is a limekiln (one of two) puffing away contentedly to the left—materials could be brought up-river to the tide-mill in the background of the landscape . . .

Limeburners lived on the job, many kilns worked continuously. In this woodcut of 1861, a mule train drags sacks of coal and limestone to the four kilns, there's plenty of furze around for firing, and water nearby for slaking the quicklime. Every kiln still has its sloping way to the charging platform, and the remains of the limeburner's hut, upwind of the dangerous gases.

Tenby's magnificent set of 'Gothic' limekilns designed by John Nash, friend of George IV, architect of Regent Street, Bath and the Brighton Pavilion; 'Buck-House' is his too, but men of the Age of Reason weren't ashamed to give of their best for industrial buildings, bridges, railways and canal architecture . . .

But there were problems. One old man we talked to described his early life in the Haverfordwest police—his first job as a young copper was to go down to the limekilns every night and turn away the tramps who had decided to sleep there, gaining thereby a whole new vocabulary of itinerant opprobrium, or tramp-eff-and-blind! None of the men turned away from this lovely warm spot ever understood it was for their own good—because the main effluent of the lime burning operation is deadly carbon monoxide, the gas used by suicides who lock themselves in their garages with the car engine running. It is quick and effective—but in the last death throes the victims' bodies twitched uncontrollably, and on the top of a limekiln that inevitably meant that the dying tramp fell into the red-hot workings, becoming a charred and unrecognisable lump by morning. This, of course, was the other gruesome task the poor police had to cope with if they didn't manage to get all the men off the kiln, or if a couple crept back later.

Industry has a lot of grim tales, but surely this must be one of the grimmest.

Limeburning was one of the lowliest jobs in early industry, and many limeburners and their families lived in abject squalor on a matter of a few pence a week. Some were itinerants, moving to a new site where temporary kilns would be set up while a new railway, canal, or factory was being built. This 1861 woodcut shows such a group and their little hut . . . the loading platform for the kiln is far left.

Their History

The history of limeburning goes back at least till 1325, when there is a record of lime and coal for that purpose arriving at Porthclais for St David's. The kilns burned a load of about a ton in two days taking 1/2 ton of coal to do it and some pot kilns (Solva, Milford) had to be cleared after that time and completely recharged. Some of these were still in use in Haverfordwest and Solva in the 1930s though, like everything else, limeburning had

changed drastically after the arrival of the railway in 1853, and cheap lime could be brought in from elsewhere. Some kilns are fine pieces of architecture, not just stone barrels—a magnificent set above Cydweli at Mynydd y Garreg look like something out of the Valley of the Kings; another set north of Swansea, at Llandybïe, were designed in full gothic by that master architect Richard Kyrke Penson, whose schools and churches make Swansea such a lovely place to explore, and who built the magnificent gothic castle of Bronwydd. Even 'Beau' Nash was not above industrial design, and his unique set of limekilns in the Gothic style still make some visitors think they have strayed into a ruined church or castle rather than something for making fertilizer and paint! . . .

And if you want a count, there are still two hundred and fifty one kilns in Pembrokeshire.

Taking the Slow Road

Modern road travel may be fast, but one sad aspect of it is that we no longer seem to have time to enjoy it as one could in the days of the horse and cart. Then there was time to muse upon the bits of roadside history we were passing—even in earlier motoring days it was still possible to find mileposts and gibbets and suicides' graves and bearbaiting rings and ancient direction finders and threats of transportation for this and that offence; enliven your journey by a glance at a little church, pretty village street or unusual shopfront. Now we bullet our way along concrete, nothing to think about except the radio and the fool on our tail. Many journeys are, in fact, just as quick and far more pleasant on the still existing trunk roads of the past and far, far more interesting; and you are still allowed to stop and admire scenery or stretch your legs. Enjoyment of travel, of course, is a fairly modern phenomenon—our ancestors found it no picnic at all:

Fishguard in 1800—Most goods were transported by water as far as possible, as the roads were so awful that prices doubled for every six miles you went inland! Another reason for the limekilns (left) being near water . . . The line of houses in the old harbour became world famous in our own days as the location for the filming of 'Under Milk Wood'.

. . . travelled by Turn pike, a road; if I may venture to call such a cursed string of hills and holes by the name of road; a causeway is here and there thrown up, but so high, and so very narrow, that it was in peril of our necks that we passed a waggon with a careful and civil driver . . .

1770

Journeys took an age—a lady visiting Pembrokeshire in the 1780s recorded in her diary that it took two days travel to get from Haverfordwest to Milford, a trip which now takes about quarter of an hour! Traders reckoned the cost of their goods doubled with each six miles they had to carry them

Marychurch's Foundry and ironworks was an important industry in Pembrokeshire's county town until well into the present century, supplying agricultural machinery, churns and other dairy and domestic ironware . . . their label is a proud memory of it all . . .

by road inland. So most trade was on water, and industries settled by rivers—canals were built, and ports thrived.

Placed along the dreadful roads were equally dreadful inns—we hear the echoes from our ancestors' dislike of such places as the fortaste of horrendously high prices for indifferent service and food which seems to characterize many motorway 'Service Areas' today! Far from the jolly coaching inn and red faced smiling Mine-Host depicted on Dickensian Christmas cards:

Long rides, miry roads, sharp weather, lousy beds . . .
Wrote a travelling parson with a refreshingly sharp tongue:

. . . cold houses to sit in with very moderate fuel, and three or four children roaring or rocking about you; coarse food and meagre liquor; lumpy beds to lie on, and too short for the feet. Stiff blankets like boards for a covering; rise at five in the morning, Break fast on Tea made with dirty water; mount a horse with boots never cleaned and then ride on, praising God for all Mercies . . .

1780

160

If poor, you walked—if rich, then you had a horse, or even a coach or carriage:

> . . . we keep a set of six horses, and a journey of thirty miles takes two days . . . the body of the coach often rests on the road; then a team of ten oxen is joined to the regular six horses, and we proceed a little farther . . .

There were the 'Flying Stages' and the Mail, grinding along with their complement of inside and outside passengers, driver wrapped impenetrably in woollen blankets, leather and tarpaulin, keeping out the cold with frequent application of spirits:

> . . . persons to whom it is not convenient to pay the full price sit on top of the coach, without any seats or even a rail . . . you constantly see numbers sitting there and in perfect safety—they pay only half of those inside

said a traveller of 1800; and from his tone one guesses he was In rather than Out! But these reflections from eighteenth century diaries give some of the flavour of travel on our Turnpikes, said to be a vast improvement on anything made by man before. It was an adventure and could be dangerous, in a way modern travel rarely is; despite savage punishment for even the most (to us) trivial offences, when you could be publicly hanged (when that meant slow strangulation rather than a quick snap of the neck) for stealing a handkerchief, or goods to the value of one shilling (5p) . . . yet the awful roads were infested by roughnecks, footpads, murderers and highwaymen in such numbers that no citizen went out unarmed and few journeys were complete without at least one forced stop, if not by the road surface then by one of the Gentlemen of the Road.

Even in the 1830s and 40s when young Isambard Brunel was surveying for the lines of rail that would kill coach travel overnight, he could write home to his bride and joke about the awfulness of his travels:

Mounting block at Nevern.

THIS PILLAR IS CALLED
MAIL COACH PILLAR AND ERECTED
AS A CAUTION TO MAIL COACH
DRIVERS TO KEEP FROM INTOXICATION
AND IN MEMORY OF THE GLOUCESTER
& CARMARTHEN MAIL COACH
WHICH WAS DRIVEN BY
EDWARD JENKINS ON THE 19 DAY OF
DECEMBER IN THE YEAR 1835. WHO
WAS INTOXICATED AT THE TIME &
DROVE THE MAIL ON THE WRONG
SIDE OF THE ROAD AND GOING AT
A FULL SPEED OR GALLOP MET A
CART & PERMITTED THE LEADER
TO TURN SHORT ROUND TO THE RIGHT
HAND & WENT DOWN OVER THE
PRECIPICE 121 FEET WHERE AT THE
BOTTOM NEAR THE RIVER IT CAME
AGAINST AN ASH TREE WHEN THE
COACH WAS DASHED INTO
SEVERAL PIECES
COLONEL GWYNN OF GLAN BRIAN
PARK, DANIEL JONES ESQ. OF
PENYBONT & A PERSON OF THE
NAME OF EDWARDS WERE OUTSIDE
& DAVID LLOYD HARRIS ESQ. OF
LLANDOVERY SOLICITOR AND A LAD
OF THE NAME OF KERNICK WERE INSIDE
PASSENGERS BY THE MAIL AT THE
TIME AND JOHN COMPTON GUARD

Bottom:
Memorial to some spectacular drunken driving in 1835—coachmen had a bonechilling, wet, cold job and kept warm with spirits . . . this was the result! The 'Mail Coach Pillar' is on the A40 near Llandovery.

My Dearest Mary,

. . . It is a blowy evening, and the last two miles were wet; I arrived, of course, rather wet, and found the *Hotel*, which is the best of 4 deplorable public houses, full—and here I am at the "Cow and Candle Snuffers" or some such sign—a large room or cave, for it seems open to the wind everywhere, old fashioned, with a large chimney in one corner; but unfortunately it has one of those horrible little stoves, just nine inches across. I have piled a fire upon both hobs but to little use, there are four doors and two windows. What's the use of the doors I can't conceive, for you might crawl under them if they happened to be locked, and they seem too crooked to open . . . The window curtains very wisely not drawn as they would be blown right across the room and probably over the two extra greasy muttons which are on the table, giving just light enough to see the results of their evident attempt to outvie each other, trying which can make the biggest snuff . . . one of them is quite a splendid fellow, a sort of black Colliflower. There is a horrible Harp, upon which really and honestly somebody has been every few minutes for the *last three hours* strumming chords always the same.

These glimpses of our ancestors' travelling adventures makes you wonder why they ever ventured out at all . . . but venture they did, not only the length and breadth of Britain but of Europe too. Many of our older roads bear vestiges of those days which are well worth looking out for, though faceless and grey bureaucracy obliterates more each year in the cause of 'efficiency', and metrication will doubtless provide further excuses for wholesale destruction of anything which still bears the British mile on it rather than the Napoleonic metre. I hope not. They cost little enough to leave where they are, and are now part of the scene, those stones by the

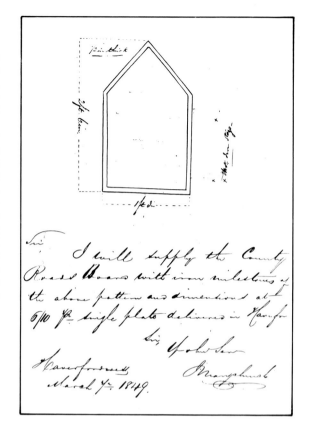

Top:
Design drawing and estimate by the Marychurch Foundry of Haverfordwest for the cast-iron milestones which are still so much a feature of the local scene.

Bottom:
One of the survivors, with its quirky insistence on accuracy to the yard.

drawing; courtesy Record Office

NOTICE.

Necessary Repairs of the ~~Toll-Houses~~ ~~and~~ Gates, on the Milford Turnpike Road, known by the names of Milford, Johnston, and Dredgman Hill, namely:—

MILFORD,—One New Gate and one New Post, both of the best Memel Deal, painted with two coats of paint, and put up complete.

JOHNSTON,—The Gates well repaired and two coats of paint.

DREDGMAN HILL,—The Gates well repaired.

Tenders for the above Work to be delivered, sealed, to Mr. Richard Wilcox, Surveyor, on or before the 22nd day of August instant.

The work to be completed within one month from the time of Contract, or other Workmen to be employed.

Aug. 10th, 1846.

J. Potter, Printer, Haverfordwest.

Carmarthen ironworks also made some fine milestones; a paper survives giving the sizes for the sand-box. 1830.

Courtesy Pembrokeshire Museums

wayside, iron finger posts, reminders of past disasters, memorials or exhortations which give each journey a unique flavour. Long may they live.

It doesn't matter where you go in these islands, you will find milestones and posts. When the Turnpike Acts were born, it was to remove some of the awful roads our travellers have described above —these could be converted farm tracks or old Roman roads, medieval drove roads for cattle (and where, more often than not you met the cattle on their way) or packhorse ways, they could be the amazingly contorted lanes the Saxons seemed to like between their scattered villages in the thick woods, or even abandoned military tracks. Whatever their origin they were terrible. The Highways Act of 1555 and the first Turnpike Act of 1663 tried to do something, but it wasn't until the Turnpike

Acts of 1766 and 1773 that real progress was made, and it is from these times that most of our street furniture and roadside history dates. Pembrokeshire milestones are in fact of cast iron, mostly made by Messrs Marychurch of Haverfordwest in a foundry that nestled between Bridge Street and the river; the original drawings and estimates for the 'stones' survive as do advertisements for strehes of Turnpike to be administered and surfaced from local resources, recouped from passing travellers— privatisation at its most extreme! The Tollgates were universally unpopular, and the Rebecca Riots are only the most violent and most remembered of all the protests against Pay as you Travel.

The first finger posts, dating from the 1694 Act, are now mostly all gone; they had to give direction and distance, and have fallen to the small boy, the

163

vandal, the badly aimed motorcar or the official sprayed-glass-plastic. But our milestones are mostly there still, accurate to the yard, Carmarthen's to the mile, and sturdy with it, and a bit more information as to locality. Parish and boundary stones nestle in the roadside grass where they have not been clipped by 'trashers' and you may also find a local eighteenth century landowner's own stone commemorating his far-sightedness and public spirit in roadmaking for the lower orders. Gibbets were also part of the travelling scene—no point in having capital punishment unless justice was *seen* to be done; so the traveller went on his scary way, looking over his shoulder for the next footpad or command to 'Stand and Deliver' while the mouldering corpse hung in irons by his path, slowly dropping to bits as it vainly tried to remind wrongdoers of their fate if caught—because then, as now, the problem was not punishment, it was catching the no-goods first.

So keep a lookout for gibbet mounds, for suicides' or witches' graves at crossroads, for packmens' rests on steep hills (we forget that even in the days of the horse a lot of goods were put on mens' backs for the arduous inland journey); the better sort had a similar stone block on which to steady themselves as they mounted their horses and remind you that, just as nowadays everybody knows how to drive, then everybody knew how to handle a horse. So in Pembroke Dock you will still find rings to tether your horse while you call or shop, and at Nevern a block to mount it. Some buildings' corners are still protected by bollards so that the fragile stonework was not damaged by a

Loading at Llandysul—In the years leading up to the first World War, the roads were beginning to challenge the supremacy of the railways, and the chug of the Motor was more often heard—but you wouldn't hear a sound from this fine steam lorry huffing with quiet good manners on its rounds from Llandysul station.

More steam haulage as a traction engine takes goods over the New Bridge, Haverfordwest, in 1906; evidence of the use of horses is still present, however . . .

badly manoeuvered cart—pillarboxes and gas-lamps enliven the roadside scene, casting marks on drain covers give a clue to long-gone foundries in the area, or street name to local hero or vanished industry. Well worth keeping slow for, allowing you to recollect in the comfort of your car the arduous but exciting journeys of your ancestors who, though they may have Travelled Hopefully, also meant to Arrive, in the days before Isambard's surveys were complete, the 'Cow and Candle-Snuffers' closed for lack of customers, and the new, fast railway whirled you from one place to another at a terrifying thirty miles an hour, which was well known as the speed at which your head would come clean off . . .

Tay and Solomon Grundy

The Story of "Black Bart", Bartholomew Roberts, the Pembrokeshire Pirate.

'Black' Bartholomew Roberts (1682-1722)—the most successful pirate of all time, born in Pembrokeshire. His fine clothes are scarlet from head to toe, his pistols are in a gold sash, he takes an orchestra to sea with him . . . yet he is teetotal, strict about Sundays and sex, and has thought up a socialised Health Service . . .

Woodcut dated 1720

As we have posters of our favourite pop stars today, so our ancestors had their heroes; in the 1720s there was no doubt who was top of the pops in Pembrokeshire. He was Bartholomew Roberts the pirate, probably the most successful one ever, clearing whole seas just by appearing in them on board his fierce little Welsh collier the *Royal Revenge*, taking four hundred ships in two years with a total value in gold of fifty one MILLION pounds . . . yet today he is almost forgotten. Why? This is his story.

The little village of Castell Newydd Bach (Little Newcastle) is a bleak spot on the southern slopes of the Preseli Hills—here, in 1682, was born Bartholomew Roberts; the writer Daniel Defoe came here researching his life, about half a century later—

'. . . tall, dark-complexioned man . . . of good natural parts and personal bravery . . .'

The 'Black' in his nickname refers to his hair colour, not his soul! Young Barty grew up in troubled times for this country; he was three when the awful events of Monmouth's rebellion shook Britain—the illegitimate son of Charles II and a Pembrokeshire girl, Lucy Walters of Roch, Monmouth claimed the throne from James II, and, was proclaimed king in Somerset, but captured by the King's troops and executed, after which a bloodbath followed as his adherents were butchered—this is the time of Judge Jeffries and the Bloody Assize. A thousand men were sent to slavery. All this would have been discussed in secret by Roberts' parents, as James proclaimed that this staunchly protestant country would henceforth be catholic . . . the revolution of 1688 was the result, William of Orange taking over as king next year, and the Irish troubles which still plague the people of that sad but lovely land are a direct result of all this religious warfare in Barty's youth.

When Barty was ten he went to sea as ship's boy, sailing from Solva in the year of the Glencoe Massacre. We were in turn at war with France, Holland and Spain; Barty would have heard of this background, though he was far from it, working his way up in the merchant service, becoming eventually third mate in a slaver, the *Princess* commuting between Africa and America with its human cargo. In turn William and Mary were succeeded by Anne, then King George, the first of the Hanovers, who could barely speak English. Barty was a brilliant navigator, a brave and fine seaman, yet he would rise no higher in the merchant service—in those days, who you knew, who you could bribe, were far more important than how good you were at your job; and Barty, with his thick Pembrokeshire accent and his working class 'chapel' background of strict nonconformity, would never make first mate, let alone captain—legally, anyway. But events were to change all that. In 1719 their lumbering ship was anchored in a steaming hell hole called Anamaboe when it was attacked and taken by pirates, led by fellow Welshman, Hywel Davies. Davies and Roberts seem to have taken a great liking for each other, and Barty was invited to join Davies' ship as first mate; the offer overcame Barty's scruples about piracy—he noted wryly:—

> What I do not like as a private man I can reconcile to my conscience as a Commander. In an honest service there is thin commons, low wages and hard labour; in *this*, plenty, even satiety, pleasure and ease, liberty and power, and who would not balance creditor on this side when all the hazard that is run for it is at worst only a sour look or two at the choaking! No, a merry life and a short one shall be my motto . . .

So Barty joined the crew of the *King James*; by now he was a tall, strapping dark man of 37, completely fearless, with a sense of humour and a splendid leader as well as master navigator. So when, six weeks later, Hywel Davies was killed in an ambush by the Portuguese, the men elected Barty Roberts to be their next captain.

Here was the success of piracy. The crew *elected* their officers, and if an officer failed to please, was a poor leader, he was not an officer for long. The mens' leader, Valentine Ashplant, who became firm friends with Barty, wrote:

> We pitch upon a man of courage, skilled in navigation; this man by his counsel and bravery seems best able to defend this commonwealth and ward us from the dangers and tempests of an instable element and the fatal consequences of anarchy. Such a man we take Roberts to be . . .

Barty must have surprised the hardened salts who formed Davies' crew as much as he was about to surprise the rest of the maritime world; he immediately made each member of the crew swear to and sign, upon a copy of his Welsh Bible, a set of articles setting out duties and responsibilities—there was to be no gambling, no quarrelling and no women on board; 'lights out' was at eight o'clock; smoking on deck only (sensible in a ship full to the gunwales with gunpowder); Barty himself was teetotal all his life, swigging instead gallons of murderously expensive china tea; he was also strictly Sabbatarian, never taking a ship on a Sunday or allowing his musicians to play . . . because the other surprising thing about Barty was his great love of music, he never went to sea without a wind-band aboard, to play his ship into battle or amuse the captain and crew in-between whiles with 'The Death of Admiral Benbow' and other pop tunes of the day.

Barty's articles set up a fairly comprehensive welfare scheme for the crew in case of injury, or to provide a pension when they decided to retire—some did indeed buy themselves islands and live out their lives as Presidents! Barty himself was obviously a born leader, flamboyant, brave, humorous and deadly all at once; his one vice was flashy clothing—he loved to dress from head to toe in scarlet:

> He made himself a gallant figure at the time of his engagements, being dressed in a rich crimson damask waistcoat and breeches, a red feather in his hat, a gold chain around his neck with a diamond cross hanging to it, and two pair of pistols hanging at the end of a red silk sling, flung over his shoulders . . .

wrote Daniel Defoe having spoken to men who knew him; little wonder the French captains, so often robbed by this laughing man dressed in red, called him 'le joli rouge', and his skull-and-cross bones flag has been known as Jolly Roger ever since.

Barty Roberts now set sail on the greatest voyage of piracy of all time. Ship after ship fell to him, usually without a battle, as he was known to be strict about giving quarter if you surrendered as soon as you heard his band mooing away, saw his black flag with death's head and hourglass break out at the topmast head. His feats of navigation became a legend, commuting as he did between one volcanic island off the coast of Africa to another off the coast of South America, before the days of longitude, three thousand miles of dead reckoning accurate to the mile time after time. His exploits sound like Errol Flynn; the papers of the Public Record Office back them up as true, however! He sailed into the Portuguese Treasure fleet, forty two fully armed merchantmen, and calmly sailed out again taking the richest ship, the *Sagrada Familia*, with him; its gold was worth twenty million pounds at today's prices, and included the entire treasure of the King of Portugal. Barty hated and despised the 'Porty-Geese' as he called them, probably as they had killed his shipmate and friend Hywel Davies. Even so, he was always polite to anybody he met, even though he be Portygeese; any captain whose ship Barty's men were busy rifling, was invited to take tea with the pirate Captain. So were His Majesty's Colonial Governors, some of whom exploded onto paper about it:

> See what the rascal does with the majesty of Government! He writes me letters inviting me to take Tay with him—A Governor of His Majesty sipping Bohea and swopping smalltalk with a pirate?—
> This day the "Experiment", Captain Cornet, master, which I was obliged to send to the bottom since the good Captain refused my offer of Tay, so we put him ashore in a small boat and less dignity.

An American paper, the *Boston Newsletter* describes the arrival of Barty:

> . . . the pirate Roberts went into Trepanny with drums beating, trumpets sounding and other instruments of music, English colours flying, the pirate flag at the topmast head with death's head and cutlass . . .

The Governor of Virginia wrote to the Admiralty:

> . . . with no more than a sloop of ten guns and sixty men, the pirate Roberts ventured into Trepanny in Newfoundland where there were twenty five merchant ships upwards of twelve hundred men and forty pieces of cannon, and yet for want of courage in the heedless multitude plundered and burned divers ships.

Governor, St Christopher to Admiralty, London:

> Only resolute action by Men of War can stop the depredations of this pirate Roberts. This day, under fire from our shore battery, he burned thirty or forty ships in the Roads, plundered several merchantmen and set fire to the town. The impudent rascal even stepped ashore to steal sheep for his larder before he took his leave. The port is now a smouldering ruin . . .

These extracts, from hundreds of documents, tell what sort of man the hapless captains and governors were dealing with. Barty at this time was captain of a sleek little collier, armed with 32 cannon and 27 swivel guns, a crew of 157—her slim hull made her faster and more manoeuverable than most other ships of the day, and Barty added to this by 'boottopping' her, which was to coat her below the waterline with a mix of tallow, redlead and sulphur.

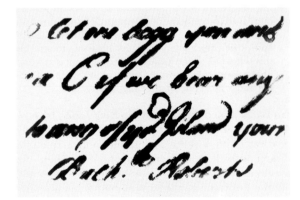

Bartholomew Roberts's signature on a threatening letter sent to a Governor who had captured one of his men—he wrote a lot, in a fine hand and with great good humour, and much can still be read in the Public Record Office.

Haslemere Museum per PRO

Here Lieth ye Body of Jane Skyrme wife of William Skyrme bfawhaden, Efq^r who died October ye 18th 1710 Aged 56.
Alfo Lyes ye Body of Thomas Skyrme of Vaynor Efq^r Third Son of ye above William Skyrme and Jane his Wife who died Sept. ye 29th 1731 Aged 40.
Here Lyes ye Body of Will Skyrme of Vaynor Efq^r only Son of ye above Thos. Skyrme and Theodosia his Wife he Married Jane only Daughter of John Hughes of Laugharn Efq^r by Johanna his Wife Daughter of Sr Edward Mansel Bar^t of Trimsaran by whom he had four Sons and one Daughter he departed this Life ye 2^d day of Feb^{ry} 1762 Aged 46. Also ANN BROWNE Daughter of the above W^M SKYRME Esqr and Relict of the late JOHN BROWNE Esqr many Years President of the island of Nevis West Indies who died Oct 26th 1816 Aged 76 Years.

The Skyrme memorial in St Mary's, Haverfordwest; Captain Skyrme is not here—he died in battle alongside his friend and fellow master Bartholomew Roberts in their final engagement against the Royal Navy in 1722. But his great niece lies here, widowed a long time after her marriage to a pirate, John Browne, who used his winnings to buy the island of Nevis and make himself President of it! . . .

The tallow made her slip through the water well, the red lead and sulphur prevented marine growth and attack by the terror of the seas, *Teredo* the shipworm. It also made his ship look extremely smart. He would sail up towards his victims, flying a 'bewildering variety of flags' as he put it to "confuse our adversary as to our intent"; then out would come the black Joli Rouge, the band would strike up, and all but four of his four hundred victims gave in straight away—with the ones that fought, Barty was murderous.

But his time was up. He swopped the little collier for a vast three decker, the *Victoire* of 100 guns, gilded in every cranny, a true flagship for a pirate king. But she wasn't as manoeuvrable as his first command. By now he had two other ships along too, the *Great* and *Little Ranger*, just to carry the loot; one commanded by another Pembrokeshire man, Captain Skyrme from Milford. At last the Admiralty was having to respond to all the fuss made by the various colonial governors, irate shipowners, and foreign governments; trade was being seriously damaged as the seas emptied every time it was rumoured that Roberts was in the area; garrisons fled into the woods when they heard a trumpet or sackbutt, or Barty's freed negro slave banging on his drum, dressed in full war paint, a leopard skin over one shoulder (is the modern military drummer his descendant? Interesting thought . . .) The British government sent out two men o'war commanded by Captain Challoner Ogle.

Barty by this time was getting a vast army (or navy) of men under his command. They considered him 'pistol proof'—the pirates' VC—there was a belief in his total invulnerability; now, by 1721, he had taken nearly four hundred ships, beaten garrisons of fully trained troops, armadas of foreign shipping . . . he was beginning to get to believe it himself. But he could not manage his crew as he had done; there was more drunkeness on board, though he still kept his men free from the scourge of syphilis by strict laws about sex

Any man who brings a woman on board disguised shall suffer death

Ogle must have envied Barty his hold over his men's sex lives, as his ships were crippled for months while the ship's surgeon struggled to cope with wave after wave of venereal disease; Surgeon Commander Atkins has left a diary from which much of Barty's later exploits are taken. Barty had heard of Ogle's coming to Africa, of course, but seems not to have taken it too seriously. He had, after all, already declined a bribe from the King himself, with an Act of Grace—freedom from prosecution in return for giving up piracy:

> To my Sovereign Lord King George the First.
>
> Wee shall accept no Act of Grace, that the King and Parliament be Damned with their Acts of Grace for *Us*. Neither will wee go to Hope Point to be hanged up a'sun-drying as Kidd's and Braddish's company

were. But if we be overpowered, we shall sett fire to the powder with a pistol and all go merrily to hell together
> Bathl Roberts

One wonders if the king ever got it, and what he made of it.

When Ogle and Barty did meet, Barty was surprised at breakfast (his favourite Salmagundi, plus the inevitable Tay) and didn't bother to see who the intruder was; Ogle tricked *Great Ranger* away with a pretence of turning tail, and captured Skyrme's command after a bloody battle in which

Haverfordwest as Barty knew it, ships bringing goods from all over the world, quays bustling, warehouses bulging with exotic spices and silks, sailors telling wide-eyed boys of adventure. Barty's adventures were to be the most amazing of them all . . .

Boot topping a careened pirate ship—Barty used this slippery mixture of sulphur and red lead to protect his ships and give them an extra few knots of speed . . . woodcut 1720.

Skyrme lost a leg but kept fighting, the bleeding stump propped on a redhot cannon to staunch the blood. Then back to engage Barty, who was mortally wounded by sniper fire and, his body thrown overboard as he had always asked to be. The biggest trial in pirate history followed; a hundred and sixty nine men were charged, forty five of them freed negroes. Fifty six were acquitted, the rest were hanged or imprisoned. Ogle sailed for home and the biggest mystery of all; what ever happened to Barty's gold? The government never seems to have asked Captain Ogle for it, and after his inevitable knighthood he bought a largish chunk of the Midlands and lived like a king for the rest of a fairly long life. I wonder what *did* happen to the gold?

Barty has left us a legacy—of chivalry, daredevil humour, of death defied with a grin in the best Fairbanks or Flynn manner. The Jolly Roger. His navigation set standards which made for the supremacy of later navies and merchant fleets and adventurers.

His record for sheer cheek, and the piles of gold, have never been equalled. The Pembrokeshire lad from Little Newcastle made a dent in the maritime history of the world which nobody else will ever equal. His toast, always drunk in tea on deck with his men before an engagement, is his best epitaph:

Let's drink a Damn to the Halter, lads, and them that lives to wear it.

Misericord, lunch break during the building of a
medieval boat. St Davids Cathedral.

A Pirate's Present . . .
In 1768, Capt. John Worsley caught
this lovely view of his ship and an island
in the South Seas, where it was tempo-
rarily moored, by sticking tiny pieces of
his own hair to a piece of ivory, then
mounting it in stolen gold. An incredibly delicate task, it must have
needed a good eye and lots of patience;
not a spare-time occupation you'd
associate with a buccaneer!

Piratical Haunts . . .

Top Left: Newport, a famous seaport for centuries; in 1566 Queen Elizabeth sent a government Commission here, among other places, to investigate accounts of rampant piracy.

Top Right: This medieval pele tower is at Angle, its top just the right height so that a man keeping a lookout to sea over a rise in the land, won't *himself* be seen . . . by pirates.

Lower Right: Solva, fine hiding place for pirate or smuggler (Tobacco Cave is just round the corner). . .

Carew Castle, home in turn to the most beautiful princess in medieval Wales, the man whose power and friendship put Henry Tudor on the British throne, and "Good" Sir John Perrott, Queen Elizabeth's bastard half-brother (Henry VIII was their father). Sir John was chief of the Commissioners to Suppress Piracy . . . gossips pointed out he was also chief among local pirates,—that way you couldn't lose.

Centre Left:
Pimples on a farmscape show the site of ''bellpits''
where Tudor miners slaved to get out the finest
anthracite in the world.

Bottom Right:
Another sole survivor, a forlorn stack, marks one of
twenty six collieries which bustled and smoked along
the coast at Newgale, Pembrokeshire, loading their
''black gold'' into sturdy little ships which took the
anthracite as far afield as Hong Kong, for the tin-
trade; the miners at the coalface would hear the waves
crashing above their heads as they worked.

Top Left:
The Gwili railway is one of the latest bits of line to be
saved from oblivion by hard-working enthusiasts
(Bronwydd Arms). Industrial archaeology is one of the
fastest growing branches of our new found fascination
with history.

Top Right:
''Margaret'', sole survivor from the tiny North
Pembrokeshire and Fishguard Railway, is now the
centrepiece of the Railway area at Scolton Manor
Museum, Haverfordwest.

The miners took their midday meal to the pit either in a spotless linen "Tommy Bag" (there was great competition among the wives to see whose was whitest), or in these tinplate boxes, each area having its own special shaped box to match the local loaf. This box is from Hook; the tinplate came from Kidwelly Tinplate Works (Carms), one of the oldest in Wales.

Bottom: If coal mining was dangerous, then slate quarrying was even more so, no job more hazardous than that of the blaster. This drum-shaped building at Aber Eiddi is often taken for a limekiln or even a shepherd's hut; but it's a powder house to store the explosive, its turf roof designed to come off easily should the building's contents detonate, the blast wall to try and protect passers-by!

A Word from your Writer

If you have enjoyed these outings, or the programmes which gave rise to them, the chances are that you like whatever-it-is that history does for you. But what is it? For a start, of course, it should never be dryly academic! We've been accused of many things, but never that. History gives a perspective, you see people just like you in a different set of circumstances separated by hundreds, or sometimes thousands, of years. That can be a comfort, or it can be scary. But every one of the places we visited has written into it, somehow, the result of an individual's life here, under pressures of disease or war, political or religious forces, but who managed to express his or her personality in something tangible . . . it is by their work you know them.

The man who carved this misericord was probably often hungry; if he stepped out of line with the church he might suffer mental if not extreme physical discomfort. If he displeased his master he might very easily be killed. What we take for granted as our 'freedom' was not his. But he has left us, anonymously, a marvellous portrait of his age, two people he knew, making a boat; near it is another carving, from the same hand, of a group of travellers being mightily seasick in the same boat, a bit later, and we laugh with the carver at their misfortune. It is that nameless man's sense of humour, his laughter we hear down the centuries, his ability to be an individual despite the pressure all around him. And it is the story of individuals we have tried to tell in this book. They built churches, cromlechs, railways or canals, they mined for riches in the bowels of the earth, they fought each other, or the elements, they struggled through mountains for slate or gold or iron or coal, to make tunnels.

Each of the places we visited in this book is a monument to some person or people like you or me, who had an idea, and decided it was worth fighting for, and come hell or high water did something about it, even though it might fail. We can admire their courage for trying, if nothing else.

In this new Dark Age we can, most of us, rely on material comfort; indeed, half our trouble may be that we demand it at any price—the 'wage round' is taken for granted, the 'Standard of Living' is replacing the 'Quality of Life'. Jobs, when there are any, are done in bleakly boring surroundings—but there may *be* no jobs . . . a dismal prospect for Man, because he is a Hunter. Our most primeval instinct is to provide for our family and ourselves . . . and if the State gives us reasonable comfort from cradle to grave, but provides nothing upon which the hunter part of us can feed his ego, is it any wonder we riot? That we act crazily or join any little quasi-political group if it gives us identity, makes us a pack once again, enables us to say, 'I AM'.

One thing coming up again and again is that until now a man *was his* job; he was a carpenter, fisherman, shepherd or soldier . . . a smith, maybe, so valuable to the community that he could answer back a king and keep his head, or have his grave marked with his vital calling. His surname was his trade, often enough; so the many proud Smiths, which since the Iron age was such a central trade. So too the Glovers, Mercers, Carpenters, Ropers, Drapers, Cutlers, their jobs so much a part of them they and their families were known by them. And now? We see the identity of cities squashed as is our own. Our lives are dominated by faceless towers. We are born in one, schooled in another, live in yet another and work in another still. Our very education is designed to stop us thinking too much, to make us conform whether at shopfloor level, on the administrative or business ladder, in the services or the bureaucracy. We live in a monolithic society. We are under pressure to drive the same cars, wear the same jeans, and read the same papers to ensure we think the same thoughts. Yet inside each of us is the spark which made that anonymous wood carver at St David's joke about his friends, and keep *us* smiling, several centuries later.

Depressing stuff, you may think, for the end of a book; but it was not necessarily meant to be—we are on the brink of another revolution, this time as profound as that which the Neolithic farmers introduced in 3400 BC or so; as with the coming of the canals and railways and factories of a century and a half ago, now—the 'chip'. This book was started on

173

an ordinary electric typewriter, it was finished on a Word Processor, the central part of which is a chip to which you can 'speak' in English or French, Italian, German or other European languages, and it understands them all. This allows you to make perfect copies of your thoughts, quickly and accurately, change your mind if need be, and do all sorts of fancy tricks with all sorts of lettering . . . but the thoughts have to be human; there is no substitute for your soul, the bit of you that is 'You'.

Maybe this omnipresent little grain of silicon which is so altering our lives, will give us freedom to think again, as those Neolithic astronomer priests were enabled to think once there was a food surplus in three thousand or so BC. With or without a 'job', it is in what we do and in what we *are* outside our everyday dullnesses which makes us real people, which helps keep us sane, off the bottle or the tablet or the syringe. With something going on in your mind, you can once again say 'I am', and that is most important; you may be planning fishing expeditions, a walk, ships-in-bottles, reading or music, carving owls from balsa wood . . . it has to be *Something*.

And maybe history will *be* that something. It gets you out. Your feet get wet and your mind stretched. You read. Remember. Note. Get interested in following a clue; and suddenly—you're a hunter again! You've broadened yourself in mind and stature as a human being and can once again say 'I *Am* . . . I *matter* . . .'

We are not here long. We own nothing; we are temporary custodians of our surroundings for seventy years or so, then we are part of it again, and somebody else takes over. Our ancestors knew this in their bones, now the Welfare State pushes it out of sight with attempts to convince us that Someone, in some Ministry miles away, Knows Best. They, those mysterious nameless faceless ones, know best about motorways and planning high-rise, we need not worry, indeed shall receive no thanks if we do poke our nose inconveniently in. They do not like it at all if we suddenly make mouselike protests about our patch, that we liked it better the way it was. Is sterile orange juice to a sterile world the answer? Shall the Shopping Precinct always replace the shop on the corner? Is Big Always Beautiful? Is the

motorway better than the lane? Farms expand, hedges diminish, leaving less room for the flowers and insects and mice; the sense of scale vanishes. We travel from Here (wherever that is) to There in aircraft it is impossible to see out of . . . and when you reach that airport, it is virtually identical to the one we just left. Same shops and goods and hotels. We might as well have stayed at home.

History provides an outlet from this nightmare. Britain, and especially Wales, is so rich in remains of our past, even though more hedges and fields vanish for the convenience of the machine, each walk may reveal yet more old ways carved into nice straight superhighways, and like the Jumbo, you get from one place to another identical place in less time. Now is the time to stop. There is still plenty to see, plenty to love and cherish in this land of ours; you can still chase up an old canal, castle or church or come upon the ghost of a port. Stop and muse about highwaymen (and women) by an old milestone, there are buttermarkets and bear-baiting rings and odd corners which still proclaim the 'I Am . . .' -ness of people as mortal as we, frightened, loving, cross, laughing, as perplexed to find themselves where they were as we are to find ourselves here. The world may seem a mad place now; imagine what it must have been like in the Black Death . . . at the time when we executed the first King Charles . . . at the arrival of some Viking pirates or the Normans or the time when bronze was replaced by iron. We may groan at the speed of change and of modern life generally, then smile in recognition of a protester about railways in 1830, assuring his audience that their heads would most certainly come off at any speed in excess of thirty miles an hour. Bronze age man would have shrugged and said no good would ever come of travelling on horseback. Flint knappers no doubt shook their heads at that newfangled alloy of tin and copper; it would never catch on. We are the same now about pylons or Concorde or atomic power. My grandfather would never have a 'wireless' in the house, and worried about its effect on the weather.

Yet history shows that some of our ancestors' reactions proved to be right, potty though some of them appeared to be at the time. Luddites smashed

Pentre Ifan, Wales's most famous ancient monument; a fine New Stone-age burial chamber in the shadow of magnificently brooding Carn Ingli, a vast sprawling Iron age hill fortress with stone banks measured in miles rather than yards, where our local saint, Brynach, talked to angels and got the hill its Welsh name. If anywhere sums up my love for a place, this is it . . .

machinery when they saw their jobs going in the sacred cause of 'productivity' (though it wasn't called that then); jobs are going again, and at an increasing rate as robots take over . . . who was right? Towns with housing of a 'human' scale were erased from the map in a way that the might of Hitler never managed, tower blocks took their place, we boggled at the Centre Points and the Post Office Towers, miracles of technology . . . now the Jeremiahs appear to have had something. The towers were not much fun to live in, the lifts didn't always work, the insulation was poor and the underfloor heating was cripplingly costly to run. Now some of these awful places are being—

expensively—demolished after ten years' use. And they took no more people-per-acre than the comfortable, homely back-to-backs they replaced.

We'd see, if we were to look, the same factors which have tottered other civilisations before our own. The Roman bureaucracy, high taxation, inflation, deserted city centres as the richer folk

Thirsty Work in Church . . .—Tongue hanging out for more *cwrw*, this medieval priest sadly turns his tankard upside down to show its emptiness—a lovely bit of quiet humour from medieval times, in St Mary's church, Haverfordwest—nearby is a monkey playing a harp, lots of dragons, and a man who simply couldn't STOP getting married . . .

moved to the suburbs (the Romans *invented* suburbs) . . . their world got too big to administer. Their world had barbarians inside and out, waiting in the wings to destroy it. And yet we still get bigger, whether it be the E.E.C., or to talk of billions of pounds or of megadeaths or to watch, apparently with no power to act, as multinationals get more power than governments . . . yet all this has happened before, albeit on a smaller scale. Can we do better this time round?

So while I hope you have enjoyed this book as sheer entertainment, as outings for the family, to stimulate walks with the dog or as a pocketable answer to the childrens' 'Why? . . .', let's hope it does something extra. We hope it lets you dream, raise an eyebrow or two at our more amazing assertions; I hope too that the message comes through that man succeeded best when he didn't over-reach himself, accepting a challenge while acknowledging his limitations.

And for the younger members of the party—you are, all of you, born archaeologists. We hope this book gets you out and about hunting some Open Secrets of your own.

A Walk Along a Hedgerow

Hedges are all we have left of long vanished forests, those wild and frightening places our Neolithic ancestors started clearing in about 3400 BC., and which we have been steadily encroaching upon ever since—but never with such ruthless efficiency as we are now doing. Bigger machines seem to mean smaller patches of hedge, field systems vanish, and there are good reasons for thinking that irreversible damage is being done to our landscape, just as the Bronze age farmers made much of upland Britain into acid peaty moorland by their "cut-and-burn" methods of forest clearance.

A hedge, then, is a refuge of all the plants and animals which once lived in a forest; more than that, it provides shelter, a windbreak, prevents soil erosion and is a living piece of history. What more could one want? If you picture some of our West Wales hedges as they were built, imagine a team of men and women laboriously clearing an area of stones, pushing them by hand to the side of their "patch", straightening up the line, then piling on some turves and sighing with relief that it was all over . . . but it *wasn't* all over. As the years went by, first grasses, then shrubs, then small trees seeded themselves at about the rate of one species a century. So if you walk along a hedge and count the number of tree species—oak, ash, hazel, blackthorn, alder, yew and so on—seven species mean that hedge was probably started about the time Edward I (when not hanging people who lit up a coal fire) was building Harlech Castle, or Beaumaris, or signing away Wales as a nation with the Statute of Rhuddlan. Ten species of tree (and there are several lengths of hedge with more than this) and we are back before the Conquest—you can look at that hedge and think of the men and women who planted it, looking fearfully over their shoulders, out to sea, lest the terrifying sight of a long fierce ship with beaked prow, red-and-white striped sail, and the sound of pirates yelling in Norse . . . Vikings! It has lasted all this time—what a pity to destroy it now.

However, that hedge has got more to offer than mere antiquity. In it lie ragged robin, pennywort boldly holds its polished round leaves to the sun, there's St. John's Wort and Dandelion, a wisp of Broom on its top, maybe, thick greeny blue stems of Burdock in among the grasses and the blackberry thorns. Our ancestors had a use for every plant in the hedge. You cut the Broom to sweep the house (that's how the household article got its name) and made a diuretic wine cordial from its flowers. The herbalist Gerarde says:—

". . . That woorthie Prince of Famous Memorie Henry Eight King of England was wont to drinke the distilled water of Broome flowerys against surfets . . ."

Well, if anyone knew anything about surfeits, including wives, it must have been Bluff King Hal. Another Henry, loved Pembrokeshire's Broom so much he wore sprigs of it in his hat, and as it was called in latin the Planta Genista, so we got the dynasty of kings called the Plantagenets.

Burdock, of course, still occurs with Dandelion in a cordial, though one suspects it isn't quite so natural from Corona as it was from the old wives. I wonder if the cordial manufacturers realise that their product, according to Gerarde, ". . . ys a pleasaunt herbe, doth increase seed and stir up Lust . . ." Lusty Elizabethans used to chop it up in salads or munch it like celery after dipping it in salt. The other half, Dandelion or "Dent de Lion" (Lions Teeth) is another apothecary's herb; *Taraxacum officinale* was made into a cleansing beer which workers in iron foundries used to drink, as it did the world of good to their insides, and it is good to have the leaves in salads still. Celandine is very common all over this part of Wales, though it is not native and was probably introduced by the Saxons as a herb "To take away the mistiness of the eyes . . ."; you mixed it with fennel, wormwood and honey. One of its folk names is Kennings, which means "sore eyes" in Saxon. The bright yellow flowers were squeezed for their juice to cure warts, which would be charmed away when the swallows came— the flower opens in the light and closes when the power of sun wanes, another example of the Doctrine of Signatures.

It's hardly surprising that Bluebells have more Welsh names than any other local plant; their ancestors came with ours, the first Welsh in Wales brought Bluebells with them, and *Scylla nonscripta* has been with us ever since. Botasen y gog (Cuckoo's Boots), Croeso haf (Welcome summer) and Glas y llwyn (Blue of the woods) are just three of its names. But its use? The only clue comes from a paper of medieval date which tells of the plant's use in glue. As we know that Iron age man stuck poisoned tips on the shafts of his arrows, are the bluebells which grow so abundantly on Skomer and within some of the hillforts, as warlike in origin as they are? . . .

Blood of the Raven—Medieval floor tile with the arms of Sir Rhys ap Thomas, the man whose lifelong friendship and powerful private armies put young Henry Tudor on the British throne; Rhys's power won Bosworth in 1485, his friendship with the Welsh king brought Britain from medieval feudalism into modern times . . . he is buried in Carmarthen, these tiles were made for his castle at Carew, but are now in Carew Cheriton Church.

Place Names

Looking at the name of your village, farm, town, or the field where your house was built, at the lane or clifftop or little hill . . . any landmark, in other words, which your ancestors might have wanted to pinpoint by giving it a name . . . in this way you can follow more clues to our history, and an amazing tangle it is too! For one thing, as has already been seen, we have been speaking a torrent of different tongues over the last couple of thousand years or so, and each of these must have meant that a knoll on a skyline, a river bend or burial, woodland or cliff may have had several different names in its time. The odd thing is how conservative we are about these names; a harking back, perhaps, to the thought that names in themselves were magic, that Naming Names conferred a special meaning, almost a soul on a place, as baptism does on a person.

So we have, as might be expected, Welsh place-names; in the Celtic north half of Pembrokeshire, in Cardigan and Carmarthen—at any rate, inland —we have Welsh pure and simple. Often the coming of the Christian church meant that the local chieftain handed out a parcel of land, called a 'Llan', to his own priest. The priest was usually related by blood or marriage *to* this powerful chief, and in time gave his name to the religious site— where, like as not, the chief would end up buried, on the north side of the chancel (the Right Hand of God). Thus the 'Llan' place-names, Llanboidy, Llanfyrnach, Llanwnda or Llandeilo, are called after celtic holy men some of whom—like Brynach or Teilo—are found in several dedications, indicating the power of their patron as much as their own holiness . . . some, like Gwyndaf or Wrw, get only a single mention from history.

A description was often enough to pinpoint the place; 'the bare hill where the three burials are . . .'; you can still see the trio of tumps wherein reputedly lie some Bronze-age kings—the Welsh name is Foel Drygarn, a literal translation of the description. The Black Mountain became Mynydd Du, the Red Wall became Fagwyr Goch, the little pool at the bottom of the hill was Pwll Gwaelod, the Moor where the Stones are becomes Rhos y

Clegyrn, and so on. Personal names, of famous or infamous people, remain as firmly attached today as they were when that man or woman was alive; thus Clegyr Boia recalls an Irish pirate who befriended St David, just as Porthlisky remembers Lliski, who murdered Boia. Trefasser remembers the man who was born here, on the bleaker side of Strumble Head, and who became friend and counsellor of King Alfred—Bishop Asser helped the king found places of learning, including Oxford. Great names and small, then; you are as likely to find the name of a long forgotten farmer as you are to reveal the place named after a king. In general, though, Welsh place-names describe, accurately and often poetically, what the place looks like—or once looked like.

Over the centuries, the land was owned by men and women who came from different lands and who spoke different languages; Saxons, Flemings, Norman French, the Church's official language was Latin, some of which got into Welsh (ffenestr for window, Eglwys for church, for example; we talk of fenestration as we speak about ecclesiastical matters, both words from the same root). But there is no doubt about which language apart from Welsh principally influences West Wales's place-names—it is Norse . . . the fierce Scandinavian pirates who harried this coastline, and paddled their shallow draughted longships up our rivers as far as they could, have left a thick covering of -dales and -tuns and-holms, and no-one who wants to chase up this kind of history can ignore the men who named Haverford, Fishguard, Freystrop and Dingstopple, Stackpole and Hubberston. Their genes are here in fair hair and blue eyes—their names live on too, even their pronunciation is still about in places.

Following the course of a place name is not always easy—admittedly, the prominent landscape feature may be obvious, but who named it, and whose language are we to take as the final one? Keeston has a fine rath, or hill-slope fortress; rath is Irish, but Keeston may come from the Middle/Low German/Saxon Kuse = club, or it may come from the Middle Dutch Cuse = (mod. Dutch Kuis) 'lump', as the hill *is* somewhat lumpy. Related to this is the Norse, from those pirates; Kus there is 'Hump' or 'Hunch' but the Swedish Kuse means

'bun' or 'loaf', or at any rate that shape. So Kees-tun probably means a settlement on a bun-shaped or lumpy hill. There are lots of other examples, and it is often hard to decide which one is most likely for your quest. Hook, now, is a common enough name; there is South Hook near Milford, there is Hook, the colliery area south of Haverfordwest, and there is West Hook near Spittal in the middle of the county. Now Hook can be Norse, or Saxon, and mean 'corner, bend'; but it can be Welsh and mean 'Sow' (Hwch). To complicate matters further, it can be a Norse personal name—Hucca. It is these multiple derivations which give place names such headaches. You have to follow up each name to its source, if you can, link it to the topography, land use, even the geology, and then ask yourself, 'which was most likely?'

The best place to make a start is by writing up the local field names and lanes and houses, giving them a possible derivation; which language seems to be dominant? Welsh in the north . . . French or Saxon in the south . . . Scandinavian all around the edge, near water. The church may have old maps, and in any case the vicar, rector or schoolmaster are all people to talk to; they will probably all recommend a list of the oldest people in the parish; always the ones to know about the area . . . before the era of universal and continuous entertainment, stories were told around the fire of a night; you went with your father or grandfather and were shown the boundaries, the fields, the old stones and landmarks, each of which had a name . . . and it is those we are after, just catching some of them at the very instant they are vanishing for ever. After you have seen the local experts, the next place to go is the library, where general reference books, or publications by the various societies whose members are mad keen on this aspect of local history; some counties have County Histories, and some already have 'place-name . . .' research in book form. The next port of call is the museum and the record office. Once you know your 'patch' a little, you'll have spotted clues such as a great number of young people all buried at much the same time, or one family represented much more than the others in the local grave yard. Why? Were there just more *of* them, or was there an epidemic—typhoid, say, or diptheria, or TB? The church registers are a gold-mine of local information, and old names for renamed farms, fields and houses turn up here. Solicitors sometimes clean out their over-stuffed offices of old family papers, and these, too, often end up at the record office; so do parliamentary plans for railways and canals, when local names, fields, boundaries and such like, turn up in their early 19th century context. And for earlier work, there are Pipe Rolls, Hearth Tax documents and Tithe Maps, all of which give you invaluable information and a variety of spellings, linguistic clues and so on. Remember this interest has been others' too, and a lot of published work will be useful to your enquiries; in connection with West Wales you may wish to consult *Archaeologia Cambrensis* (it's abbreviated as a rule to *Arch Camb*), the Bulletin of the Board of Celtic Studies, or such specialist papers as 'Scandinavian Settlement, the place-name evidence' (Ed. by Clemoes and Hughes, Place Name Society 1971); your museum, library and record office will know what is helpful, and will probably be able to lay their hands on most of them for you. Look at old newspapers; and sales of farms and land. Eventually you will end up with masses of information collated and with conclusions drawn. The last, and very important stage, is writing it up for possible publication; otherwise someone else will, one day, have to go through all the same hullabaloo you have. Your local area may have a natural history or archaeology society whose bulletin will take your work, or one of the bigger publications may jump at it. But every bit of research should lead to publication somewhere, in the end. It is, after all, by reading a lot of other peoples' work that *you* got to where *you* are!

Short reading list

Significance of British Place-names, Israel Gollancz Memorial Lecture, British Association.
Signposts to the past, Margaret Gelling, 1978. Dent.
Place name evidence for Anglosaxon & Scandinavian settlements, Cameron and Gelling English Place Name Society, 1975.
Concise Oxford Dictionary of English Place-names (including Welsh), 1960.
And someone whom you may be surprised to see in this context:
English and Welsh; Angles and Britons, J. R. R. Tolkein, Cardiff, 1963.

Welsh Place Names

There seems to be a special blockage when it comes to Saxon or Norman tongues getting around Welsh sounds; yet it is really not too hard to make a brave stab at the right sort of pronunciation—and it is a lot easier once you know what the sounds *mean*. Welsh is pronounced as it is written—there are no silent 'W's or 'P's; words like wrought or Pneumonia, mnemonic or knight or throughout. 'Oh, no,' we hear the cry, 'but what about all those double-L's and double D's and no vowels for ages and . . .' Calm down! Follow a few rules, and not only will you learn some Welsh painlessly, but get a new view of the places you visit. Remember, all Europe was Wales once, so we all have a little Celtic blood in our veins!

GUIDE TO THE RIGHT SOUNDS

letters *b d h l m n p t* = same sound as in English; C is *always* hard (as in cat)

ch is a throat clearing sound like you find in the Scottish *loch* or German *Bach*

dd is a softer D, made by tongue against teeth and breathing out, as in '*those*'

f one at a time, pronounce as 'V'; two at a time, pronounce as 'F' (i.e., fawr (large) is pronounced vowr, Ffynnon (well, spring), as funnon)

g is always hard as in game, not as in geography

r's should roll on the tongue; rh (as in Rhys) should start with an 'h' breath

s should be hard and hissing as in snake, never hard and like a 'z'

ll; the most worrying Welsh sound; try putting your tongue ready to say 'l', then breathe out hard through your mouth, keeping the tongue there. It should then make a sound a bit like 'thl'; Llandeilo

We have 2 more vowels in Welsh than English; *A : E : I : O : U : W : Y* Put the stress on the last but one syllable; Pwll*croch*an, Lland*ei*lo, Eglwys*w*rw. And once you can pronounce Eglwyswrw with confidence, you are an honorary Celt!

A SHORT PLACE NAME DICTIONARY

Aber	mouth of, estuary (of river)—Abergwaun (mouth of the Gwaun)
Allt	slope, woodland (Allt y Cnap = woodland by the tump)
Awel	breeze (Bryn Awel = Breezy Hill)
Bach (fach)	small (Castellnewydd Bach = Little Newcastle)
Bedd	grave (Bedd yr Afanc = the Monster's Grave)
Brân	crow (Llys-y-frân = Crow's court)
Brenin	king (Stacen y Brenin = the king's rocks)
Preseb	manger Carn Breseb (Presely Hills)
Bwch	he-goat (cf. 'buck')
Bwlch	pass, gap in hills (Tan-y-bwlch = below the gap)
Cadno	fox (Maes Cadno = Fox's Field)
Cae	field (Cae Hwch = Sow's field)
Caer (pl. caerau)	fortress (Carew is a corruption of Caerau; Caerbwdy)
Capel	chapel (Capel Colman)
Carn (pl. carnau)	mound, or mass of rocks
Carnedd(au)	cairn, tumulus (Carnedd Lleithr, St David's)
Carreg	stone, rock (Carreg Coetan Arthur = Rock of Arthur's quoit)
Castell	stronghold, castle (Castell Mawr = Great Stronghold)
Cefn	ridge (Pen y Cefn = head of the ridge
Cei	quay (Ceinewydd = New Quay)
Gelli	grove, small woodland (Pen Gelli, Nevern; 'wooded head-land')
Cemais	bends in river, stream, coastline (old name of Nevern area)

181

ci (pl. cŵn)	dog (Tre-cŵn = settlement with the dogs)
Cigfran	raven
Cil (pl. ciliau)	corner, hideaway, retreat Cil-fynydd = hidden mountain)
Cledd (pl. Cleddau)	sword; the twin rivers slashing through the county.
Clegyr	cliff, crag (Clegyr Boia = Boia's crag (camp; St David's))
Cnwc	small hill (Cnwc y buwch = Cow Hill)
Coch, goch	red (Croes-goch = red cross, named from bloody battle)
Coetan	quoit, burial (Quoit in Goidelic language e.g., Scots, irish)
Colomendy	dove-cot (St David's)
Cors, Gors	bog (Gors Fawr = Great Bog)
Craig (pl. creigiau)	rock (Criag y Ddinas = Rock of the Fortress)
Crochan	cauldron; so Pwllcrochan = Pool like a cauldron
Croes	cross, crossroad; e.g. Croes-goch
Crug (pl. crugiau)	tump (burial or topographical) Crug y Gwrach = Hag's Tump)
Cwm	valley (Cwm Gwaun = Meadow Valley)
Dafad	sheep (Carn Ddafad las = hill of the blue sheep)
Derwen	oak (Clunderwen)
Dinas	hill fort; township
Du	black (Mynydd Du = Black Mountain)
Duw	God
Dŵr	Water; Glandŵr = bank by water
Dyffryn	valley e.g., Dyffryn, Goodwick
Eglwys	church (Cwm yr Eglwys = Valley of the Church)
Eryr	eagle (Foel Eryr = Bare Hill of the Eagle)
Esgob	bishop (Carreg yr Esgob = Bishop Rock, St Justinian)
Fagwr	wall (Fagwr Goch Fach = little red Wall, Presely)
Ffordd	road, track (Ffordd y Pererinion = Pilgrims' track)
Ffos	ditch (Ffos y Mynach = Monks' ditch)
Ffynnon	well (Ffynnon Dewi = David's well)
Moel, foel	bare (bald) hill (Foel Drygarn = Bare Hill of three burials)
Glas, las	blue, green
Glyn	deep, steepsided valley (Glyn Rhosyn = Rose Valley)
Gof	blacksmith (Cerrig y Gof, Newport)
Gwaelod	bottom (Pwll Gwaelod = Pool at the bottom)
Gwastad	flat, plain (Carreg Gwastad = flat rock)
Gwaun	moor, meadow
Gwylfa	lookout point (Penrhyn Gwylfa = Lookout headland)
Gwyn, gwen	white, (Hendy Gwyn = Hen-tŷ-Gwyn = old white house)
Gwynt	wind, smell (Tre-gwynt = windy village)
Gwyrdd	green
Hafod	summer dwelling
Hen	old
Hir	long (maen hir = long stone)
Hwch	sow (Ysgubor Hwch = Sow's Barn)
Llan	enclosure for church. (Bryn Henllan = old church hill)
Llech(i)	slate (Llech Isaf, Dinas)
Llethr	slope
Llwyn	grove (Llwyn Onn = Ash Grove)
Llys	court (Llys-y-frân = Crow's court)
Maen (pl. meini)	stone (Carn Meini)
Maes	open field (Maes y bont = fields near the bridge)
Mawr, fawr	large, dramatic (Castell Mawr = Great castle)
Mêl	honey (Pig y Mêl, Dinas)

Melin, felin	mill (Aberfelin = mill near the river mouth)
Melyn	yellow
Moel, foel	bare hill (Foel Goch = bare red hill)
Morfa	salt marsh (Mynydd Morfa = mountain near salt marshes)
Mynach	monk
Mynydd	mountain (Tegfynydd = fair mountain)
Nant	brook (Nant-y-moel = brook by the bare hill)
Newydd	new (Tŷ-newydd = New house)
Ogof	cave (Ogof Tobacco, a smuggler's' cave near Solva)
Pant	hollow, valley (Blaen Pant = head of the valley, hollow)
Parc	field (Parc y Meirw = field of the dead, Fishguard)
Pen	headland, promontory (Pen Clegyr)
Penglog	skull (Penybenglog, Nevern)
Penrhyn	headland
Pig	beak (Pig y baw = dirty beak, Nr. Fishguard)
Pistyll	spring (Pistyll Cleifion = spring of the sick)
Pont, bont	bridge (Pont yr Henffordd = bridge of the old road)
Porth	harbour entrance (Porth-gain)
Preseb	manger (Carn Breseb)
Pwll	pool (Pwll Deri = pool by oak trees, Strumble Head)
Rhaeadr	waterfall
Rhiw	hill
Rhos	moor, acid plain (Rhos y Clegyr)
Rhyd	ford (Rhyd y Brwyn = ford by the rushes)
Sant, san	saint
Traeth	beach The Welsh name for Newport is Trefdraeth, or settlement by the beach; Saundersfoot was Coedraeth, or Woodland by the beach; Whitesands is Traeth Mawr, great sand

Tre(f)	homestead = group of houses
Troed	base, foot (Troed y Rhiw = bottom of the hill)
Trwyn	headland, point (Trwyncastell = promontory fortress)
Tŵr	tower (Tŵr y Felin = tower mill)
Tŷ (pl. tai)	house; Tŷ bach (little house, euphemism for loo)
Tywyn	sand-dune (whole area near Whitesands, St David's)
Uchaf	higher, upper
Ynys (pl ynysoedd)	island
Ysgubor	barn (Ysgubor Gaer = Barn fort; mis-spelled Skeibir)
Ysbyty	hospital, hospice (for pilgrims) Ysbyty Tre-Prior, St David's

See *Rhestr o Enwau Lleoedd: A Gazeteer of Welsh Place-names* (ed. Elwyn Davies), University of Wales Press, 1957.

Home-made butter pat, about 1890. West Wales is a countryside of small dairy farms—those who live there hope and pray the Eurocrats and their quotas will not kill a five-and-a-half thousand year tradition . . .

Pembrokeshire Museums

NORSE PLACE NAME INDEX

Ambleston	hammil (pers.); tun = settlement
Angle	angle = hook
Hasgard; Asgard	as = a god; gardr = enclosure. Scandinavian examples have a flavour of Olympus about them, with important circle/alignment sites nearby (e.g. Asgard, Iceland)
Barnslake	Barna = child (cf. Bairn); laekr = brook, stream
Barry	Berr = bare; Oy = island
Bletherston	Bladr (cf. blathering = bleat; tun(sax) = enclosure
Brandy Brook	Brandr (pers.)
Brother Hill	Brodir = brother, used as surname
Buckston	Bukki (pers.); tun = settlement
Butter Hill	Budar (pers., also brother)
Caldy	Kald = cold Oy = island
Coleby	Kollr = hilltop; by = house
Crackwell	Krakr = crow
Crundale	Kroen = crown Daelr = valley; "the chieftain's valley"
Dale	Daelr = valley
Derby	Dyr = deer (american pron?) by = house
Drussleton	Trostr = thrush (cf. Germ drossel, old Eng. throstle); tun (sax)
Erickshill	Erik (Pers.)
Fishguard	Fiski = fish; gardr = enclosure
Frayneslake	Frain = glittering; laekr = lake
Freystrop	Freya (Freyr) fertility goddess (cf. Friday, friend) thorp = village
Gander's Nest	Gandir = mythical monster; nes = point
Gateholm	Gata = gap, passage (it is cut off at high tide) Holmi = island
Gelliswick	Geli (cold; prob. from Latin gelidus??); vik = Bay
Goodwick	Gud = good; vik = Bay
Giltar	Geul = wide bay; tar = tump
Goscar	Goth = god = skare = rock
Goulthrop	Geul = wide bay; thorp = village
Grassholm	Gras = grass; holmi = island; also known as Gwales = 'place of strangers' of Mabinogi and Brân
Greenala	Grun = green ; hollr = slope
Gumfreston	Gudmar or Gunarf (pers.); tun = settlement
Hakin	Hakon = bachelor
Haven	Havn = harbour
Haverfordwest	Havr = corn (c.f. haversack); fjord = inlet
Hellswick	Helli = cave; vik = bay
Herbrandston	Herbrandr (pers.)
Honeyborough, Honeyhill	Hogni (pers.) burgh = burial (sax)
Hubberston	Hubba, the Danish leader, who brought a Viking fleet to winter in the Haven in 877 AD; he and his two brothers Halfdene and Hinguar had spent the last fourteen years raiding Britain; though Hubba had only 23 ships, he had command of the banner called a Dannebrog, woven by the King's sisters, and this makes Hubba someone of importance . . .
Knock (rath)	Knok = mound
Lambston, Lamborough	Lammaston; Lambi (pers.) or could be Llan = church (Lampeter)
Lundy	Lundi = puffin
Milford	Mildr = middle; fjord = inlet
Mireston	Myrr = moor; tun (sax) settlement or tun (norse) enclosure
Musselwick	Mos = moss; fellr = upland area; vik = bay (cf. the village of Mossfellsheath, Iceland)

Newton Noyes	Naze; ness = nose or promontory
Newgale	Gaelr = hollow place
Ramsey	Hrams = garlic; Oy = island (or Hrammr = ram?)
Rinderston	Rinda = outer crust of the earth (cf. orange rind); tun
Skomer = Scalmey	Skjel = piece cut off OR sword; Oy = island
Skerries	Skare = rock or Skera = ploughshare
Skerry back	Skare and bakki = bank
Skokholm	Skogar = copse doubtful; but Owen and others call it Stockholm where stokkr = boat yard (cf. on the stocks)
Snailston	Snjllr = land cut clean off, isolated; tun = settlement now called Wood Field
Skrinkle	Kringla = circle (cf. cringles, the little rings in sailors' hammock ends)
Solva	Solvaar (pers.) or Solvaer = Samphire, which grows on the cliff thereabouts; there is a Solva in Denmark and a Solvaer in the Lofoten islands
Stackpole	Stakr = tall rock (and see Stack rock, south Stack, and the Welsh version Stacen y Brenin, St Elvis); pollr = pool
Steynton	Stan = stone; tun (settlement)
Studdock	Studdi (pers); dokk = pit
Tenby	Some authorities give it as Dinbych (din bach = little fort) others as Dan = dane; by = house i.e., Dane's house. Early pronunciation as 'Denby' doesn't help either case!
Temperness	Timbr = timber; nes = promontory
Thurston	Thor = God of thunder (cf. Thursday); tun = enclosure
Wathwick	Vad = wading; vik = bay
Worm's Head	Ormr = long slinky animal like a snake, worm, Orme

Nevern cross among its yews, one of which is said to bleed in mourning for the death of the last Welsh Prince of Wales, and which will go on bleeding until we have another. The cross is made from Preseli Bluestone—did it start off in a prehistoric sacred stone circle? . . .

FURTHER READING AND BIBLIOGRAPHY

Archaeological books have mushroomed over the past few years as the popularity of the subject has gained ground—due initially to the TV series' like 'AVM', 'Chronicle', and latterly Michael Wood and his confreres in magnificently produced and richly budgetted series' like 'Doomsday'—all these are now backed up by publications. But to start with some

CLASSICS

If you can get hold of a second hand copy (sadly, new copies seem no longer available), one of the best general guides for a keen beginner is

Collins Field Guide to Archaeology (Eric Wood)
> Splendidly eclectic about the bits and bobs you find about the townscapes and countryside, clear description of time-scales, artifacts, techniques; a good start and still good reference.

Field Archaeology (R. J. C. Atkinson; pub. Methuen)
> Good general guide for beginners to fieldwork.

Archaeology in the field (O. G. S. Crawford, pub. Phoenix)
> Another classic, from one of the 20th Century masters of the archaeological craft.

Personality of Britain (C. F. Fox, 1959)

Language and History in Early Britain (K. H. Jackson, 1953)

Archaeology and Place-names in History (F. T. Wainwright; R & KP)
> Two solid guides to the 'sounds' of history, should be read in conjunction with a modern 'Classic'.

Words, an illustrated history of Western Languages (Ed. Stevenson)
> An amazing book packed tight with intriguing evidence about how the language you, I and the rest of Europe speaks are tied in with our history and archaeology. Have it by you as you read *anything* else! Macdonald 1983.

Archaeology is a science, and the scientific side of it is well reviewed and explained in

Science in Archaeology (Ed. Brothwell & Higgs; Thames & Hudson)
> Pollen analysis, dendrochronology, thermoluminescence and much else in one hefty volume; oldish now but a mine of useful references.

Plants in Archaeology (Geoffrey Dimbleby, pub. John Baker)
> The 'father of pollen analysis' introduces the importance of plants to man, and to the study of man, and explains some of the techniques which have advanced our knowledge of what grew where, and why, in the past.

Archaeology and the Microscope (Leo Biek; pub. Lutterworth)
> Early book on the subject, clear and well written introduction; good especially if you may be involved in a 'dig' and wish to know what the experts are doing. And . . .

Physics and Archaeology (M. J. Aitken)
> Interscience; he has written a lot on various aspects of science in archaeology in 'Antiquity' and 'Archaeometry'.

Archaeology, History and Science (R. J. C. Atkinson, Cardiff)

More specialised books abound; some favourites include:—

Prehistoric Chamber Tombs of England and Wales (Glyn Daniel)
> Now decidedly out of date, especially in dates, but you won't find our marvellous clutch of cromlechau explained and discussed with such scholarly enthusiasm anywhere else but in this pioneering book; gives many references back to classical early archaeologists and antiquarians.

Neolithic communities of the British Isles (Stuart Piggot, Camb U. P.)
  Good general survey, clearly explained.
The Northern World (Ed. David M. Wilson; T. & H.)
  History and heritage of Northern Europe; meticulous scholarship combined with lavish illustration
  —all contributors are top in their field, the Editor is Director of the British Museum.

Getting more parochial, you'll find the following useful:—
Prehistoric and early Wales (Foster and Daniel, R & KP)
Welsh Antiquity (National Museum of Wales)
Welsh Archaeological Heritage (Cambrian Arch. Assoc.)
Prehistory of Wales (W. F. Grimes; Cardiff, 1951)

The archaeological journals have many fine papers well worth searching out in your local library; a few examples are:—
Prehistoric and Roman Frontiers in Wales (Nash Williams, 'Antiquity', 1954)
Hill slope forts and related earthworks in S. W. England and S. Wales (Lady E. Fox; Archaeological Journal, 1970)
A.B.C. of the Iron Age (Christopher Hawkes, Antiquity, 1959)
Late Bronze Age in Wales (H. N. Savory, 1958, Arch. Camb. CVII 3-63)
  'Antiquaries' Journal', 'Archaeologica Cambrensis', 'Antiquity', 'Archaeological Journal', 'Archaeometry', are well worth searching through for specialized articles and for further references, as are some of the older magazines such as 'Folk Lore', 'Notes and Queries' and even the 'Gentlemens' Magazine'. Back numbers of local papers often provide intriguing paragraphs, stories about shipwrecks or murders or smuggling or robberies on the highway.

Art and Artifacts occur in all the above, specialised works are:—
Early Christian monuments of Wales (Nash-Williams)
Celtic Ornament in the British Isles down to AD 700 (E. T. Leeds, Oxford, 1933)
Picture Book of Ancient British Art (1951)
Art in Britain under the Romans (Toynbee, 1964)
Anglo-Saxon Art to AD 900 (T. D. Kendrick, 1938)

But how about ancient science? For a general view Colin Ronan's *'Cambridge Illustrated History of the World's Science'* (1983) gives an overall background . . . and for special cases?—

What were stone circles? What do they show about *how* our ancestors viewed their surroundings, *how* they thought?
Circles and Standing Stones; (Evan Hadingham, pub. Heinemann)
  It is now almost respectable to talk of the possible uses of stone rings and rows as astronomical instruments, indeed a new science has grown up, with its own name, Archaeo-astronomy. This book explains basically and with fine illustrations and diagrams, how we think our ancestors used the sky, what for, and why.

If you wish to go further into this fascinating subject, then you should read the Master's own works— Alexander Thom and his entire family seem to have been quietly pioneering this branch of our knowledge about our ancestors, and a line of impressive publications as long as your arm is the result—it is hard to know how the doubters CAN still doubt, but they do! Try:—
Megalithic remains in Britain and Brittany (A. & A. S. Thom, Oxford)
  Expects some mathematical know-how on the part of the reader but otherwise takes you painlessly through the astronomy you need to know, and the archaeology, as well as the maths., of our amazing stone circles.

Megalithic sites in Britain (A. Thom, pub. Clarendon, Oxford)
Megalithic Lunar Observatories (Thom, Clarendon)
>   Rather more maths, lots of his evidence clearly set out for the general reader with a scientific background.
Sun, Moon and Standing Stones (John Wood, O.U.P.)
>   Another general introduction, well researched and written.
Stone Circles of the British Isles (Aubrey Burl, Yale)
>   Goes over much the same ground, worth reading for its alternative views on some conclusions.
Megalithic Science (Douglas C. Heggie; pub. T. & H., 1981)
>   Compendious paperback packed with information—with this, you need no others! But for an enjoyably quirky read, try
Megalithomania (John Michell, T. & H., 1982)
>   This book answers the question—what did our ancestors think of the old stones? Poets, artists, antiquarians, and the lunatic fringe have all had their say—and here it is in book form!

For particular periods in our history, there are mountains of books, good, bad and awful; it is hard to thread one's way through the bibliographic minefield. A few will be found above, but closer inspection of the following is recommended:—
The Celts (T. G. E. Powell, Thames & Hudson)
>   If you want to get to know your Iron age ancestors, this is the book—superbly illustrated and richly written, it brings the Celtic people alive as few do. The 1958 edition has been updated and is in paperback.
Anglo Saxon Chronicle; ed. D. Whitlock (Eyre & Spottiswoode)
The Towns of Medieval Wales (Ian Soulsby, pub. Phillimore, 1983)
Town defences in England and Wales; Normans in south Wales (Nelson)
Medieval Religious houses in England and Wales (Knowles and Hadcock, 1971)

Hogg and King wrote two monumental works on *Welsh Castles* in 'Arch. Camb.' (1963, 1967); and David Cathcart King wrote a splendid book more recently (1983) but the *flavour* of castles is well caught by *'Castles in Wales'* (AA/Wales Tourist Board, 1983) just as Wales itself is encapsulated in Wynford Vaughan Thomas's fine books, specially *'Wales, a History'* (Michael Joseph, 1985). More local still, George Owen (1603) and Richard Fenton (1809) have both written books about Pembrokeshire, and there the (literally) weighty *'History of Carmarthenshire'* (John E. Lloyd, pub. by London Carmarthenshire Society 1898); the *Royal Commission on Ancient Monuments* in England and Wales have done county histories, which should be consulted for individual sites, and the *Dyfed Archaeological Trust* has computorized site and subject references to make a comprehensive research tool available at their HQ (Bishops Palace, Abergwili).

INDUSTRIAL ARCHAEOLOGY

A newish branch of the subject, with libraries—full of books on canals, railways, mines, Victoriana, cast iron, tinplate and copper . . . you name it, and there will be shelves of books about it! The NATIONAL TRUST publishes excellent books about its own properties (e.g., Aberdulais, Dolaucothi), various LOCAL HISTORY SOCIETIES have researched and written up their own areas; BRUNEL and the GWR have a mountainous literature (e.g. MacDermott's 3 volume *'History of the Great Western Railway'* or L.T.C. Rolt's lovely biography *'Isambard Kingdom Brunel'* (Orig Longman's, now Penguin, 1983); Canals are covered in Hadfield's *'Canals of South Wales and the Border'* (D. & C.), a good general outline of the area in Morgan Rees's *'Mines Mills and Furnaces'* (HMSO), *'Mining for Metal in Wales'* (F. J. North, pub. Nat. Mus. Wales), *'Metal Mines in Southern Wales'* (G. W. Hall, pub. Author) . . . the list lengthens daily.

SPECIAL PLEADING

Various sections in this book meant a lot of specialised reading such as masses of original papers in the Public Record Office for 'Black Bart', Bartholomew Roberts the pirate—he also turns up in Daniel Defoe's 'Generall History of Pyrates': Trellyffaint's toad turns up in Giraldus Cambrensis' medieval 'Itinerary through Wales' (so does the Flood at Newgale) now translated in paperback, small local railways often have their very own books e.g. 'Pembroke and Tenby Railway', 'Gwendraeth Valley Railway', 'The Cardi Bach' and so on. Plant hunters and those intrigued by our living archaeology should read 'The Englishman's Flora' by Geoffrey Grigson (Phoenix) as those who want to find out more about dialect and folk lore should try and get hold of a copy of Elizabeth Wright's vintage book 'Rustic Speech and Folk-Lore' (Milford, 1914) as well as 'Welsh Folk-lore and Folk Custom' (T. Gwynn Jones, pub. Brewer, 1930) and 'Welsh Folk Customs' (Trefor M. Owen, pub. Nat. Mus. Wales, 1978). What the bureaucrats and planners would call our 'Housing Stock' and its early history is well reviewed and surveyed in 'The Welsh House' (Iorwerth Peate, pub. Brython Press, 1940) as the sea-beacon is in Douglas Hague and Rosemary Christie's fine book 'Lighthouses' (Gomer Press, 1975). Coins, tokens, silver and gold, ceramics, furniture, pewter, all have marks to search for and identify; 'Dictionary of Marks' by Margaret MacDonald Taylor (Connoisseur, 1965), and Seaby's Coin catalogue will give the dates and interesting points about this branch of archaeology, subject of vastly increased interest since the advent of the metal detector! . . .

RESEARCH

This book, and the further reading, may encourage you to speculate on how you might go about some historical detective work of your own—something fairly simple, like the name of your street or village . . . a bit more complicated, like that of your family, or a whole local industry or historical event. Back numbers of newspapers can be found on microfilm in some libraries, as the preserved originals in Record Offices, or in the Newspaper Library at Colindale. Record offices also hold borough and town records, census returns, Parliamentary plans for railways and canals, Turnpike toll sheets, details of medical emergencies such as cholera or Black Death, as well as more prosaic documents such as church records, Baptisms, burials, marriages and the like . . . Go and explore your church, it has far more to tell than the history of the faith in your area—eccentrics, or crimes, or odd happenings, even prehistoric custom and myths seem to stick obstinately to those ancient stones . . . well worth looking into closer to find some 'Open Secrets' of your own!

Roger Worsley

INDEX

A

Aberdulais — Copper works, 16, 94, 94-6

Aber Eiddy — slate quarry, powder house; railway, 154

Aber Mawr — Rems Brunel railway terminus 1848, 1, 45; Drowned forest

Adders — Norman noble and, see Roch, 64

Amroth — Sunken forest; lost land legend, 1, 154

Angle — Saxon strip fields, pele tower, 18

Anthracite — Pembrokeshire coal industry

Arsenic — Works; Watson's Flue see Clyne, 143, 144

Arthritis — Cure for, see Meadowsweet, 140-41

Astronomy, prehistoric — 34, 37>

B

Bacon Hole — Palaeolithic cave, 29

Barti Ddu, 'Black Bart' — 'Black' Bartholomew Roberts, world's most successful pirate, 166-71

Bluestones — see Carn Meini, Stonehenge, 6, 34-5

Boia — Roughneck who befriended St David, 9, 92; see Clegyr Boia

'Boston Newsletter' — USA account of Welsh piracy, 168

Bowdler — Dr. Thomas; cleaner-up of Shakespear, and see Oystermouth, 133 et seq 135

Bronwydd — Gothick mansion now ruined (R. K. Penson); pure Welsh Dracula, 158

BRONZE AGE — 2000 BC—600 BC; metal users; round barrows; plough; stone circles, 4, 5, 12, 19; palstave, 21; Roman scent vessels, 14

Brunel — I. K. Railways, 'Great Eastern', 16, 94; Neyland, Aber Mawr, Milford, 118-125; Great Western, South Wales Railway, 118; letter about road conditions, 161-63

Buckland — Dean; little blue bag, 29; Red Lady of Paviland

Burry Port — Harbour/canal basin/Railway, 98; 'and Gwendraeth Valley Railway', 100, 101

C

Caldey — Ogham Stone; priory, 44; cattle, walked to, 45

Canals — See Stepaside; Llechryd, Gwendraeth valley; Kymers Inclined planes; converted to railway furniture for; basin at Burry Port, 16, 92, 97-101. 97-8, 98

Cantre'r Gwaelod — drowned lands of, 1, 19, 45>

Capel Isaf — Inclined plane for canal, 99

Cardigan — Railway station, 'Cardi Bach railway, 130

Carew — Castle, cross, Cheriton ch, tidemill, 13, 81-85, 81, 82, 85

Carmarthen — seaport, 15; Romans at, 9; lead at* 60-1

Carn Alw — Amazing mini-fort I. A., *cheveaux de frise* anti cavalry defence, 50, 51

Carn Ingli — Enormous fort, 5 miles stone bank defences, *cheveaux de frise*, 52, 175

Carn Meini — Source of Preseli Bluestones used at Stonehenge; Golden Road, 3, 19, 34-5, 52, 86, 32

Castell Mawr — strong I. A. fort, 17

Castle Flemish — Roman fortlet, 87

Cleddau — pair of stupendous rivers awash in history, 36

Clegyr Boia — Irish chieftain's stronghold, 9, 92, befriended St David, 179

Clyne valley, Swansea — Industrial valley; old railways, 143-4; arsenic works, 143, 144; with Watson's flue and furnaces

Collieries, old — Pembrokeshire; Trefran, 16; Begelley, Newgale, Hook Colliers, 'Druke and Beam', 39;

Copper — works, see Aberdulais, Swansea, 16; Burry Port, 94-6; mines, St Elvis, St Justinian

Corpse Road — Mathry, St Edrin, 86, 87

Cosheston — fine strip field system, 13; quarry yielded 1 Stonehenge; 'Bluestone, 36

Cromlechs — 19; Parc le Breos Cwm, 145, 147, 148; Pentre Ifan, 175

Crusader — St Davids, portrait of, 18

Crymych — Railway at, 131-32

Culver Hole — Wreckers' 'False light'; and see 'Phebe and Peggy', 16, 70-73, 71, 72

Culwch and Olwen — romantic tale? Iron age? Bluestones story, 36

Cydweli (Kidwelly) — port, canals at, castle, 15, 97; arsenical death at, 144

D

Dale — Landing place of Henry Tudor (Brunt Farm, Mill Bay); Viking name; limekilns, 9, 154, 12

DARK AGES — 410 A.D. to 1066 A.D. coming of Christianity; see Nevern, Ogham, St Davids, Boia, Saints, etc., 9, 92

Dendrochronology — Dates got from tree rings, 25

Doctrine of Signatures — signs from God for early medics, 140, 177

Dog — Man's best and first friend, 1; mesolithic; whippet New Moat, 151-3; curing bite of made, see St Edrin, 86

Dolaucothi — Roman Gold mine, biggest ever, 9; in ownership of Nat. Trust., 54-9; aqueduct, hushgulleys, coffin adits, 54-9

Dragons — Origins of; horses and St George, 21, 50, 52

Drovers — roads; journeys of; geese; superstitions, 87

Drowned valleys — geology of ports and harbours, 31

Druidston — 18th C. report of wreck at, 74-5

E

Eclipses — predicting, Parc y Meirw, 37

Eglwyswrw, — Castell Mawr camp, 17; 'Railway built by Russians', 130; Motte at, 11

F

Fenton, Richard — Pembrokeshire historian, 75, 138

Fields — and hedges; dating; importance of plants in; 'Celtic', strip; open; med enclosure, 13, 17, 177-8

Fishguard — Viking name; Invasion by French, 120; GWR at, 123; limekilns at, 155, 159; prehistoric computor nr, 37

Flood, the — Mesolithic origin for 'Genesis'? 19, 33, 45-49

Foel Drygarn — Impressive I. A. Fort with over 220 hut circles; Mabinogi connection, 7, 8, 34, 50; —and sphagnum moss, 142

Freshwater — Sailors' burial mounds, cross, 76

Frosse — Herr Ulrich, the mad German, 16, 94-6; see Aberdulais

G

Gateholm — Early Christian settlement, 11

German — the mad, see Aberdulais, Frosse, 16, 94-6

Giraldus Cambrenis — Gerald de Barri, medieval scholar, 92; source of much enjoyable gossip about his life and time, and for Wales generally; see Trellyffaint, St Davids, Stackpole Elidor, 12, 46, 138

Glogue — slate quarry, Cardi Bach railway, 131

Gold — See Dolaucothi, Treffgarne, 54-9

Golden Road — Prehist. trackway; see Carn Meini, 5, 52, 86; Bluestones, Foel Drygarn, 32

Gors Fawr — Stone circle, observatory, stone row, much prehistoric activity, 3, 19, 35, 38-9, 38, 39

'Great Eastern' — Brunel's giant steamship, 18

GWR — and see Burry port, Fishguard, 'Cardi Bach', Brunel, Treffgarne, 131, 132

H

Hallowe'en — iron age connections with, Crundale, 53

Haroldston — much ruined mansion once home of Sir John Perrott, Queen Elizabeth's half brother and pirate . . . see Carew, Haverfordwest, 81-85

Haverfordwest — County town, inland seaport, piracy (see Perrott), 12, 15, 16; Castle; Vikings; 82, 120; plague at, limekilns, 155; 'Brunel' candelabra to mayor of, 123

Heads — Losing of . . . see Wells, Crundale, St Justinian, Strumble stone head, Llanwnda, 53, f7p

Hedd and Isaac, bishop's sons — murder of by Vikings, 9, 12

Hedges — importance of; and see fields, 177>

Herbs — and herbalists; plants used in medicine; hedges; Dark age/med

Horses — and dragons; St George patron saint of—wells to cure ills of, 51-3

Hoyle's Mouth — Palaeolithic cave, Tenby, 31-2

Hook — colliers at (Druke & Beam), 61

Hush Gulleys — see Dolaucothi

I

INDUSTRIAL ARCHAEOLOGY — ind. revolution; various refs under canals, railways, Brunel, Abermawr, Porthgain, Solva, collieries, Trefran, Hook etc., 12-3, 53>, 130-32

Ireland — Potato Famine in; see Treffgarne, Navvies, see Treffgarne; Perrott governor of, 84; Wicklow Hills and eclipses, 37

Irish — invasion and establishment of kingdom; Ogham stones and alphabet, 9, 41-4

IRON AGE — 600BC—43AD (but in Pembs carries on through Roman period), see Carn Alw, Carn Ingli; forts, heads, losing; Treffgarne, 7, 8, 50, 51-3, 17, 20, 27, 119

J

Johnston — Collieries; see Hook; limekilns, 155
Justinian — Beheaded saint; well; copper mine, 9, 52

K

Kenfig — med. town smothered in sandstorm, 12, 66
Kymer — Canal built by indomidable ladies, 16, 97

L

Lady Eliza — Lead mine engine house; kibbles, 63
Landore, Swansea — Copper capital of the world, 102, 103
Landsker — Pembrokeshire Linguistic Divide drawn by Normans, 64, 150-61
Limekilns — vital part of early industrial landscape; Dale, Solva, Porthclais, etc., 154-8
Little Newcastle — Birthplace Barti Ddu, 166
Llandeilo — Blende Street (zinc), 18
Llandovery — Drunken coachman at, 161
Llandybie — Gothick limekilns by R. K. Penson, (see Bronwydd, Cockett), 155
Llandysul — Steam lorry at Station, 164
Llanfyrnach — impressive leadmine, railway, 131
Llangunnor — leadmines by riverside, Carmarthen, 9, 60-63
Llanpumpsaint — gold pestle acquires five saints, 57
LLawhaden — Castle, Hospitium, pilgrims, 12
Llechryd — Ben Hammett's 1799 tinplate works rems canal less than 1m long now partly destroyed by modern vandalism, 16
Lubbock — Sir John, inventor of the Bank Holiday, archaeologist, social reformer, 34, 145-9

M

Mabinogi — Celtic folk tales, 36
Maenclochog — railway; tunnel (Dam-busters), 130
Mansell, Sir Rice — wife murdered in Oxwich castle, 71-72
Margam — Abbey; industrial Cistercians, inscribed stones coll, 16, 143
Marros — best place to see drowned forest and Cantre'r Gwaelod story; low tide, 1, 2, 45<, 46
Marychurch — maker of milestones, 160
Medicinal plants — see herbals, hedges, Arthritis, 140-41, 177-8
Merlin — and Stonehenge bluestones, 34; and his pig, 63

MESOLITHIC — Middle Stone age, 1, 2, 19; c8,000-3,400 BC hunters invent house, witness great flood and acquire DOG, 20, 46-9, 46
Mesur y Dorth — 'Bread-measure Stone' on pilgrims' road, St Davids, 89, 87
Milestones — Pembs—accurate to yard, 160; Carms—informative but chatty
Milford — Hamilton's New Town; Great Eastern Whale oil; Quakers; Vikings; dock, 9, 18, 15, 16
Misericords — 'mercy seats' for aged clerics, carved with medieval cartoons, 172, 15
'Mister Morris's Castle' — Colliers flats complex, Morriston, 16, 102-3
Monmouth, Geoffrey of — writer of Stonehenge and Bluestones, 34
Monmouth, Duke of — connections with Roch, 64
Motte & Bailey — earthwork castle, Norman; Wiston, Rudbaxton, Wolf's Castle etc., 10, 64
Myddfai — Physicians of; lead mines at, 87
Mynydd y Garreg — 'Valley of the Kings' limekilns, 155, 158

N

Nab Head — Meso flint working site; I. A. cliff fort, 1, 19, 20
Nash, John — Architect, Regent St., Ffynnone; limekilns at Tenby, 157, 158
Neath Abbey — Cistercians; iron working; tiles; furnaces, 143
NEOLITHIC — 3400BC—2000 BC; cromlech builders; first farmers; astronomy; navigation; see, Pentre Ifan, Trellyffaint, Parc y Meirw, Gors Fawr, Carn Meini, 2, 3-4, 4, 12, 19, 34, 53, 138, 145-9, 175
Nevern — Great cross; pilgrims way and X; ch; 7, 64, 88; Ogham stones at; fortress of great character and interest, bleeding yew, 89, 11, 9, 42-3, 139, 161,
Newgale — Collieries at; sunken forest at; 1, 43, 48; (See Giraldus Cambrensis)
New Moat — Ch contains Scourfield monuments, story of dog faithful unto death, 10, 150-54
Newport (Pem) — Inscr stone; cromlech; med port; cas., 1, 12, 45
Neyland — Railway terminus I. K. Brunel, 16, 18
Nicholaston — St George Well; horses & dragons, 55
NORMANS — see castles; motte and bailey, 9, 150; Giraldus Cambrensis; Pembroke
Norse, Old — Place names index, 9, 150, 184-5

O

Ogham stones — and alphabet for decoding; Brawdy, Clydai, Bridell, St Dogmaels, Nevern, 41-4, 40, 42, 43, 44

Overton — Wartime wreck; wrecking in 18th C. See Port Einon, Culver Hole, Phebe and Peggy, 70-72, 71, 16, 71-3

Oxwich Castle — Wrecker's wife murdered by brick, haunts castle still . . . 66, 71

Oystermouth — Home of Bowdler; world's first passenger railway commem in ch., orig now a cycle track, 133, 134-5, 136

P

Palmerston — Follies (Haven forts 1852-70), Stack, Chapel Bay, West Hook, Dale, Pembroke Martello Towers Hubberston, St Catherine's fort, 104-9

Parc le Breos Cwm — Neo tomb; origins Bank Holiday (Lubbock), 4, 145-9

Parc y Meirw — Unique Neolithic eclipse predictor, 3, 34, 37-41

Paviland — Red lady of; Buckland, Palaeolithic 'Bone cave', 28, 29-31

PALAEOLITHIC — 'Old Stone Age' c. 1½ m BC-10,000 hand axe, 2, 19, 28-33

Palliser cannon — Victorian ultimate weapon, Stack, 105

Pembrey and Burry Port — canal; Bowser's mem., 9, 7-9; good stretch of Gwendraeth valley railway (once canal; hawser scratched bridges)

Pembroke — Castle, best in the west; town walls med port; birthplace Henry Tudor 1457, 12, 36

Pembroke Dock — Fine industrial housing early 19 C, 107; town plan, dockyard, 'Martello' Towers seaplane hangars and 3rd W.W., 17

Penally — limestone quarries; ch yd X, 154

Pennard — haunted Castle lost in sand, 66-7

Pentre Ifan — most famous cromlech in Wales, 3, 4, 175

Perrott, Sir John — Hard swearing Elizabethan, half-brother to Good Queen Bess; see, Carew Haroldston; Haverfordwest; Piracy; Ireland, 16, 71, 81-85, 83

'Phebe and Peggy' — 18th C pop song printed in Solva commemorates shipwreck and murder, 72, 74

Philadelphia — connections with Wales, 'Phebe', 74, 73-5

Pilgrims — Road, steps and cross, Nevern, 88, 89

Pirates and piracy — Iron age; Vikings; Angle; Perrott; 9, 16, 20; Commissioners to Suppress 1566, 31; Bartholomew Roberts' millions, 166-71

Place-names — Norse, Saxon, Norman, Welsh, Irish, 178-80; importance of, to historians, 184-5

Plague — bubonic; Haverfordwest; (Rudbaxton Howard tomb); yellow (Nevern Ogham stone); remedies against, 188-9, 44

Pollen — grains, analysis, 24, 25

Pont Henry — Canal inclined plane and adjacent, 16, 97-101; inn sign, 99

Port Eynon — see Culver Hole; Wrecking; Phebe and Peggy

Porthclais — Limekilns, small harbour. Pirates, warriors, St David and holy well invasion of Ireland by Henry II Boia; med boat building, 15, 90-93, 154-5, 158, 173

Porthgain — Slate, granite, bricks all exported from this unique industrial site, now under aegis of National Park, Industrial archaeologists' mecca, 110-117, 16

Preseli — mountains, packed with ghosts and archaeology; cromlechs, circles, cairns, bluestones, Mabinogi assoc., see Carn Meini, Gors Fawr, Foel Drygarn, Parc y Meirw, 6, 50

Q

Quakers — Whaling, see Milford; Nantucket Avenue, Starbuck Road, 18

R

Rabbit — and Crusaders, 12; and 'Cardi Bach' railway, 131

Radiocarbon — dating method, 23

Railways — development of, mania for, 16; Brunel's at Treffgarne, 118-126; Burry Port and Gwendraeth Valley, 98-9, 101; Cardi Bach, 130-132; GWR, 127; built by Russians, Eglwyswrw, 130; North Pemb and Fishguard, 127; Oystermouth, 134-5; Porthgain's multi-gauge, 110-116

Roch — Castle, home of Adam 'de la Roch' a reptile-haunted nobleman . . . Lucy Walters & Duke of Monmouth, 64-5, 166

ROMAN — 43AD-410AD—see Roads; Castle Flemish, Nevern (Vitalianus stone), 9, 12, 87, 41, 43; Dolaucothi, 54-9; lead mining, Llangunnor, 60; bronze scent bottles, lamp, glass, 9, 14, 24; Samian ware, 24

Roads — Prehistoric—'Golden Road', 86; Roman, medieval Drove, pack-horse, 87; pilgrims', 87-9; corpse, 86; Turnpike (tolls and milestones) 159-65.

'Royal Charter' storm — 400 ships lost in a single night, 49, 79

S

St Bride — Brigid in Ireland; originally Brigantia Celtic fertility goddess; cousin of Freya, Eostre (Friday, Easter), 3, 4, 20, 72

St Davids — Cathedral, city; saint helped by Boia the irish pirate; misericords; pilgrims; Giraldus Cambrensis, 9, 12, 18, 15, 52, 89, 158

St Decuman — saint had head cut off . . . 52

St Dogmaels — Ogham's 'Rosetta Stone', 42, 43

St Edrins — small ch in 7 sided ch yd (now in private hands); grass from ch yd once 'cure for mad dog bite'. Corpse road, 86

St Elvis — 'Phebe and Peggy' was wrecked here, copper mine, rather ruined cromlech, 73-4

St Justinian — well, losing head; Viking; Ramsay, 9, 52

Saundersfoot — Extensive rems coal industry; railways, port; incline, 154

Siemens, Sir Wm. — Open hearth furnace; pioneering metallurgical lab at Landore, Swansea, 16, 103

Skokholm, Skomer — Islands with viking names, for bird-people and archaeologists, 9

Smalls — rocks, lighthouse with tragic tale, 76-9, 77, 78

Smuggling — see Solva, Wrecking, 16

Snakes — Adders, prophesy of death to noble, 65

Solva — Small but important port; smuggling; piracy; wrecking; vikings; Barti Ddu; Phebe & Peggy; Smalls light house, 16, 72, 154

Sphagnum moss — used in dressing wounds 300BC-1987AD, 142

Stack Rock — very complete Victorian fort, 104-9

Stepaside — ironworks, colliery, limekilns, 16

Stonehenge — Bluestones for, 6, 7, 19; chipping bits off as medicine, 35, 38; Merlin and Geoffrey of Monmouth, 140

Strata Florida — Cistercian abbey, lead mining, 143

Szlumper, J. W. — Railway engineer, 131

T

Talley — Cistercian—leadmines and see Dolaucothi, 16, 143

Taf Vale — start of Whitland and Cardigan Railway and the ghost of Driver Pugh, 131

Tenby — Coal and herring port turned watering place; escape of Henry Tudor; town walls (Jasper Tudor); Palmerston Folly (St Catherine's) 'P & T' (Pembroke and Tenby Railway); Hoyles Mouth, 31-2

Thermoluminescence — method of dating pottery by measuring stored energy from nuclear breakdowns, 23>

Thorn Island — Victorian fort, now a hotel, 108

'Toad Men' — for controlling animals; see Trellyffaint, 138-9

Tobacco — cave, for smuggling; see Solva, 16

Tree rings — see Dendrochronology

Treffgarne — I. K. Brunel's unfinished broad gauge railway; gorge lined with I. A. forts, gold mine; Owain Glyndwr b. 'Spyplane strip' (1942-3), 7, 16, 130, 118-125, 17

Trellyffaint — Neolithic tomb with cupmarked capstone; toad men made here . . . 4, 138-9

Turnpikes — see roads, 159-165

Ty pwpdwr — see Aber Eiddy, Rosebush

V

Vikings — place names, influences, 9, 42, 92; Old Norse, 179, 184>

Vivian, Henry, Lord Swansea — see Lubbock, Parc le Breos, Cwm, Swansea, 145-9

W

Watson, Bishop — patent flues to deal with Arsenic, 143

Wells — holy, cursing; worship at, heads thrown into, 9, 53

West Williamston — limestone quarry, canal-like 'cuts', see limekilns, 155

Whitesands Bay — End of Golden Road; pilgrims; chapel David.

Whitland — fair, 132; and Cardigan Railway, 130-41

Wicklow Hills — Parc y Meirw and the eclipses, 40

Wiston — Motte and Bailey fortress, 11

Wolfs Castle — motte, 11

Wrecking — see Phebe and Peggy, Culver Hole, Solva (St Elvis); Druidston, 16, 69-73

194

Y

Y Pigwn   Roman fort on exposed site, 9, 87
Ysbaddaden   giant king, Olwen's father; was Foel
           Drygarn his castle? 8

Bottom:

Cadaver Tomb, Tenby—All that is mortal of Thomas Danby, brave priest who helped hide two famous fugitives at risk to his life, half a thousand years ago. He knew Jasper Tudor well—Earl of Pembroke, the man who built Tenby's town walls to their present strength . . . the youth with him was to kill a king and end the Plantagenet dynasty at Bosworth, and become Henry VII—but he wouldn't have done so without the help of this fearless man of God . . . a man humble enough to have his tomb made not in the image of a pompous priest in full regalia, but of a semi-naked, decomposing corpse, with its stark message to us all—

'As I Am Now, So Shall Ye Be'

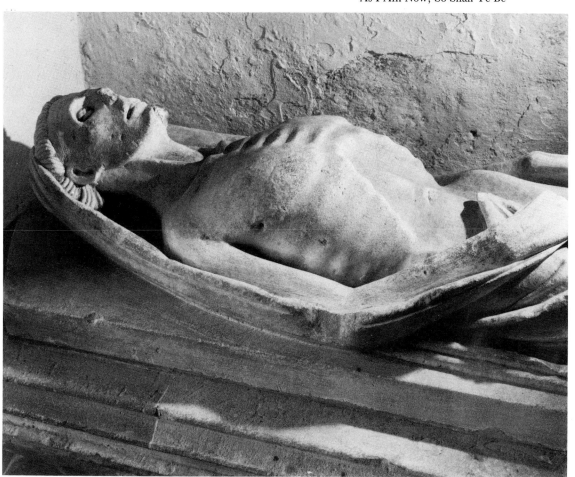

Ring a Ring o' Roses . . .—Victims of the Black
Death, the Haywards stare at us clutching their
symbolic skulls, on their fine tomb at Rudbaxton
Church, Pembrokeshire. You got to the village across a
little ford, in Welsh 'Rhyd Bach'—Saxon tongues
could not get around this, which they altered to 'Rud-
Bax', adding their own 'Tun' to mean 'Settlement'. A
good example of how our place-names evolve . . .